Lecture Notes
in Business Information Processing   187

Series Editors

Wil van der Aalst
Eindhoven Technical University, Eindhoven, The Netherlands
John Mylopoulos
University of Trento, Povo, Italy
Michael Rosemann
Queensland University of Technology, Brisbane, QLD, Australia
Michael J. Shaw
University of Illinois, Urbana-Champaign, IL, USA
Clemens Szyperski
Microsoft Research, Redmond, WA, USA

Sofia Ceppi · Esther David
Vedran Podobnik · Valentin Robu
Onn Shehory · Sebastian Stein
Ioannis A. Vetsikas (Eds.)

Agent-Mediated Electronic Commerce

Designing Trading Strategies and Mechanisms for Electronic Markets

AMEC 2013, Saint Paul, MN, USA, May 6, 2013, TADA 2013, Bellevue, WA, USA, July 15, 2013, and AMEC and TADA 2014, Paris, France, May 5, 2014
Revised Selected Papers

 Springer

Editors
Sofia Ceppi
Microsoft Research
Cambridge
UK

Onn Shehory
IBM Haifa Research Lab
Haifa
Israel

Esther David
Ashkelon Academic College
Ashkelon
Israel

Sebastian Stein
University of Southampton
Southampton
UK

Vedran Podobnik
University of Zagreb
Zagreb
Croatia

Ioannis A. Vetsikas
National Center for Scientific Research
Agia Paraskevi, Attikis
Greece

Valentin Robu
Heriot-Watt University
Edinburgh
UK

ISSN 1865-1348   ISSN 1865-1356   (electronic)
Lecture Notes in Business Information Processing
ISBN 978-3-319-13217-4   ISBN 978-3-319-13218-1   (eBook)
DOI 10.1007/978-3-319-13218-1

Library of Congress Control Number: 2014956503

Springer Cham Heidelberg New York Dordrecht London

Printed on acid-free paper

Springer International Publishing AG Switzerland is part of Springer Science+Business Media
(www.springer.com)

Preface

Electronic commerce and the design of automated trading agents have been at the core of research interests in the multi-agent systems (MAS) and artificial intelligence (AI) communities since the beginning of these fields. In the past decade, the number of areas in which a form of automated trading is employed has steadily increased. These range from bidding in keyword auctions in online advertising, to algorithmic trading in financial markets and energy acquisition in decentralized electricity markets.

In order to design mechanisms and strategies for such automated marketplaces, researchers from the MAS and AI communities have used techniques from a variety of disciplines, ranging from game theory and micro-economics to machine learning and computational intelligence. The automated Trading Agents Competition (TAC) has served to supply the community with a number of benchmark problems and trading platforms, in which different strategies can be independently tested and validated.

In this volume, we group together revised and selected papers from three leading international workshops in this area: the Agent-Mediated Electronic Commerce (AMEC 2013) workshop, colocated with the AAMAS 2013 conference in St. Paul, Minnesota; the Trading Agents Design and Analysis (TADA 2013) workshop, colocated with the AAAI 2013 conference in Bellevue, Washington, and the joint AMEC/TADA 2014 workshop, colocated with the AAMAS 2014 conference in Paris, France. All papers included in this volume have been thoroughly peer-reviewed, and represent updated versions of the papers presented at the three workshops, revised by the authors in line with reviewers' comments.

Given the breadth of research topics in this field, the range of topics addressed in these papers is correspondingly broad. These include the study of theoretical issues related to the design of interaction protocols and marketplaces; the design and analysis of automated trading strategies used by individual agents; the deployment of such strategies, in times as part of an entry to the Trading Agent Competition (TAC).

Four of the papers deal with acquisition strategies and tariff design in energy markets, an area that has received increasing attention within the AMEC/TADA research community. Babic and Podobnik present an overview and analysis of the results of the 2014 PowerTAC. Liefers et al. present the energy broker which they developed, as part of their successful runner-up strategy submitted in the 2013 and 2014 editions of PowerTAC. Ntagka et al. propose a different approach to designing tariffs in the energy market, using particle swarm optimization techniques, while Yasir et al. present an intelligent learning mechanism for trading strategies for local energy distribution. Also in TAC-related work, Toshniwal et al. consider the detection of opportunistic bids in the Trading Agent Competition, but using the supply chain management game of TAC.

Other papers consider the problem of designing negotiation protocols and strategies. Fatima and Wooldridge study how the agenda influences the outcome of sequential, multi-issue negotiations, and discuss how to set the optimal agenda in such settings.

Di Napoli et al. propose a protocol for market-based negotiation for QoS-aware service selection. Moreover, a range of papers consider novel market settings, where agent-based and automated bidding techniques can be applied. deCastro and Parsons propose a model in which securities markets are modeled as a society of heterogeneous trading agents. Jumadinova and Dasgupta model distributed prediction markets through weighted Bayesian graphical games, while Greenwald et al. provide an empirical analysis of profits in QuiBids in penny auctions. Hafizoglu and Sen consider the problem of fairness and incentives of profit sharing schemes in group buying. Finally, Miyashita investigate the design of an online double auction for perishable goods, motivated by the practical problem of designing fresh fish markets in Japan.

We hope that the papers included will offer the reader an insight into the state of the art in research on electronic markets, performed in the multi-agent systems and artificial intelligence communities in the past 2 years.

To conclude, we would like to thank everyone who contributed to this volume, including the paper authors, the members of the program committees of the three workshops, who provided comprehensive reviews to ensure the high quality of the selected papers, and the participants themselves, who engaged in lively discussions during the workshops.

October 2014

Sofia Ceppi
Esther David
Vedran Podobnik
Valentin Robu
Onn Shehory
Sebastian Stein
Ioannis A. Vetsikas

Organization

TADA&AMEC Workshop Organizers

Sofia Ceppi	Microsoft Research, UK
Esther David	Ashkelon Academic College, Israel
Vedran Podobnik	University of Zagreb, Croatia
Valentin Robu	University of Southampton, UK
Onn Shehory	IBM Haifa Research Lab, Israel
Sebastian Stein	University of Southampton, UK
Ioannis A. Vetsikas	NCSR Demokritos, Greece

Program Committee

Bo An	University of Southern California, USA
Michal Chalamish	Ashkelon Academic College, Israel
Maria Chli	Aston University, UK
John Collins	University of Minnesota, USA
Shaheen Fatima	Loughborough University, UK
Enrico Gerding	University of Southampton, UK
Maria Gini	University of Minnesota, USA
Amy Greenwald	Brown University, USA
Minghua He	Aston University, UK
Gordan Jezic	University of Zagreb, Croatia
Patrick R. Jordan	Microsoft, USA
Radu Jurca	Google Inc., Switzerland
Wolfgang Ketter	Erasmus University, The Netherlands
Christopher Kiekintveld	University of Texas at El Paso, USA
Jérôme Lang	LAMSADE, France
Kate Larson	University of Waterloo, Canada
Ignac Lovrek	University of Zagreb, Croatia
Peter McBurney	King's College London, UK
Pericles Mitkas	Aristotle University of Thessaloniki, Greece
Jinzhong Niu	City University of New York, USA
David Pardoe	Yahoo! Labs, USA
Simon Parsons	Brooklyn College, USA
Zinovi Rabinovich	Bar-Ilan University, Israel
Juan Antonio Rodriguez Aguilar	IIIA-CSIC, Spain
Alex Rogers	University of Southampton, UK
Harry Rose	University of Southampton, UK
Jeffrey Rosenschein	The Hebrew University of Jerusalem, Israel

Norman Sadeh   Carnegie Mellon University, USA
Alberto Sardinha   Carnegie Mellon University, USA
David Sarne   Bar-Ilan University, Israel
Lampros C. Stavrogiannis University of Southampton, UK
Andreas Symeonidis   Aristotle University of Thessaloniki, Greece
Krunoslav Trzec   Ericsson Nikola Tesla, Croatia
Michael Wellman   University of Michigan, USA
Dongmo Zhang   University of Western Sydney, Australia

Contents

An Analysis of Power Trading Agent Competition 2014

Jurica Babic[✉] and Vedran Podobnik

Faculty of Electrical Engineering and Computing, University of Zagreb,
Unska 3, HR-10000 Zagreb, Croatia
{jurica.babic,vedran.podobnik}@fer.hr
http://agents.tel.fer.hr

Abstract. This paper provides insights into performance of competing agents in Power Trading Agent Competition finals held in May 2014. Firstly, the paper gives the description of the Power TAC post-game data set and presents our analysis process. Furthermore, paper discusses the analysis output: indicators about brokers performance in energy retail market, energy wholesale market as well as the balancing process. Results of the analysis identified diverse approaches in the design of competing agents strategies.

Keywords: Trading agents · Energy markets · Competition · Analysis · Power Trading Agent Competition

1 Introduction

The current electrical power systems switch from the traditional producer-centric grid to the advanced consumer-centric grid called the smart grid [1,2]. Not only will consumers with installed smart metering equipment be able to adjust their consumption habits according to market price signals received from the smart grid, but also, thanks to new technological solutions, will those consumers become an essential element in real-time alignment of energy demand and supply within the local area. To allow for efficient control of such complex system, retail consumers will be aggregated in the virtual power plants. An example of a planned virtual power plant project is the four-year, 21 million EcoGrid project for the Danish island of Bornholm [3].

However, in addition to technical aspects of the smart grid, the establishment of a supporting market system is crucial. Consequently, what smart grid ecosystem currently lacks in addition to technical infrastructure is an efficient set of market mechanisms. In order to avoid bad market design once smart grids

---

This paper uses Power Trading Agent Competition (Power TAC) analysis framework originally described in the paper "An Analysis of Power TAC 2013 Trial" presented at the "Workshop on Trading Agent Design and Analysis (TADA 2013) @ AAAI 2013" for analysis of the Power TAC 2014 finals.

© Springer International Publishing Switzerland 2014
S. Ceppi et al. (Eds.): AMEC/TADA 2013 and 2014, LNBIP 187, pp. 1–15, 2014.
DOI: 10.1007/978-3-319-13218-1_1

are going to be widely deployed, it is necessary to provide a risk-free environment for testing market policies. The Power Trading Agent Competition (Power TAC, http://powertac.org) is an open, competitive market simulation platform that addresses the need for policy guidance based on robust research result on the structure and operation of retail electrical energy markets [4]. Power TAC extends the portfolio of TAC games [5], open simulations that have counterpoised agent-based computational economics (ACE) [6] as alternative to traditional game-theoretic approaches for testing policies for complex systems [7,8]. The trading agent in Power TAC game is business entity (or broker) that can fulfill the real-life role of energy retailer in the smart grid environment. Agents task is to provide energy to consumers through tariff offerings, and then manage its consumer portfolio loads by trading in a wholesale market.

This paper describes our approach to Power TAC game analysis and provides insights into performance of each of the competing agents in Power TAC 2014 finals. The remainder of this paper is organized as follows. Firstly, we provide brief description of the game scenario in Sect. 2. Afterwards, Power TAC data set used as input for analysis, as well as steps in processing Power TAC data to provide performance indicators, are described in Sect. 3. Derived performance indicators are presented and discussed in the Sect. 4. Section 5 concludes the paper with the final remarks about the Power TAC 2014 finals.

2   Power Trading Agent Competition

The traditional power systems are defined through the *energy layer* that includes functionalities of energy *production, transmission, distribution* and *consumption.* The vertical extension of the single-layered traditional power systems with the *information and communications technology (ICT) layer* enables real-time integration of smart grid components and synchronous two-way communication among stakeholders in the power systems. It is believed that the "Internet of energy" [9] will be developed due to use of ICT in energy distribution systems. Consequently, the smart grid ecosystem extends the traditional power grid with various advanced functionalities that are superior to the traditional energy layer functionalities: new client-side functionalities are *smart metering* and *demand-side management,* while the grid operator can benefit from new functionalities such as *grid balancing* and *real-time monitoring* of the grid.

Multi-layered smart grid architecture along with its functionalities and correspondent resource flows is depicted in Fig. 1. However, to facilitate the evolution from traditional power systems towards smart grid ecosystem, establishment of the supporting market system is of great importance.

Power TAC is a simulation platform which deals with the market layer of the smart grid architecture. The major elements of its scenario are shown in Fig. 2. The main element, a competitive trading agent, is a self-interested *broker* that aggregates energy supply and demand with the intent of earning a profit. The majority of brokers' energy supply is obtained through the use of a *wholesale market.* Brokers must build a good-quality portfolio of *retail customers*

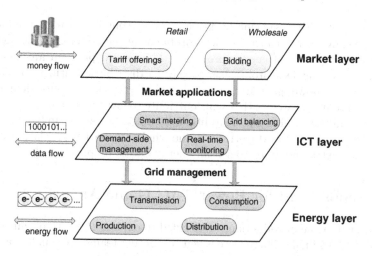

Fig. 1. A multi-layered smart grid functional architecture.

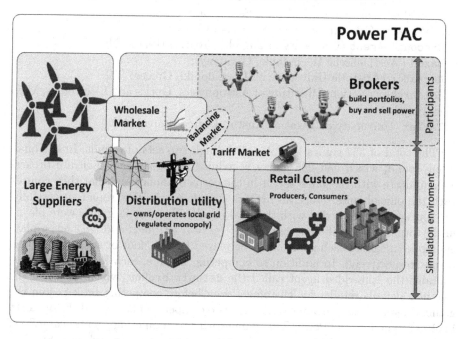

Fig. 2. Elements of Power TAC scenario.

(i.e. consumers and producers) by offering carefully designed tariffs through *tariff market* [10]. Good-quality portfolio implies having tariff subscriptions that are profitable and can be real-time balanced. However, the specific consumption and production capacities broker has acquired through the tariff market will almost certainly cause imbalance in brokers' energy supply and demand, causing two negative impacts. First, specific broker imbalance contributes to the imbalance of the whole power grid, causing serious problems in the power grid management and lowers the quality of energy provision. The second problem are less-than-attractive balancing fees broker has to pay to distribution utility for causing imbalance of the power grid. Because of described reasons, a profit-oriented broker will tend to use strategies that will contribute to low energy imbalance caused its activities in the tariff market. Additionally, to tackle energy imbalance problem, brokers are encouraged to trade in the wholesale market by placing bids to acquire some extra energy or to sell an energy excess by placing asks.

3   Methods Used for Power TAC Game Analysis

As mentioned in the introduction, we decided to explore the data obtained from Power TAC 2014 finals. There were seven competing teams (hereinafter a *broker* or *agent* are used interchangeably) participating in finals:

- AgentUDE (Universitaet Duisburg-Essen, Germany);
- cwiBroker (CWI Amsterdam, Netherlands) [11];
- CrocodileAgent (University of Zagreb, Croatia) [10, 12–14];
- Maxon (Westfaelische Hochschule, Germany);
- Mertacor (Aristotle University of Thessaloniki, Greece) [15];
- coldbroker (National Institute of Astrophysics, Optics and Electronics, Mexico); and
- TacTex (University of Texas at Austin, United States) [16].

   The total of 357 games was played through two sets of rounds. In the qualifying round, which had 285 games scheduled, the goal was to ensure brokers communicate with the game server in the correct manner and that they comply with the official rules. Since all brokers completed the first round successfully, the tournament proceeded with the final round. The next 72 games were played in the form of three different game sizes: *(i) two*; *(ii) four*; and *(iii) seven* players mode (meaning each game could be played by two, four or seven competing teams, respectively). In addition to competing brokers, each Power TAC game contains the embedded agent called the default broker, which serves in the role of a default retailer for customers even before competing brokers join the game. Therefore, we use *gameSize3* (i.e., two competing players and the default broker) to denote the Power TAC game with two competing agents, *gameSize5* to denote the Power TAC game with four competing agents and *gameSize8* to denote the Power TAC game with seven competing agents.

   Additionally, we observed that there were five different game sizes instead of three as described earlier in this paper. The reason for this is the way tournament scheduler works in case there are some problems with one of brokers (i.e. the game will continue without the malfunctioning broker). Careful investigation showed that Mertacor broker failed to participate in a couple of games. Even so, those games were included in the tournament level analysis.

The output of each Power TAC game is a set of logs for debugging (i.e., trace log) and game exploration (i.e., state log) purposes. As the name implies, the state log keeps track about all changes to the game state and enables ex-post analysis of brokers, customers and markets. The chosen input for the analysis process are state logs from all games of the final round of Power TAC 2014 finals.

It is important to mention that the TacTex had some issues in the tournament and was therefore excluded from the final rankings. Nevertheless, state logs contain data from all games and thus the analysis presented in this paper takes into consideration performances of all brokers.

Power TAC research community developed an open-source database model called the Power TAC Logfile Analysis (PLA)[1] for storing the data from completed games. The PLA contains a script for state log conversion and a procedure for importing the data from converted state logs. In the analysis process we used:

- PLA as means to represent the data from Power TAC 2014 games in a structured manner; and
- R^2 for calculating Key Performance Indicators (KPIs).

The discussion on the selected KPIs is given in the next section.

4 Power TAC 2014 Results and Discussion

Brokers performance can be observed from various perspectives. The overall performance of the competing brokers is measured through the *profit* they achieve in the end of the Power TAC game. However, in order to facilitate comparison of brokers performances in games of different sizes, results are normalized for every game size and the final winner of the tournament is the broker with the highest total (normalized) score.

Table 1. Official normalized scores of the Power TAC 2014 finals

Broker	*gameSize3*	*gameSize5*	*gameSize8*	Total
AgentUDE	1.976	1.499	0.279	3.754
cwiBroker	0.600	1.026	1.557	3.183
CrocodileAgent	−0.560	−0.893	0.952	−0.501
Maxon	−0.643	0.142	−0.921	−1.423
Mertacor	−0.865	−0.492	−0.945	−2.302
coldbroker	−0.509	−1.281	−0.922	−2.712

---

[1] Power TAC Logfile Analysis is developed by Markus Peters, Rotterdam School of Management, Erasmus University. The software is available on http://bitbucket.org/markuspeters/pla.

[2] R is a free software environment for statistical computing and graphics. The software is available on http://www.r-project.org/.

Table 1 shows the official normalized scores of the Power TAC 2014 finals and reveals that brokers `AgentUDE` and `cwiBroker` performed the best. The aim of this work is to complement official normalized scores for the 2014 tournament with a set of KPIs to provide more detailed insights on competing brokers. That being said, in the remainder of the section we will explain reasons that stand behind presented final results by examining brokers performance in several categories: *retail market, wholesale market* and *balancing process*.

4.1 Retail Market

Retail market is a place where brokers offer their services to retail customers. Since the typical game configuration tends to have much more consumers than producers, brokers are expected to focus on making attractive consumption tariffs which are suitable for various types of consumers. The attractiveness of consumption tariffs offered by various brokers is presented in Fig. 3.

The aforementioned figure presents the total energy consumed by customers from each of brokers. The consumption shares correlate with the final rankings because the consumption share sizes follow the order of the official normalized scores. The exception is `TacTex` which was excluded from the final rankings and `coldBroker`. This insight is somewhat expected because the majority income from the brokers comes from the retail consumption.

Figure 4 present the total energy produced by customers from each of brokers. Since the pie chart only consists of shares from `CrocodileAgent`, `AgentUDE`

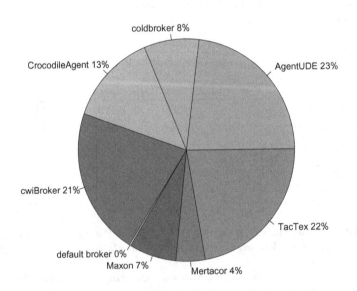

Fig. 3. Brokers energy consumption shares in the retail market.

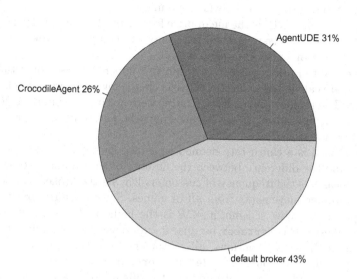

Fig. 4. Brokers energy production shares in the retail market.

and `default broker` it is interesting to point out none of remaining agents were able to secure at least one retail production transaction. This means other brokers were forced to acquire all of the needed energy on the wholesale market exclusively.

Table 2. Brokers retail performance

Broker	$\mu_{retPriceCons}$ [€¢/kWh]	$\mu_{retPriceProd}$ [€¢/kWh]	CR [%]	$N_{tariffs}$	TPG
AgentUDE	6,0	1,5	9,41	3725	90,9
coldbroker	4,6	NA	15,30	606	14,8
CrocodileAgent	7,8	1,6	12,41	1073	26,8
cwiBroker	6,7	NA	10,92	1041	25,4
default broker	50,0	1,5	1036,03	142	2,0
Maxon	7,9	NA	15,11	1394	34,0
Mertacor	6,6	NA	60,16	2636	73,2
TacTex	5,8	NA	11,69	1617	40,4

Further insights regarding brokers performance on retail market can be explored with the help of Table 2. The $\mu_{retPriceCons}$ KPI indicates what was the mean price for the retail energy sold to customers. The brokers which have a high consumption share (see Fig. 3) also have lower mean prices for the consumption. Despite the fact this behaviour may infer the lower profit margins, judging from the final rankings (see Table 1) the key to success on the finals was, along with the high consumption share, the balance between broker's portfolio management and trading on the wholesale market.

The $\mu_{retPriceProd}$ KPI is the mean price for the production tariffs. The values suggest the same conclusion as the Fig. 4: only two competing brokers were able to secure at least one retail production trade.

The mean retail prices presented within this paper are based on retail transactions and are calculated as a ratio between charge for the energy bought or sold and energy. The periodic payments for tariffs were not included in the calculation of $\mu_{retPriceCons}$ and $\mu_{retPriceProd}$ because periodic payments are represented as separated transactions.

The CR KPI is a churn rate defined as a ratio between the number of lost customers and the difference between the number of gained and lost customers. This KPI measures the frequency of customers leaving the broker by taking into account customer movements from all of games. Since `default broker` has a non-competitive pricing scheme, its CR is the highest. The competing broker with the highest CR is `Mertacor` because it experienced a few of disconnections during games. In such situations, all customers from the disconnected agent switch to default tariffs offered by `default broker`.

The $N_{tariffs}$ KPI is a total number of tariffs offered by brokers while the TPG KPI is the average number of tariffs offered by broker per game. It is worth mentioning that `AgentUDE` as the best performing agent had the most aggressive strategy on the retail market: the TPG value of 90.9 suggest `AgentUDE` on average published a new tariff specification every $16\,h^3$.

The final remark about the retail performance is about the evolution of the retail price depending on the game size. Results from Table 3 indicate all competing agents decrease their retail consumption prices with the increase of the game size. This is not the case with production retail prices as all agents offer similar prices in all game sizes.

Table 3. Mean retail prices per games sizes

Broker	Consumption			Production		
$\mu_{retPrice}$ [€¢/kWh]	gameSize3	gameSize5	gameSize8	gameSize3	gameSize5	gameSize8
AgentUDE	8,4	5,7	5,2	1,5	1,5	1,5
coldbroker	5,7	3,9	3,5	NA	NA	NA
CrocodileAgent	8,1	6,9	6,6	1,6	1,6	1,6
cwiBroker	12,9	5,8	5,4	NA	NA	NA
default broker	50,0	50,0	50,0	1,5	1,5	1,5
Maxon	9,1	7,2	7,8	NA	NA	NA
Mertacor	6,8	6,6	6,5	NA	NA	NA
TacTex	8,0	5,8	5,0	NA	NA	NA

---

[3] Based on assumption the game on average lasts for 60 days or 1440 h.

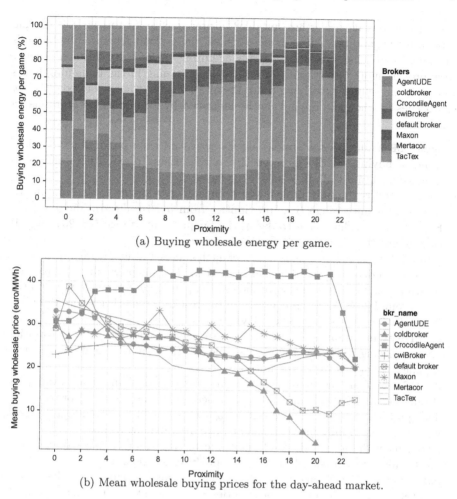

(a) Buying wholesale energy per game.

(b) Mean wholesale buying prices for the day-ahead market.

Fig. 5. Wholesale buying patterns.

4.2 Wholesale Market

Reliable wholesale price predictions as well as the ability to anticipate the net load from customers are the prerequisites for successful trading in a day-ahead wholesale market[4]. The variety of strategies used can be identified by inspecting brokers total net volume of traded energy decomposed over the 24 h interval.

Figure 5 provides insights on wholesale buying patterns each of brokers usually performed during one game. The rightmost values on horizontal axis suggest best performing agents, i.e., AgentUDE, TacTex and cwiBroker managed to secure most of the energy for their customers at an early stage. Under assumption

---

[4] In the day-ahead market, contracts are made between seller and buyer for the delivery of power in the next 24 h (i.e. the price is set and the trade is agreed).

that such wholesale trades are suitable[5], a prerequisite for this kind of trading pattern is the good prediction model for both energy load generated by broker's customers and wholesale prices. Early acquiring of majority required energy gives brokers more opportunities for fine-tuned trading in the remaining hours and even for selling extra energy at the price higher than acquired. Diverse approaches in wholesale buying can be identified by examining both graphs on Fig. 5:

- AgentUDE maintains the similar shares across all time proximities. It has a trend of buying slightly more energy at the closing proximities which is in contrast with most of other brokers.
- coldBroker is the only broker which buys energy almost exclusively in the middle proximity range (i.e., proximities from 5–16 h ahead). Judging from Fig. 5(b) it even has some trades in the far proximity range (16–23 h ahead) at very low (i.e., less than 10 €/MWh) prices.
- CrocodileAgent [14] tries to secure enough energy in the far proximity range and it has a declining trend of energy share as the time proximity goes to zero. Its wholesale buying trades were the most expensive in the whole tournament (i.e., around 40 €/MWh in contrast to the rest of the market where the price is usually set at less than 30 €/MWh).
- cwiBroker maintains similar buying shares across majority time proximities and its pricing pattern is the most stable as prices on average do not change significantly across time proximities.
- default broker has most of trades in close and medium time proximities (from 0 to 16 h ahead) and its prices increase towards closing proximities. This pattern suggest there were quite a few games where competing brokers were not able to fully lure customers away from default tariffs.
- Maxon have the lowest share of wholesale buying trades and its prices were mostly higher than rest of brokers except CrocodileAgent.
- Mertacor have a strong peak of trading at time proximity 22. Its prices increase towards the closing proximities and it is interesting to notice that Mertacor was not able to score a single trade at time proximities 0, 1 and 23.
- TacTex have most trades at the furthest time proximity and it maintains its buying shares across most of time proximities. Consistent with most of brokers, its prices increases as the time proximity goes to zero.

Since the main purpose of the wholesale market is for brokers to match energy load from their consumers by buying on the wholesale market, wholesale selling patterns are different than corresponding buying patterns. Figure 6 supplements previous graphs by giving insights on wholesale selling patterns:

- AgentUDE, along with CrocodileAgent, is the only competing broker which offers wholesale energy at the furthest time proximity.
- coldBroker scores selling trades in the close proximity range (i.e., up to time proximity 8) and its prices are the second best.

---

[5] Wholesale trades are suitable if they match the energy load generated by the customers and the price follows the mean wholesale price.

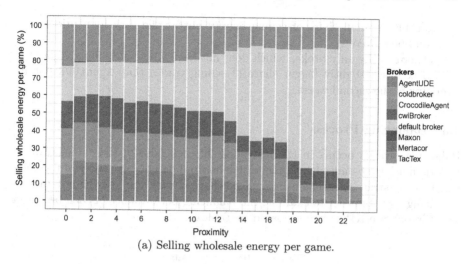

(a) Selling wholesale energy per game.

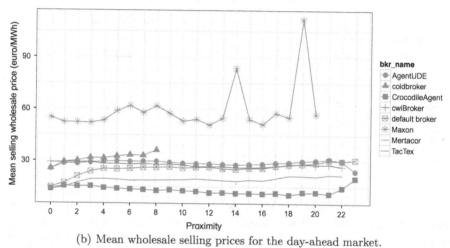

(b) Mean wholesale selling prices for the day-ahead market.

Fig. 6. Wholesale selling patterns

- CrocodileAgent increases its selling share towards closing proximities and prices are the lowest of all other brokers.
- cwiBroker has among best selling shares and, similar to its buying pattern, its prices seem to be pretty constant across all proximities (i.e., around 30 €/MWh). Also, by comparing its buying and selling prices one can conclude that cwiBroker is making a profit on the wholesale market since on average selling prices are higher than correspondent buying prices.
- default broker has the majority share of selling trades on the wholesale markets and its prices are pretty constant with a slight decline towards the close proximity range.

- `Maxon` has a small share of selling energy but at the very high prices (i.e., around 60 €/MWh).
- `Mertacor` is the only broker which does not have wholesale selling trades.
- `TacTex` has a slightly bigger share of selling trades than `AgentUDE` but its pricing is the second worst.

4.3 Balancing Process

Balancing process occurs in the last phase of each hour of the game. Brokers that do not have balanced customer portfolios and do not have successful wholesale bidding strategy mechanisms will be charged with the less than attractive balancing cost. In order to examine the balancing performance of each broker, a set of imbalance KPIs were prepared in Table 4.

Table 4. Imbalance stats

Broker	$\mu_{imbalance}$ [kWh]	$\mu_{imbalancePrice}$ [€¢/kWh]	$RMS_{imbalance}$ [kWh]
AgentUDE	60	3,9	6110
coldbroker	−9766	5,7	12077
CrocodileAgent	−4715	5,2	7357
cwiBroker	−1730	4,2	5103
default broker	−267	4,5	2589
Maxon	−2943	4,2	9660
Mertacor	−221	4,1	4694
TacTex	−2123	4,2	4335

The $\mu_{imbalance}$ KPI is the mean per-hour imbalance each of brokers had during the 2014 finals and it is measured in kWh. This KPI provides a good insight on whether the broker was mostly negatively (i.e., energy deficit) or positively (i.e., energy surplus) imbalanced. The results suggest `coldBroker`, `CrocodileAgent` and `Maxon` were the most negatively imbalanced. A reasonably imbalanced were `default broker` and `Mertacor` although results may sound better than they were since both of brokers had very little shares on the retail market. Top performing brokers in the retail market and wholesale market; `TacTex`, `cwiBroker` and `AgentUDE`; also dominated in the balancing process.

$RMS_{imbalance}$ is the root mean square per-hour imbalance measured in kWh. This KPI complement the first one since it neglects the importance of positive and negative values but it is more sensitive to outliers. With the $\mu_{imbalance}$, a broker can have a good score even it has extreme negative and positive imbalances. The results are consistent with prices being paid for imbalances and the KPI confirms that best performing brokers `AgentUDE`, `TacTex` and `cwiBroker` indeed had the best energy balancing.

The $\mu_{imbalancePrice}$ KPI is the mean per-hour price brokers paid for one kWh of imbalanced energy. Due to the use of balancing algorithm in which brokers

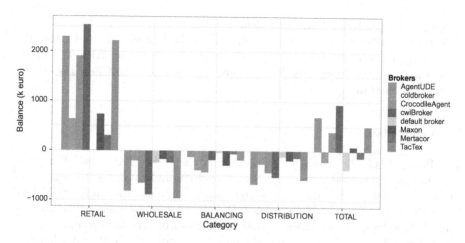

Fig. 7. Brokers balance profiles per game.

with the bigger imbalance pay more, mean imbalance prices are consistent with corresponding imbalance energy. Best performing broker `AgentUDE` had by far the lowest imbalance price (i.e., 39 €/MWh) while two worst imbalanced brokers `coldBroker` and `CrocodileAgent` had to pay 57 €/MWh and 52 €/MWh respectively.

Dependencies among discussed performance on wholesale market, retail market and balancing process can be seen in Fig. 7. All brokers achieved positive retail balance (i.e. sum of all tariff transactions, both with consumers and producers) meaning they were actually making profit on the retail market. This is expected since the majority of retail population is consumption-driven, meaning most of customers pay to brokers for using the electricity. Retail balance also correlates to final rankings: best ranked brokers topped the retail balance, and vice versa. It is also interesting to see how the best performing brokers had large costs on the wholesale market which paid off during the balancing process. In contrast, `coldBroker` had lower costs on the wholesale market but experienced substantial costs for the imbalance. `Mertacor` and `default broker` had lowest balancing costs, due to the fact they had a limited market share. `AgentUDE` was able to win the finals over `cwiBroker` and `TacTex` thanks to better wholesale performance and consequently lower balancing cost. A quick observation of retail balance and distribution costs from these brokers confirms `cwiBroker` had a larger positive retail balance and lower distribution cost than `AgenUDE`, meaning `cwiBroker` has managed to charge bigger margin for its services than `AgentUDE`. This all leads to a clue that `cwiBroker` had somewhat more optimized retail strategy than `AgentUDE`. Finally, the total balance profile from Fig. 7 is somewhat inconsistent with the official final rankings. There are several reasons for this:

– The official normalized scores are calculated by combining results from various game sizes.

- TacTex was excluded from the official results.
- The total balance profile sums retail, wholesale, distribution and balancing transactions without taking into account the interest rate. Also, the graph shows average per-game results and thus do not require to follow the results from the final rankings.

5   Conclusions

The Power TAC 2014 finals have proven that the Power TAC simulation platform produces analyzable results which can help in understanding the impact of different market participants. The seven competing teams confronted their brokers in both qualifying and final rounds. We analyzed performances of competing brokers by taking into consideration all state logs from the final round.

Different brokers implemented distinct behaviours in retail and wholesale markets, as well as during balancing process. Judging from the presented analysis, AgentUDE topped the retail energy consumption share thanks to its aggressive tariff offerings (i.e., on average, AgentUDE offered a new tariff each 16 h). Interesting to note is that only two competing brokers, AgentUDE and CrocodileAgent, managed to secure shares in the retail production. The wholesale market shares correspond to both retail shares and final rankings. There also seems to be a trend of increasing wholesale prices as the time proximity goes towards zero.

The results suggest that, although retail performance correlates with the final rankings, the winning formula for a successful broker is in balancing between the portfolio management and wholesale trading strategies. This in turn helps brokers to minimize the less-than-attractive balancing costs imposed by the balancing process. Encouraging results from the analysed finals, along with the increasing number of research teams who participate in the annual tournament cycle, promise that Power TAC is on its way to become a high-quality testbed for exploring power markets of the future.

Acknowledgements. The authors acknowledge the support of the research project "Managing Trust and Coordinating Interactions in Smart Networks of People, Machines and Organizations", funded by the Croatian Science Foundation.

Furthermore, authors thank Power TAC game master for organizing Power TAC 2014 as well as competing teams for participation.

References

1. Ipakchi, A., Albuyeh, F.: Grid of the future. IEEE Power Energy Mag. **7**(2), 52–62 (2009)
2. Ramchurn, S.D., Vytelingum, P., Rogers, A., Jennings, N.R.: Putting the 'smarts' into the smart grid. Commun. ACM **55**, 86 (2012)
3. Kumagai, J.: Virtual power plants real power. IEEE Spectr. **49**(3), 13–14 (2012)
4. Ketter, W., Collins, J., Reddy, P.P., Weerdt, M.D.: The 2013 Power Trading Agent Competition, May 2013

5. Collins, J., Ketter, W., Sadeh, N.: Pushing the limits of rational agents: the trading agent competition for supply chain management. AI Mag. **31**(2), 63–80 (2010)
6. Shun-kun, Y., Jia-hai, Y.: Agent-based computational economics: methodology and its application in electricity market research. In: 7th International Power Engineering Conference (IPEC 2005), pp. 1–5 (2005)
7. Mohsenian-Rad, A.H., Wong, V.W.S., Jatskevich, J., Schober, R., Leon-Garcia, A.: Autonomous demand-side management based on game-theoretic energy consumption scheduling for the future smart grid. IEEE Trans. Smart Grid **1**, 320–331 (2010)
8. Babic, J., Podobnik, V.: Energy informatics in smart grids: agent based modelling of electricity markets. In: Third Conference on Future Energy Business and Energy Informatics, Rotterdam, The Netherlands, pp. 1–15 (2014)
9. BMWi: E-Energy - IKT-basiertes Energiesystem der Zukunft. Stand (2008)
10. Matetic, S., Babic, J., Matijas, M., Petric, A., Podobnik, V.: The CrocodileAgent 2012: negotiating agreements in a smart grid tariff market. In: Proceedings of the 1st International Conference on Agreement Technologies (AT 2012) (2012)
11. Liefers, B., Hoogland, J., La Poutr, H.: A successful broker agent for power TAC. In: Proceedings of the 2014 Workshop on Agent-Mediated Electronic Commerce Trading Agent Design and Analysis (AMEC/TADA 2014) @ AAMAS 2014 (2014)
12. Babic, J., Matetic, S., Matijas, M., Buljevic, I., Pranjic, I., Mijic, M., Augustinovic, M.: The CrocodileAgent 2012: research for efficient agent-based electricity trading mechanisms. In: Special Session on Trading Agent Competition, KES-AMSTA 2012, Dubrovnik, Croatia (2012)
13. Buljevic, I., Pranjic, I., Mijic, M., Babic, J., Petric, A., Podobnik, V.: The CrocodileAgent 2012: reaching agreements in a simulation of a smart grid wholesale market. In: Proceedings of the 1st International Conference on Agreement Technologies (AT 2012), pp. 111–112 (2012)
14. Babic, J., Podobnik, V.: Adaptive bidding for electricity wholesale markets in a smart grid. In: Ceppi, S., David, E., Robu, V., Shehory O., Vetsikas, I. (eds.) Proceedings of the 2014 Workshop on Agent-Mediated Electronic Commerce Trading Agent Design and Analysis (AMEC/TADA 2014) @ AAMAS 2014, Paris, France, pp. 1–14 (2014)
15. Ntagka, E., Chrysopoulos, A., Mitkas, P.: Designing tariffs in a competitive energy market using particle swarm optimization techniques. In: Proceedings of the 2014 Workshop on Agent-Mediated Electronic Commerce Trading Agent Design and Analysis (AMEC/TADA 2014) @ AAMAS 2014, Paris, France (2014)
16. Urieli, D., Stone, P.: TacTex'13: a champion adaptive power trading agent. In: Proceedings of the Twenty-Eighth Conference on Artificial Intelligence (AAAI 2014) (2014)

Towards Modeling Securities Markets as a Society of Heterogeneous Trading Agents

Paulo André Lima de Castro[1]($\boxtimes$) and Simon Parsons[2]

[1] Technological Institute of Aeronautics - ITA, São José dos Campos, SP, Brazil
pauloac@ita.br
[2] Department of Computer and Information Science, Brooklyn College,
City University of New York, 2900 Bedford Avenue, Brooklyn, NY 11210, USA
parsons@sci.brooklyn.cuny.edu

Abstract. In recent article, Farmer and Foley [1] claimed that the agent-based modeling may be a better way to help guide financial policies than traditional mathematical models. The authors argue that such models can accurately predict short periods ahead as long as the scenario remains almost the same, but fail in times of high volatility. Another real world problem that is rarely addressed in agent-based modeling is the fact that humans do not make decisions under risk strictly based on expected utility. This context inspired the goal of this work: modeling trading agents to populate an artificial market and use it to predict market price evolution in high and low volatility periods. We developed a set of simple trading agents and executed a set of simulated experiments to evaluate their performance. The simulated experiments showed that the artificial market prediction performance is better for low volatility periods than for higher volatility periods. Furthermore, this observation suggests that in high volatility period trading agent strategies are influenced by some other factor that is not present or is smaller in other period. These facts lead us to believe that in high volatility period human agents can be influenced by psychological biases. We also propose in this paper one simple trading agent model that includes prospect theory concepts in his decision making process. We intend to use such model in future work.

Keywords: Multiagent systems · Artificial markets · Prospect theory · Agent based computational finance

1 Introduction

Farmer and Foley [1] stated that agent based modeling could be a better way to help guide financial policies, than traditional models. They have grouped such traditional models in two big groups: (1) empirical statistical models that are fitted to previously collected data and (2) dynamic stochastic general equilibrium. They argue that the first group methods can successfully forecast short periods ahead "as long things stay more or less the same", but they fail when there are

© Springer International Publishing Switzerland 2014
S. Ceppi et al. (Eds.): AMEC/TADA 2013 and 2014, LNBIP 187, pp. 16–25, 2014.
DOI: 10.1007/978-3-319-13218-1_2

great changes in the market scenario. The second group methods adopt convenient assumptions ("...assume a perfect world..." [1]) that simplify the problem. This way, they avoid two much complexity, that could make such problem cumbersome or intractable mathematically. However, the authors [1] claim these assumptions can make such models almost useless in high volatility periods, because these assumptions would be far from reality at the time.

In fact, as stated by Phelps et al. in [2], "...in traditional mechanism design problem, analytical methods are used to prove that agents' game-theoretically optimal strategies lead to socially desirable outcomes...however, there are many situations in which the underlying assumptions of the theory are violated due to the messiness of the real-world..." This real-world messiness makes analytical methods hard to use or even impossible. However, the acceptance of suboptimal solutions and the use of iterative refinement methods can hopefully treat this complexity. In fact, significant research work has been carried out in automated mechanism design to overcome the complexity of creating mechanisms with some desirable features for situations inspired by real-word. Niu et al. in [3] simulate agents able to trade in several possible markets.

However, several problems may be identified in agent based modeling. For instance, it is hard to know how to specify the rules agents should use to make their decisions. Furthermore, it is possible that in volatile periods the rules are different or at least, slightly altered by components that are not present in normal periods. In order to address this question we developed a set of simple trading agents and simulated an artificial stock market in order to predict market price evolution. The rest of this paper is organized as follows. The next Sect. 2, describes our simple artificial market model and the trading agents that were used in the simulated experiments. These experiments are explained in Sect. 3 and their results are presented in Sect. 4 and analyzed in Sect. 5. As a result of this analysis, we propose a new approach to modeling trading agents in Sect. 6. It is interesting to note that the main motivation for such approach is reduce the market price prediction error by a better description of how human traders act rather than achieving better financial results in trading.

2   Our Simple Artificial Market Model

Our approach for modeling markets is based on the following assumptions. The market price behavior is defined by the interactions among trader agents, i.e. their buy and sell orders. The trading agents' strategies may be classified in two big groups: fundamentalist and technical strategies. The first group assumes that the stock prices reflect the company's economic fundamentals, such as profit, market share and so on. The second group assumes that stock prices change according to some patterns and therefore it is possible to identify price trends analyzing past price behavior. Furthermore, the time is modeled as a discrete value that increases through the simulation session. The amount of resources traded by the agents and their orders define the stock price at each instant t as described in Sect. 2.1.

We implemented three types of traders — **fundamentalist** traders, who have a fixed idea of the value of a good based on historical data, **technical** traders, who trade when the direction of price change alters (so, for example, they sell when the price stops raising) and **market making** agents who provides liquidity to the market. They do that using the last market price to establish a buy order at the last price minus a certain spread and a sell order at last price plus the same spread. This way market making agent provides a lower and upper limits to the price, but the main reason for those agents are the same that makes some companies hire market makers in real stock markets, which is to avoid that someone that wants to buy or sell the stock is forbidden because there is no counterpart to close the deal.

In our model, we compare the price defined by our artificial society, a set of fundamentalist, technical and market making agents, with actual prices obtained real stock exchange. The difference between the simulated and actual price is a prediction error (Sect. 2.2). We use an algorithm based on hill climbing algorithm to adjust the artificial society parameters in order to reduce this prediction error, as detailed in Sect. 2.3.

2.1 Market Price Formation

The price predicted by the artificial market, $\overline{P_t}$, is determined by the buy and sell orders given by the set of trader agents present in stock market that acts as a continuous double auction. The clearing process is performed by the Four heap algorithm described in [4]. In order to execute a deal, the sell price needs to be lower than the buy price and the transaction price is defined as the average of both prices. The transaction volume is the smaller volume, but higher volume order remains in the book for posterior execution, see [4] for further details.

The market price for a given instant of time is defined as the average of all transaction prices weighted by the volume of each transaction. That way, one agent that gives a higher volume order is more relevant to the market price formation than other agent that submits small volume orders. One order is defined by its price, purpose (sell or buy) and volume. For simplicity, the volume is defined as an integer number of shares.

2.2 Prediction Error

The absolute difference between the price defined by the simulated transactions, that we call *internal price* and the price observed in the corresponding instant t at the real market, the so called *external price*, is the prediction error for a given instant of time t. The Fig. 1 presents a example of simulation session with historical prices from one real market. However, the prediction error of a period of time is much more relevant than just one moment to state that one artificial market specification is better adapted than other one. Therefore, we need to define formally what a better prediction in a defined time period, in order to make possible the comparisons among artificial market specifications. We define the prediction error at a given instant t, as:

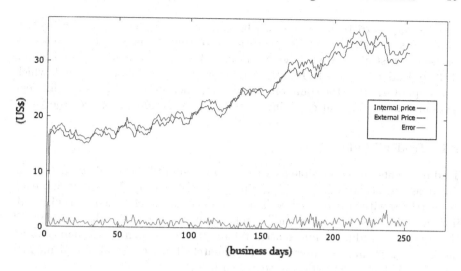

Fig. 1. Simulation session example with price evolution and error

$$E_t = |\overline{P_t} - P_t| \tag{1}$$

In Eq. 1, $\overline{P_t}$ refers to the price predicted by one artificial market in instant t, while P_t refers to the price observed in the real market. For a given time period, we define the **session prediction error** (E), as the sum of the quadratic error at each round, Eq. 2. If one artificial market specification M provides a smaller session error (E), than another artificial market specification, then we may say that artificial market M is a better description or predictor than the other.

$$E = \sum_{t=1}^{N} (\overline{P_t} - P_t)^2 \tag{2}$$

It is worth noting that any change in the market specification does not alter traders' strategy, but their relevance to the market price definition as described in Sect. 2.1. Given any trading strategy, it is possible to perform market adjustment, and such a process is described in Sect. 2.3. We describe our trader model and trader agent optimization in Sect. 2.4.

2.3   Artificial Market Adjustment

We use the fact that traders with higher volume have more relevance to the market price formation as described in Sect. 2.1 to adjust the market population (i.e., the set of the agents) to fit data previously observed in real markets. For simplicity, each agent type has just one instance, and it trades one specific share quantity at each round. The **artificial market specification** is defined by three parameters: the share quantities of each one of the three kinds of agents: fundamentalist, technical and market making agents. The objective function is the session prediction error, defined in Eq. 2.

It is very hard to know a priori how a change in one of the specification parameters may affect the predicted price $\overline{P_t}$ or the session error (E). Therefore, we used as first alternative an efficient general method to find minimum points of the objective function E. It is the random-restart hill climbing method, which is a simple variant of the common hill climbing method [5], that uses a different random starting point at each time it finds a local minimum for the objective.

2.4   Trader Model

Trading agents are responsible to decide and to submit buy or sell orders to their target assets, according to their specific trading strategies. For simplicity, each agent trades with just one stock. Trader agents can be classified as **technical**, if they decide based on price and/or volume time series, or **fundamentalist**, if they decide according to information related to the company performance in its market, e.g., profits. In order to avoid unmatched orders, we also implemented a market making agent which is described below.

Market Makers. The market making agent is responsible to offer buy and sell orders in order to facilitate trading to occur at every round. Their presence is important to guarantee that it is defined an internal market price for each round. As explained in Sect. 2.1 this price is determined by one or a set of business transactions weighted by the volume of each transaction. The market maker order price is defined by yesterday's price plus a **spread**, a small percentage, in case of a sell order or minus the spread in case of a buy order. Therefore, it defines a lower and upper limit for the price. The spread was defined as 0.5 % in our simulated experiments. However, the internal price is really defined by the technical and fundamentalist agent's orders and their respective volumes.

Technical Traders. There are many technical strategies used in the stock market [6]. One of the simplest and most well-known strategies is the moving average (MA). The moving average index tries to identify trends in stock prices. The average is defined by an observation period, usually defined between 14 and 60 days, and a calculation method that can be simple average (sum of all prices and divide it by the number of values) or exponential average to give more relevance to newer prices rather than older prices. The moving average is interpreted using graphics with lines of moving average and prices. The moving average line is a resistance for high trends and down trends. When prices are in high trend (or down trend) and the price line crosses the moving average line, it means a warning to trend reversal. Therefore, when the moving average is crossed by the price line in a high trend, it means a sell signal and similarly when the moving average line is crossed by the price line in a down trend, it is a buy signal. We used MA and adapted it to provide order price based on the last market price.

Fundamentalist Traders. The modeling and implementation of fundamentalist traders may be much more complex than technical trader [7]. The data used by fundamentalist traders may be economic information about the company (such as profit, dividends policy and so on), about the economic sector (size and growth projections) and/or general economy (growth projections, volatility analysis, etc.). We used on this paper a very simple approach to fundamentalist trader based on the profit time series. We used this to predict a profit on a given future time t through simple linear regression. Then we assumed that the relation price/profit holds along the time, so it is possible to estimate the price at time t.

3   Simulated Experiments

We performed a set of simulated experiments in order to test our simple model and evaluate the quality of predictions using real market data of several years. We implemented our trading agents using an adapted version of auction simulator called JASA [8]. JASA runs over an Agent-based modeling toolkit called JABM [9]. The real market data includes nine years of Intel stock prices between 2003 to 2011 from Nasdaq exchange. The Fig. 2 presents two graphs each one shows the simulated price, actual market price (or external price), the error at each round and the cumulative error for the whole simulation session. The left graph represent the results in a low volatility period and the other in high volatility period. It is possible to realize that the cumulative error line is steeper in the high volatility period graph.

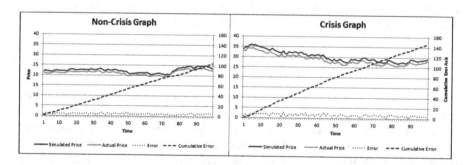

Fig. 2. Examples of simulation sessions in low and high-volatility periods

4   Simulation Results

We expected that artificial markets achieve smaller errors in low volatility periods than in volatile periods. We believe that this may happen because in volatile periods, human trader may let their emotions and feelings guide their decisions. The simulation results are presented on Table 1. We simulated nine years of operation using historical prices of Intel Corporation stock from Nasdaq Exchange.

Table 1. Simulation results of years 2003 to 2011.

Year	Variance	Volatility	Error	Performance
2003	542.3	high	344.3	good
2004	365.1	high	501.0	bad
2005	167.7	low	407.1	bad
2006	284.1	low	289.3	good
2007	269.9	low	349.0	good
2008	1116.6	high	263.4	good
2009	542.1	high	449.8	bad
2010	254.5	low	296.3	good
2011	292.6	low	234.5	good
High volatility average	641.5	high	389.6	bad
Low volatility average	253.7	low	315.2	good

The variance of arithmetic returns were calculated for each year and used to classify the years from 2003 to 2011 as high or low volatility years (*situation column*). We simulated artificial markets as described in Sect. 2.3 and calculated the smallest session error for each year after several execution of the artificial market adjustment process as explained in Sect. 2.3. The smallest session **error** achieved for each year are presented in Table 1. According to such errors, we classified artificial market performance as good and bad performance as shown in performance column. We used the average error (348.3) as limit to define between good or bad performance. The low-volatility average error is 315.2, while the high-volatility average error is 389.6, as shown in Table 1.

5   Result Analysis

The predictions done by the artificial market presented good performance on four of five low volatility years, but only two good performance of four possible for high volatility years. On the last two rows of Table 1, we may realize that the prediction performance (315.2) is better for low volatility periods than for volatile periods (389.6 of prediction error). Therefore, we can conclude that the predictions made by our artificial market presented significantly better performance in low volatility periods than in volatile periods, as we expected. One may argue that it is according to common sense, because more volatile periods are usually harder to predict. However, it is important to remark that as argued by Farmer and Foley [1], we believe that agent based models may bring more accurate predictions than traditional models specially when there are big changes in the market, but it will require better understanding about how agents reason in high volatility periods. This fact leads us to believe that in volatile period trading agent strategies are influenced by some other factor that is not present or at least it is weaker in other period. We believe that human agents can be influenced by psychological biases as described in Kahneman and Tversky's work [10] in high volatility periods. We discuss this idea and how it can be used in trading agent modeling in Sect. 6.

6 Prospect Theory and Trading Agent Modeling

One real-world problem that is not often addressed in artificial markets is the fact that human beings don't make decisions under risk strictly based on expected utility. In fact, some alternative models are available, as for example Prospect Theory. This theory was proposed by Kahneman and Tversky [10] and it can be seen as alternative to model and describe human decision making under risk. Kahneman and Tversky claim that several observed behaviors cannot be predicted or explained by expected utility theory [10]. For instance, people usually underweight outcomes, which are merely probable in comparison with outcomes that are obtained with certainty. This tendency is usually called the certainty effect, contributes to risk aversion in choices involving sure gains and to risk seeking in choices involving sure losses. Another effect pointed by Kahneman and Tversky, describes the observed preference in their experimental studies with human beings for guaranteed small gains over uncertain large gains, and conversely for uncertain large losses over small certain losses, called reflection effect.

Auctions can be seen as decision making under risk, including continuous double auctions as observed in stock market. Prospect theory was developed for prospects with monetary outcomes and stated probabilities, but it can be extended to more complex options. The theory establishes one phase of editing and a subsequent phase of evaluation and selection. The **editing phase** consists of an analysis of the offered prospects, which may eliminate some possible outcomes to create simpler representation of the initial prospects. In the **evaluation phase**, the remaining prospects are evaluated through a value function proposed by the authors and the highest value prospect is chosen.

6.1 Trading Agent Modeling and Prospect Construction Phase

$$Outcome = (M_t - P_t * \theta_t) + (Q_t + \theta_t) * P_{t+1}$$
$$-[M_t + P_t * Q_t]$$
$$Outcome = (P_{t+1} - P_t) * (Q_t + \theta_t) \tag{3}$$

As described in Sect. 2.4, our trading agents are able to define and submit orders to the market. Furthermore, each trading agent is able to make price prediction and use it to define one order among three possibilities: buy, sell or hold. As explained in Sect. 2.3, the order volume is not defined by the agent itself, but by the artificial market adjustment process. Furthermore, the trading agent selects the option that seems to him that it is going to bring the best outcome.

Such an outcome is the difference between the position at time t and the next time, after an order is executed. This outcome may be calculated as stated in Eq. 3, where P_t refers to the price, M_t is the amount of money, Q_t is the number of shares at time t and θ_t is the number of shares, positive for buy orders or negative for sell orders, to be transacted by the order given at time t. Each order defines changes in Q_{t+1} and the market behavior defines the change in P_{t+1}. The price cannot be defined a priori, but it is estimated by our trading agents ($\overline{P_{t+1}}$), so we can calculate $\overline{P_{t+1}} - P_t$. Any order may bring different outcomes according to the market price in the next round P_{t+1}. In order to establish prospects given the possible orders, we would need to determine the probabilities given each possible outcome considering two possible decisions: buy or sell. The future price $\overline{P_{t+1}}$ is a continuous value and θ_t is a non-linear parameter, it is dependent of the trading strategy and the artificial market adjustment, so the outcome is itself a continuous non-linear function which would require a probability density function to represent the associated probabilities. The definition of such functions would be extremely complex or even impossible.

Therefore, we initially intend to use a simple approach based on the discretization and arbitrary reduction of the possible outcomes. The future price P_{t+1} may be approximately equal to the estimated price $\overline{P_{t+1}}$, i.e., P_{t+1} is in the interval $[\overline{P_{t+1}} - \delta, \overline{P_{t+1}} + \delta]$ (likely outcome). Furthermore the real price may be slightly higher or lower than the estimated price. It is slightly higher, if it is in the interval $(\overline{P_{t+1}} + \delta, \overline{P_{t+1}} + 2 * \delta]$. It is slightly lower, if it is in the interval $[\overline{P_{t+1}} - 2 * \delta, \overline{P_{t+1}} - *\delta)$. Assuming that the provided estimated $\overline{P_{t+1}}$ is usually close to the real price P_{t+1} and it is not biased to higher or lower values, we can assume a higher probability to the first scenario and two equal and smaller probabilities to the other two scenarios. The parameter δ may be defined according as percentage of the initial value of the stock and the probability that real price is outside the interval $(\overline{P_{t+1}} - 2 * \delta, \overline{P_{t+1}} + 2 * \delta)$ is assumed to be zero.

We believe that using these simplistic but reasonable assumptions, it is possible to construct one prospect to each possible action of the trading agent. Such a *prospect construction phase* takes place before the editing and evaluation phases and provides the information needed for them. The selected prospect in the evaluation phase is assigned to one action, which will be selected by the extended trading agent as his decision. We intend to use the proposed trading agent modeling based on prospect theory in future work.

7   Conclusions and Further Work

Traditional economic models include dynamic stochastic general equilibrium models and empirical statistical models that are fitted to previously collected data. These models may successfully forecast short periods ahead or "as long things stay more or less the same" [1], but they are not reliable for volatile periods. Agent based modeling may become a better way to help guide financial policies, than traditional models according to some researchers [1]. However, several problems may be identified in agent based modeling. For instance, it is hard to know how to specify the rules agents should use to make their decisions. Furthermore, it is possible that in volatile period the rules are different or at least, slightly altered by components that are not present in normal periods. In order to address this question we developed a set of simple trading agents and simulated an artificial stock market in order to predict market price evolution.

The simulated experiments showed that the artificial market prediction performance is better for low volatility periods. Furthermore, this observation suggests that in volatile period trading agent strategies are influenced by some other factor that is not present in other periods. We believe that in volatile periods human agents can be influenced by psychological biases as described in Kahneman and Tversky's work [10]. Prospect theory may be seen as an alternative account of individual decision making under risk. The theory was developed for simple prospects with monetary outcomes and stated probabilities, but as the authors claims it can be extended to more involved choices [10].

We proposed a simple trading agent based on prospect theory that can be used to simulate artificial markets with this kind of agent. The model uses a prospect construction phase to be used within the trader agent reasoning process. Such phase happens before the two traditional prospect theory phases: editing and evaluation (Sect. 6). We intend to use the proposed trading agent modeling based on prospect theory in future work to verify if artificial markets populated with this kind of agent may achieve better prediction performance.

Acknowledgments. Paulo A.L. Castro is partially funded by FAPESP, Brazil (grant N. 2011/18325-8).

References

1. Farmer, J.D., Foley, D.: The economy needs agent-based modelling. Nature **460**, 685–686 (2009)
2. Phelps, S., McBurney, P., Parsons, S.: Evolutionary mechanism design: a review. J. Auton. Agent. Multi-Agent Syst. **21**, 237–264 (2010)
3. Niu, J., Cai, K., Parsons, S., Sklar, E.: Some preliminary results on the dynamic behavior of traders in multiple markets. In: Proceedings of the Workshop on Trading Agent Design and Analysis, Vancouver, British Columbia (2007)
4. Wurman, P.R., Walsh, W.E., Wellman, M.P.: Flexible double auctions for electronic commerce: theory and implementation. Int. J. Decis. Support Syst. **24**, 17–27 (1998)
5. Russell, S., Norvig, P.: Artificial Intelligence A Modern Approach, 2nd edn. Prentice Hall, Englewood Cliffs (2003)
6. Castro, P.A., Sichman, J.S.: Towards cooperation among competitive trader agents. In: Proceedings of 9th ICEIS, Funchal, Portugal, pp. 138–143 (2007)
7. Araújo, C.H.D., de Castro, P.A.L.: Towards automated trading based on fundamentalist and technical data. In: da Rocha Costa, A.C., Vicari, R.M., Tonidandel, F. (eds.) SBIA 2010. LNCS, vol. 6404, pp. 112–121. Springer, Heidelberg (2010)
8. Phelps, S.: Jasa - java auction software simulator API (2007)
9. Phelps, S.: Applying dependency injection to agent-based modeling: the JABM toolkit (2012)
10. Kahneman, D., Tversky, A.: Prospect theory: an analysis of decision under risk. Econometrica **47**(2), 263–291 (1979)

A Market-Based Coordinated Negotiation for QoS-Aware Service Selection

Claudia Di Napoli[1], Dario Di Nocera[2], Paolo Pisa[3], and Silvia Rossi[3(✉)]

[1] Istituto di Calcolo e Reti ad Alte Prestazioni - C.N.R., Naples, Italy
claudia.dinapoli@cnr.it
[2] Dipartimento di Matematica e Applicazioni,
University of Naples "Federico II", Napoli, Italy
dario.dinocera@unina.it
[3] Dipartimento di Ingegneria Elettrica e delle Tecnologie dell'Informazione,
University of Naples "Federico II", Napoli, Italy
silvia.rossi@unina.it

Abstract. The provision of Service-Based Applications (SBAs) will be driven by market-oriented mechanisms, and the market value of an application will depend not only on its functionality, but also on the value of "Quality of Service" (QoS) parameters affecting its performance. These parameters are not static properties since they may vary according to the provision strategies of providers as well as the demand of users having their own preferences on the application QoS values. In this paper we propose a market-based negotiation mechanism among service providers and a user requesting a QoS-aware SBA. It allows to take into account the variability of service QoS attribute values typical of the future market of services, as well as to dynamically set the length of the negotiation process that is usually very time-consuming especially in the context of SBAs.

Keywords: Service-oriented architectures · Artificial economies/markets · Negotiation · Quality of service · Service selection

1 Introduction

It is well recognized that Service Based Applications (SBAs) will be provided with Quality of Service (QoS) attributes that take account of service not functional properties (NFPs) such as price, response time, reliability, reputation, and so on [1]. QoS-aware SBAs are composed of autonomous and independent services that are provided with different quality attributes representing their NFPs, and they are required by users that have their own preferences over the values of these attributes. Hence, in order to deliver QoS-aware SBAs, the attribute values of their component services have to meet the user requirements, once aggregated.

© Springer International Publishing Switzerland 2014
S. Ceppi et al. (Eds.): AMEC/TADA 2013 and 2014, LNBIP 187, pp. 26–40, 2014.
DOI: 10.1007/978-3-319-13218-1_3

Nevertheless, different users may have different QoS requirements for the same application, as well as QoS attribute values for the same service may change in time according to dynamic circumstances affecting service provision strategies.

In this context, it becomes crucial to provide service-oriented infrastructures with mechanisms enabling the selection of services with suitable QoS attribute values so that QoS requirements can be satisfied when forming new value-added applications through service composition. Such mechanisms should allow to manage the dynamic nature of both provided QoS values, and user's QoS requirements.

In this paper we propose a negotiation-based mechanism among service providers and a service consumer to select the suitable services to compose QoS-aware SBAs through a market-based provision mechanism. The negotiation-based selection mechanism allows for the selection of services according to the values of their quality attributes so that, once aggregated, they meet the user quality constraints/preferences. The use of a negotiation-based mechanism allows to take into account the variability of service QoS attribute values typical of the future market of services since service providers may change these values during the negotiation according to their own provision strategies.

Since negotiation can be computationally expensive, a set of experiments was carried out to assess the impact of such coordinated negotiation mechanism on the success rate of the composition process, and to collect useful information to drive service consumers decisions about whether to proceed with the negotiation under specific conditions, or not.

The paper is so organized: Sect. 2 introduces the problem of QoS-aware service composition and provides some related works. Section 3 describes the proposed coordinated negotiation mechanism, together with the adopted strategies for the negotiators. Section 4 presents the case study and discusses the collected experimental results. Conclusions and future work are reported in Sect. 5.

2   QoS-Aware Service Composition

In a market of services, users will issue a request for an SBA specifying the functionality of each service component, their functional dependence constraints, and the value(s) of the quality attribute(s) they want the application to provide. The request is described by a directed acyclic graph, called an *Abstract Workflow* (AW), and by a quality attribute value representing the required *QoS* for the application. AW nodes represent the required functionalities, called *Abstract Services* (ASs), and AW arcs represent control and data dependencies among nodes.

It is assumed that for each AS a set of *Concrete Services* (CS) will be available on the market, each one provided by a specific *Service Provider* (SP) with QoS attributes whose values are set by the corresponding SP dynamically.

The user request is managed by a software entity, named *Service Compositor* (SC), responsible for the selection of CSs whose attribute values, once aggregated, satisfy the QoS required by the user. The selection is modeled as a negotiation process over the service quality attributes among the SC and the SPs available to provide their services. SPs issue their offer to the SC by specifying a reference to the CS together with the value of the QoS attribute they can provide the service with at that time. If the negotiation is successful, then the user request can be satisfied by instantiating the AW with the CSs having the suitable QoS value. The *Instantiated Workflow* (IW) represents the requested application ready to be executed.

2.1   Related Works

Several efforts have been carried out in the areas of QoS-based service selection for Service Based Applications [2].

Some works propose algorithms to select service implementations relying on the optimization of a weighted sum of global QoS parameters as in [3] by using Integer Linear Programming (ILP) methods. Nevertheless, ILP-based algorithms for selecting services are suitable when QoS data are accurate and the problem size is small (i.e. with a limited number of nodes for the Abstract Workflow and a limited number of potentially available services for each node) due to the ILP high complexity [4]. In such cases, instead of optimal solution procedures, heuristic algorithms are have been proposed in the literature [5]. In this context also Genetic Algorithms have been proposed to address scalability problems as in [6,7]. Approximation-based approaches are more efficient than linear approaches as they can handle large number of services better than linear methods. However, they suffer from lack of ability to find optimal solutions since they can be discarded during the elimination process using these approaches.

In [8] local constraints are included in the linear programming model used to satisfy global QoS constraints. In [9] Mixed Integer Programming is used to find the optimal decomposition of global QoS constraints into local constraints representing the service skyline for each service class, so allowing to prune the service candidates that are not likely to be part of the optimal solution.

Typically, these works rely on static approaches assuming that QoS parameters of each service do not change during the selection process, i.e. they are predetermined, and focus on optimality and performances of the provisioning methods. Such approaches do not take into account the possibility to dynamically change the provided QoS values during the selection process that represents the basic motivation for the approach proposed in our work. Other approaches rely on negotiation mechanisms to select services according the QoS values [10,11]. In most of these approaches negotiation occurs when the service provider has already been selected, and it negotiates the values of the service parameters values it provides for the service. So, the negotiation process is one-to-one between service requester and the selected service provider [3].

Other negotiation-based approaches use negotiation as a mechanism to dynamically select the appropriate the service provider whose provided services best matches the service requester's non-functional requirements [12]. But usually negotiation is carried out for each required service independently from the others. So negotiation consists of multiple negotiation sub-processes each one associated with one once of the required composite service. Each negotiation sub-process, in turn, may include multiple negotiation threads, one for each candidate provider, to choose the best service for the specific component service.

The work presented, in this paper, proposes a coordinated negotiation mechanism, where negotiations occurs concurrently with all providers of the different required services in the composition. Coordination occurs at each negotiation step when the aggregated QoS values offered by different SPs are collectively evaluated to decide whether to accept or not a set of offers, so to take into account the dependencies among different negotiation processes due to the fact that in a composition of services the attributes values for one services cannot be determined independently from the other services in the composition.

3   The Coordinated Negotiation Mechanism

The negotiation process between two agents x and y is a bilateral interaction that consists of an alternate succession of offers and counteroffers. The process continues either until an offer is accepted by the other agent, or one of the agents terminates the interaction (e.g., because of a deadline). An agent x accepts an offer j of y if the value of the utility the agent x obtains for that offer is greater than the utility value of the counteroffer the agent x would send back, i.e. $U_x(j_y(t)) \geq U_x(j_x(t+1))$ [13].

In order to prepare a counteroffer, an agent uses a set of tactics to generate new values for each negotiated object [14]. Of course, both agents must be provided with strategies to formulate offers and counteroffers, and they must be equipped with algorithms to evaluate the received offers.

In this paper we consider a modified negotiation mechanism, based on an iterative protocol, allowing only the SPs to formulate new offers, and the SC only to evaluate them. The rationale of this choice is twofold: on one hand it makes it possible to simulate what happens in a real market of services where an SC does not have enough information on the SPs strategies to formulate counteroffers; on the other hand it takes into account that the offers for a single functionality cannot be evaluated independently from the ones received for the other functionalities. In other words, negotiating over the attributes of the single AS cannot be done independently from each other. In fact, the proposed negotiation mechanism allows both to negotiate with the SPs providing services for the same required functionality in the AW, and, at the same time, to evaluate if the aggregated QoS value of the received offers meets the QoS requirement specified in the user request, to decide whether or not to accept the offers.

3.1   The Negotiation Protocol

In order to meet the user's requirements, an iterative negotiation protocol, based on the Contract Net Iterated Protocol [15], is adopted. The negotiation occurs between the SC, that is the *initiator* of the negotiation, and the SPs available for each AS of the AW, and it may be iterated for a variable number of times until a *deadline* is reached or the negotiation is successful (see Fig. 1). Each iteration

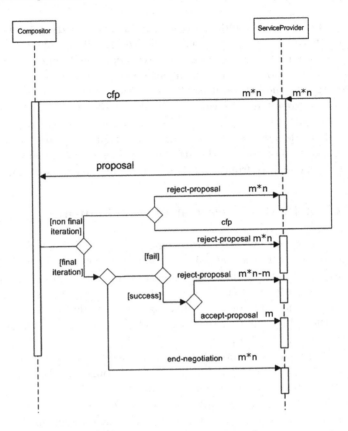

Fig. 1. The negotiation protocol.

is referred to as a negotiation *round*, and the deadline is the number of allowed rounds. In this protocol the SC may set the deadline according to estimates of parameters influencing the negotiation progress (see Sect. 4), so the negotiation takes place for a variable number of iterations based on the specific situation occurring when a request is issued.

As shown in the Fig. 1, the SC prepares m call for proposals (*cfp*s), one for each AS in the AW to send to the set of n SPs available to take part in the negotiation for that AS. So, the total number of *cfp*s sent at each round is $m*n$.

After waiting for the time set to receive offers (*expiration time* of a negotiation round), the SC checks if there are offers for each AS; if not, it declares a failure since it is not possible to find a CS corresponding to each AS. Otherwise, it evaluates the received offers, and, according to the result of the evaluation (see Sect. 3.2), it performs one of the following actions:

– if the aggregated QoS value of the received offers does not meet the user's QoS requirements, it asks for new offers by sending again $m*n$ *cfp*s, so starting another negotiation round;

- if the aggregated QoS value of the received offers meets the user's QoS requirements, it selects the best set of offers, in terms of its own utility, i.e. it accepts
  the offers sent by the corresponding SPs (one for each AS), so ending the
  negotiation successfully.
- if the deadline is reached without a success, the SC declares a failure to all
  SPs that took part in the negotiation.

3.2   Service Compositor

The SC receives service offers at each negotiation round and, once checked that
there is at least one offer for each AS, it evaluates if the global QoS constraints
specified by the user are met. The constraints are intended to be upper bounds
for the aggregated values obtained by the offered QoSs, and the evaluation function is a solver of a Integer Linear Programming problem. We decided to use
this global optimization approach, and not to investigate sub-optimal approaches
since we are mainly interested in the evaluation of the impact of the coordinated
negotiation approach on the probability to succeed. The ILP problem is formulated as follows. There are $n * m$ decision variables $x_{i,j}$ where i identifies one of
the m ASs and the j identifies one of the n SPs compatible with the i-th AS.
Such variables assume value 1 if the j-th SP is selected for the AS i, 0 otherwise.
Exactly one SP has to be selected for each AS, and so the sum of $x_{i,j}$ for a
specified AS i, must be equal to 1. This constraint holds for all ASs, so:

$$\sum_{j=1}^{n} x_{i,j} = 1, \forall i = 1, \ldots, m \tag{1}$$

Assuming a multidimensional QoS $(Q_1, \ldots, Q_r)$, the r-tuple $(q_{i,j}^1, \ldots, q_{i,j}^r)$ of
offered values is associated to each corresponding SP identified by $x_{i,j}$.

To check whether each QoS constraint has been satisfied, the values of the
parameters $q_{i,j}^k$ offered by each selected SP, once aggregated, must not exceed
the user upper bound Q_k:

$$aggrFun_i(\sum_{j=1}^{n} x_{i,j} * q_{i,j}^k) \leq Q_k, \forall k = 1, \ldots, r \tag{2}$$

The aggregation function $aggrFun$ for the QoS parameters depends on the
type of the parameter. Typically, additive (e.g., price and execution time) and
multiplicative (e.g., reliability and availability) parameters are considered [3], so
$aggrFun$ is either a sum or a multiplication over the m ASs.

Once solutions that satisfy the constraints of Eq. 2 are found, the SC evaluates
the overall utility [9]:

$$U(SC) = \sum_{k=1}^{r} \frac{Q_{max'}(k) - aggrFun_i(\sum_{j=1}^{n} x_{i,j} * q_{i,j}^k)}{Q_{max'}(k) - Q_{min'}(k)} w_k \tag{3}$$

where, w_r is a weight for the specific QoS, $Q_{max(i,k)} = max(q_{i,j}^k)$, $Q_{max'(k)} = aggrFun_k(Q_{max(i,k)})$, $Q_{min'(k)} = aggrFun_k(Q_{min(i,k)})$; i.e., $Q_{max'(k)}$ aggregates the maxima of the offers received for each AS, and $Q_{min'(k)}$ the corresponding local minima. The objective function is a maximization of Eq. 3. Hence, the SC selects the combinations of offers with the maximum utility among the ones that satisfy the constraints.

3.3   Service Provider

According to [14], time dependent and resource dependent strategies are two important classes of negotiation tactics in service-oriented domains, already used for modeling B2B interactions [8]. Time dependent strategies model the interactions of agents with deadlines for making deals. Usually, as the deadline approaches the agent is more willing to concede in utility. The tactics are implemented as time dependent functions, typically exponential or polynomial functions, classified as *boulware* or *conceder* tactics [14]. In the first case, the agent proposes values near to the initial offer until the deadline approaches, then it will propose its *reservation value* that represents the offer with the minimum utility the agents is able to provide within its negotiation set. In the second case, the agent will approach its reservation value sooner than the previous case.

Resource dependent strategies are similar to the time dependent ones, but the domains of functions modelling the tactics are the available resources, so it is necessary to evaluate the available resources w.r.t. the received requests to generate new offers.

In a previous work [16], a provider agent concession strategy was modeled as a monodimensional Gaussian function where the dimension represents a single negotiated QoS attribute. The use of Gaussian distributions allows to simulate the stochastic behaviour of service providers with zero-intelligence that can be used to approximate the trends of a volatile and open market of services [17]. In the present work, the same strategies are used, that are both time and resource dependent, and take into account the *computational load* of the SP, and the *computational cost* of the provided service. The computational load accounts for the provider workload in terms of the amount of service implementations it will deliver; while the computational cost represents a measure of the service complexity, so that the more complex the service is the higher its expected cost is.

The negotiation strategy is modeled, for each SP, by a Gaussian distribution that represents the probability distribution of the offers in terms of the provider's utility. As shown in Fig. 2, the mean value of the Gaussian $maxU$ represents the best offer the SP may propose in terms of its own utility having the highest probability to be selected; the standard deviation σ represents the attitude of the SP to concede during negotiation, and it is given by $\sigma_{i,j} = maxU_{i,j} - maxU_{i,j} * percent_{i,j}$, where $percent \in [0, 1]$ represents the concession percentage of the SP with respect to its own utility.

The negotiation set for the SP is $[maxU - \sigma; maxU]$, where $maxU - \sigma$ is the reservation value. The parameter σ varies from SP to SP providing the same AS,

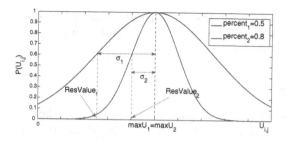

Fig. 2. An example of probability functions to compute new offers.

so that the lower its computational load (in terms of available resources) is, the more it is available to concede in utility, and the lower its reservation value is.

In Fig. 2 the functions associated to two different SPs for the same AS are reported. The best offer is the same for both SPs (i.e. $maxU_1 = maxU_2$) since it is assumed that services providing the same functionality have the same utility value for all the providers of that service, while their concession strategies are different according to their workload when the negotiation takes place. In the reported case σ_1 is greater than σ_2 meaning that SP_1 has a lower computational load than SP_2, so it concedes more in utility than SP_2.

At each negotiation round, each SP generates, following its distribution, a new utility value corresponding to a new offer. If this value is lower than the one offered in the previous round and within the negotiation set, then the SP proposes the new value. Note that values generated in the set $[maxU; maxU + \sigma]$ will be specularly mapped to the corresponding values within the negotiation set $[maxU - \sigma; maxU]$ with the same probability to be selected. If the new generated utility value is higher than the one offered at the previous round, or it is outside the negotiation set, the SP proposes the same value offered in the previous round.

This strategy allows to simulate different and plausible behaviors of providers that prefers not having a consistent loss in utility, even though by increasing the number of negotiation rounds the probability for the SP to move towards its reservation value increases.

4   A Case Study

A set of experiments was carried out in order to determine weather the coordinated mechanism affects the negotiation probability of success/failure, and to evaluate the impact of the number of SPs and ASs on the negotiation progress. The experiments were designed to extract information that can be used by the SC to understand negotiation trends according to the current market situation.

In the experiments, we considered a single QoS attribute, that is the price. So, the QoS aggregation function is additive in the number of ASs in the AW, and it does not depend on the structure of the AW, i.e., on the functional precedence relations among ASs. For this reason the nature of the arcs in the AW (representing sequential, parallel constructs, and so on) is not taken into consideration in the experiments.

4.1   The Price Parameter

Considering the price the only parameter to negotiate, the utility value for the SP is just the price of the service it offers. This means that the $maxU$ value is the $bestPrice$ in terms of the SP utility, and an SP offer is $Price_{i,j}$. The lowest price that the SP can offer is $bestPrice - \sigma$, that represents its reservation price.

With this setting, assuming there are m ASs in the required AW, and n SPs for each AS, the linear programming problem is formulated as in Sect. 3.2, where Eqs. 2 and 3 are instantiated follows:

$$\sum_{i=1}^{m}\sum_{j=1}^{n} x_{i,j} * Price_{i,j} \leq reqPrice \tag{4}$$

$$U(SC) = \frac{Q_{max'}(Price) - \sum_{i=1}^{m}\sum_{j=1}^{n} x_{i,j} * Price_{i,j}}{Q_{max'}(Price) - Q_{min'}(Price)} \tag{5}$$

where, $reqPrice$ is the maximum price the user specified as hard constraint, expressed by Eq. 4.

The SC utility for each received offer j is given by Eq. 5. If there is a combination of offers that satisfies the constraint, the linear programming solver identifies it. It is assumed that the more complex the functionality a service provides, the higher its "market price" is. This price is also the one with the maximum utility for all SPs providing that functionality, i.e., it represents the $bestPrice$ for all the SPs. It is reasonable to assume that the variability in prices for different ASs is proportional to the complexity of the provided functionality. To simulate the variability of prices for services providing different functionality in terms of their complexity, a parameter k is used. The more complex the functionality provided by a service is the higher the value k is.

The k parameter is set to be equal for all providers of the same service, meaning that services providing the same functionality have the same market price. In fact, the value k determines the mean value of the Gaussian distribution, i.e., the price that most likely will be proposed for the service that is given by:

$$bestPrice_i = \frac{reqPrice * k_i}{m} \quad i \in [1,\ldots,m] \tag{6}$$

where, m is the number of ASs in the AW, $k \leq 1$ for SPs providing less complex services, and $k > 1$ for SPs providing more complex services.

If for each AS $k \leq 1$, then the first offers will be at most equal to $reqPrice/m$ (i.e., the price is equally distributed among ASs). In this case, the QoS constraint is fulfilled at the first negotiation round. If for all the ASs $k > 1$, then at the first round there is not any combinations of offers leading to the constraint satisfaction, i.e., no *feasible* solution exists. The lack of a feasible solution implies that the SC has no chance of getting an instantiation of the workflow, so it has to iterate the negotiation.

The value of $bestPrice_i$ in Eq. 6 takes into account both the computational cost of the offered service, and that the requested price $reqPrice$ is not "unreasonable" compared to the market price of the required ASs in the AW.

4.2   Numerical Evaluation of the Negotiation Trends

In order to model reasonable market situations, we fixed the k_i values for each AS so that the average value is equal to 1.5. In fact, this setting models a market configuration where it is not possible to obtain a success at the first negotiation round, but there are still good chances to reach a success during the process.

We considered two AW configurations including respectively 5 and 10 ASs. The ASs have a different a default price, $bestPrice_i$, determined by the following values of k_i: 2.4, 2.0, 1.3, 1.0 and 0.8 for the case of 5 ASs, and 2.6, 2.4, 2.2, 2, 1.7, 1,3, 1, 0.8, 0.6 and 0.4 for the case of 10 ASs. For each AS, the corresponding SPs will send as initial offer a price in the neighborhood of $bestPrice_i$ $[bestPrice_i - 5\%, bestPrice_i]$. The concession percentage value of each SP, $percent_{i,j}$, randomly varies in the range $[0.5, 1.0]$, so including SPs

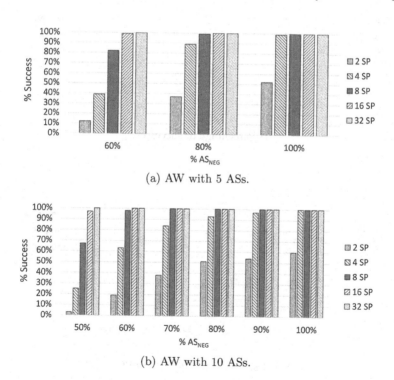

(a) AW with 5 ASs.

(b) AW with 10 ASs.

Fig. 3. Percentage of successes varying the percentage of ASs in the AW with negotiable QoS, and the number of SPs for each AS.

with the maximum computational load that are not willing to concede (i.e., $percent_{i,j} = 1$), and SPs with a low computational load willing to concede until a reservation price that is half of their $bestPrice$. The maximum number of negotiation rounds is 100, and the result of each experiment is mediated on 100 runs.

In a first set of experiments we evaluated the percentage of obtained successful negotiations in the case the negotiation occurs only for a subset of ASs (referred to as AS_{NEG}), and varying the number of SPs for each AS. This configuration models a market situation including service types whose QoS values are not negotiable.

As expected, the percentage of successes increases by increasing both the percentage of AS_{NEG}, and the number of SPs for each AS. This holds both for the case of 5 ASs (see Fig. 3a) and for the case of 10 ASs (see Fig. 3b). In particular, the fewer AS_{NEG} are in the AW, the higher the percentage of failures in the negotiation is, meaning that the probability of successful negotiations

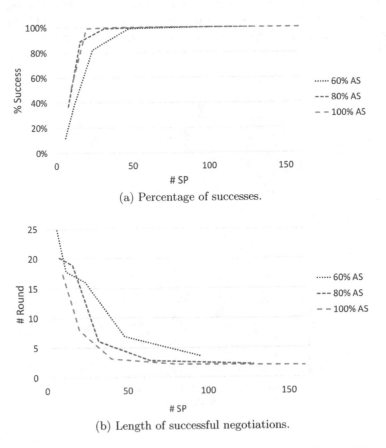

(a) Percentage of successes.

(b) Length of successful negotiations.

Fig. 4. % of successes and # of rounds w.r.t. the number of negotiating SPs, varying the percentage of AS_{NEG} in the case of 5 AS

decreases, so, if the QoS of all the types of services is negotiable such probability increases. At the same time, the probability of successful negotiations increases by increasing the number of SPs for each AS. This is due to the fact that increasing the number of SPs compensates the number of SPs that do not negotiate at all. Furthermore, in our settings, by increasing the number of ASs in the AW, the number of SPs involved in the negotiation increases. This means that, with respect to the same percentage of AS_{NEG} and the same number of SPs for each AS (see Figs. 3a and b), the percentage of success increases by increasing the number of ASs in the AW. However, this does not directly means that the success rate increases by increasing only the number of SPs because of the increasing complexity of the AW (i.e., the number of ASs). For example, in Fig. 3a in the configuration with 4 SPs for 5 ASs all negotiating (20 SPs in total) we have a success rate of 99 %, while in Fig. 3b in the configuration with 2 SPs for 10 ASs all negotiating (20 SPs in total) we have a success rate of 60 %. This is also true when not all the SPs are involved in the negotiation.

In Fig. 4a we plotted the percentage of success with respect to the total number of SPs involved in the negotiation process, varying the percentage of AS_{NEG} for the case of 5 ASs (the case of 10 ASs has similar trends). Considering a fixed number of SPs, it can be noticed that the more the negotiating SPs are spread among ASs, the higher is the probability of success. Moreover, we evaluated length of successful negotiation (i.e., the number of rounds necessary to reach a success). As shown in Fig. 4b, the length decreases by increasing the number of SPs, and for the same number of negotiating SPs (e.g., 50) the length

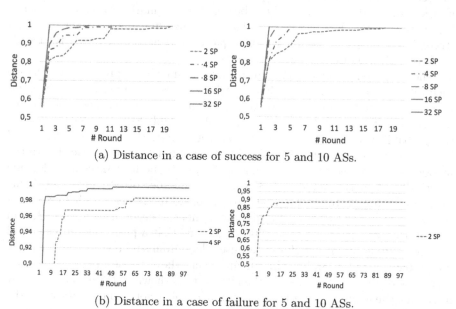

(a) Distance in a case of success for 5 and 10 ASs.

(b) Distance in a case of failure for 5 and 10 ASs.

Fig. 5. Normalized distance of the best service aggregation from the user's constraint.

of negotiation decreases increasing the number of AS_{NEG}. This confirms that it is worth negotiating, when composition of services are required, and that it is worth negotiating with all available SPs in order to increase the probability of successful negotiation.

Finally, in Fig. 5 we plotted the distance of the best combination of offers from the user's QoS constraint, at each negotiation round, normalized in the range [0,1], to analyze the negotiation trends in time. In particular, Fig. 5a reports such distance in five cases of success (respectively for 5 ASs and 10 ASs in the AW) showing that the greater the number of negotiating SPs is, the faster the success is reached. Figure 5b show the same distance in cases of failures obtained respectively with 2 and 4 SPs for 5 ASs, and with 2 SPs for 10 ASs, showing that when a plateau is reached it is very likely the negotiation ends with failure.

5   Conclusions

In the present work the use of software agent negotiation is proposed as a means to select service implementations required by a SBA by taking into account the Quality of Service that providers offer for their services, and the end-to-end QoS requirements expressed by a user requesting the application. The use of negotiation allows to address the limitations of several approaches for the QoS-based selection of services in composition of services that are based on the assumption that QoS provided for the required services are static during the selection process. This assumption is not realistic in service provision scenarios of the future that are likely to be regulated by market-based mechanisms. It is necessary to allow service providers to change dynamically their provision strategies, so changing the value of QoS parameters according to market trends while the selection takes place.

The proposed iterative negotiation mechanism allows providers to change their offers at each iteration so that, in principle, they could change their provision strategies to be more competitive in the market. The experiments carried out showed that it is worth to negotiate with all available SPs in order to increase the probability of successful negotiation. Of course, the adopted CNP-based iterative negotiation protocol have a lot of communication overhead due to the broadcast of the *cfp*s to all the available SPs, so its performances may degrade drastically when the number of SPs and the number of ASs increases. Some works in the literature [18] propose learning-based mechanisms to help selecting the most promising agents so limiting the number of negotiating agents. But, in a market of services it is not possible to assume that a promising provider will keep on sending promising offers, because a less promising provider may change its strategy in the meantime. In our approach, the increase in communication costs is partially compensated by the fact that, as shown in the experiments, by increasing the number of SPs the success rate of the negotiation increases. So, the overhead due to the communication cost is partially compensated by a decrease in the negotiation length, i.e. its overall computational cost. The analysis of the negotiation progress, in different configurations, allows to evaluate the possibility to stop negotiation if the distance of the aggregated best offers from the user's QoS constraint is not improving. This is an useful feature when adopting computationally expensive mechanisms like negotiation in service-based application settings.

Furthermore, the coordinated negotiation mechanism allows to evaluate aggregated offers through a linear programming solver, so tackling the problem that when selecting services whose aggregated QoS values have to meet end-to-end QoS requirements, the selection of one service cannot be made independently from the other services. This is even more crucial in case of multidimensional QoSs.

In order to reduce the communication overhead of the proposed mechanism, more experiments are planned to determine the "critical mass" of SPs that is worth to negotiate with in order to increase the probability of success in different market of configurations.

Acknowledgments. The research leading to these results has received funding from the EU FP7-ICT-2012-8 under the MIDAS Project (Model and Inference Driven - Automated testing of Services architectures), Grant Agreement no. 318786, and the Italian Ministry of University and Research and EU under the PON OR.C.HE.S.T.R.A. project (ORganization of Cultural HEritage for Smart Tourism and Real-time Accessibility).

References

1. Strunk, A.: Qos-aware service composition: a survey. In: Brogi, A., Pautasso, C., Papadopoulos, G.A. (eds.) 2010 IEEE 8th European Conference on Web Services (ECOWS), pp. 67–74. IEEE Computer Society (2010)
2. Zeng, L., Benatallah, B., Dumas, M., Kalagnanam, J., Sheng, Q.Z.: Quality driven web services composition. In: Proceedings of the 12th International Conference on World Wide Web, WWW '03, pp. 411–421. ACM, New York (2003)
3. Zeng, L., Benatallah, B., Ngu, A.H., Dumas, M., Kalagnanam, J., Chang, H.: Qos-aware middleware for web services composition. IEEE Trans. Softw. Eng. **30**(5), 311–327 (2004)
4. Yu, T., Zhang, Y., Lin, K.J.: Efficient algorithms for web services selection with end-to-end qos constraints. ACM Trans. Web **1**(1), 1–26 (2007)
5. Berbner, R., Spahn, M., Repp, N., Heckmann, O., Steinmetz, R.: Heuristics for qos-aware web service composition. In: Proceedings of the IEEE International Conference on Web Services, ICWS '06, pp. 72–82. IEEE Computer Society (2006)
6. Canfora, G., Di Penta, M., Esposito, R., Villani, M.L.: An approach for qos-aware service composition based on genetic algorithms. In: Proceedings of the 7th Annual Conference on Genetic and Evolutionary Computation, pp. 1069–1075. ACM (2005)
7. Liu, H., Zhong, F., Ouyang, B., Wu, J.: An approach for qos-aware web service composition based on improved genetic algorithm. In: 2010 International Conference on Web Information Systems and Mining (WISM), pp. 123–128 (2010)
8. Ardagna, D., Pernici, B.: Adaptive service composition in flexible processes. IEEE Trans. Softw. Eng. **33**(6), 369–384 (2007)
9. Alrifai, M., Risse, T.: Combining global optimization with local selection for efficient qos-aware service composition. In: Proceedings of the 18th International Conference on World Wide Web, WWW '09, pp. 881–890. ACM, New York (2009)

10. Paurobally, S., Tamma, S., Wooldridge, M.: A framework for web service negotiation. ACM Trans. Auton. Adapt. Syst. **2**(4), 14 (2007)
11. Siala, F., Ghedira, K.: A multi-agent selection of web service providers driven by composite qos. In: Proceedings of 2011 IEEE Symposium on Computers and Communications (ISCC), pp. 55–60. IEEE (2011)
12. Gimpel, H., Ludwig, H., Dan, A., Kearney, B.: PANDA: specifying policies for automated negotiations of service contracts. In: Orlowska, M.E., Weerawarana, S., Papazoglou, M.P., Yang, J. (eds.) ICSOC 2003. LNCS, vol. 2910, pp. 287–302. Springer, Heidelberg (2003)
13. Jennings, N.R., Faratin, P., Lomuscio, A.R., Parsons, S., Sierra, C., Wooldridge, M.: Automated negotiation: prospects, methods and challenges. Int. J. Group Decis. Negot. **10**(2), 199–215 (2001)
14. Faratin, P., Sierra, C., Jennings, N.R.: Negotiation decision functions for autonomous agents. Robot. Auton. Syst. **24**, 3–4 (1998)
15. Smith, R.G.: The contract net protocol: high-level communication and control in a distributed problem solver. IEEE Trans. Comput. **29**(12), 1104–1113 (1980)
16. Di Napoli, C., Pisa, P., Rossi, S.: Towards a dynamic negotiation mechanism for QoS-aware service markets. In: Pérez, J.B., et al. (eds.) Trends in Practical Applications of Agents and Multiagent. AISC, vol. 221, pp. 9–16. Springer, Heidelberg (2013)
17. Gode, D.K., Sunder, S.: Allocative efficiency of markets with zero-intelligence traders: market as a partial substitute for individual rationality. J. Polit. Econ. **101**(1), 119–137 (1993)
18. Deshpande, U., Gupta, A., Basu, A.: Performance enhancement of a contract net protocol based system through instance-based learning. IEEE Trans. Syst. Man Cybern. **35**(2), 345–357 (2005)

Optimal Agendas for Sequential Negotiations

Shaheen Fatima[1]($\boxtimes$) and Michael Wooldridge[2]

[1] Department of Computer Science, Loughborough University,
Loughborough, LE11 3TU, UK
S.S.Fatima@lboro.ac.uk

[2] Department of Computer Science, Oxford University, Oxford, OX1 3QD, UK
mjw@cs.ox.ac.uk

Abstract. One way of negotiating multiple issues is to consider them one by one in a given order. In such *sequential negotiations*, a key problem for the parties is to decide in *what order* they will negotiate a given set of issues. This ordering is called the *negotiation agenda*. The agenda is a key determinant of the outcome of sequential negotiations. Thus, a utility maximizing player will want to know what agenda maximizes its utility and is therefore its *optimal agenda*. Against this background, we focus on bilateral sequential negotiations over a set of *divisible* issues. The setting for our study is as follows. The players have time constraints in the form of *deadlines* and *discount factors*. They also have different preferences for different issues and these preferences are represented as *utility functions*. Each player knows its own utility function but not that of the other. For this setting, the specific problem we address is as follows: there are m issues available for negotiation but a *subset* of $g < m$ issues must be chosen and an *ordering* must be determined for them so as to maximize an individual player's utility. We present polynomial time methods for solving this problem.

1 Introduction

Many multi-agent systems require the agents to negotiate with each other. Examples of such systems include task allocation, resource allocation, and electronic commerce. Multiple issues can be negotiated using a variety of procedures. In this paper, we focus on one such procedure: the sequential procedure.

Results of existing research [1–3,7] have shown the key factors that influence the equilibrium outcome of sequential negotiations. One of these is the *implementation rule*, which specifies when each player is allowed to consume its share of a successfully negotiated issue. There are two main implementation rules [7]: *independent implementation* and *simultaneous implementation*. For the former, each player is allowed to consume its share of an issue as soon as it is settled. For the latter, the players can consume their shares from all the issues only when the negotiations on all the issues are completed successfully. In this paper, we will focus on the independent implementation rule. In addition to the implementation rule, the equilibrium outcome of sequential negotiations has been shown to depend on the following key factors: the *set of issues* included for negotiation,

© Springer International Publishing Switzerland 2014
S. Ceppi et al. (Eds.): AMEC/TADA 2013 and 2014, LNBIP 187, pp. 41–55, 2014.
DOI: 10.1007/978-3-319-13218-1_4

the *order* in which a set of issues is discussed, and who the *first mover* is for negotiation over each individual issue.

In many negotiations, we see that one or both players have a choice over what issues to negotiate on. In such situations, there are a certain number of issues available and the players must choose a subset of them to negotiate on. Here, a player can get different utilities from different subsets. Thus, from among all possible subsets, a utility maximizing agent will want to know the one that maximizes its utility and is therefore its *optimal set* of issues. To this end, given a set of $m > 2$ issues, one of our aims is to find a player's optimal set of size $g < m$.

Then, given the dependence of the outcome on the 'order' in which a set of issues are negotiated, it is important for an agent to know what order will maximize its utility. Form among all possible orders in which a set set of issues can be negotiated, the one that maximizes a player's utility is called its *optimal order*. Although existing work has recognized the influence of the order on the outcome of a negotiation, to date, there has been no work on how to actually find a player's optimal order. Another aim of ours is therefore to fill this gap by presenting methods for finding a player's optimal order.

Also, the outcome of sequential negotiations depends on who the first mover is for negotiation over each individual issue. Given this, our aim is to study the combined influence of the ordering of issues and the choice of first movers on the outcome of a negotiation. To this end, we consider two different settings: one where each player knows, in advance of the negotiations, who the first mover for each issue will be, and another where neither player has this information in advance (the players only know that the first movers will be chosen randomly). For each of these two settings, we show how to compute a player's optimal set of issues and an optimal ordering for that set.

In more detail, the setting for our work is as follows. There are m *divisible* issues available for negotiation. The players have time constraints in the form of *deadlines* and *discount factors*. They also have different preferences for different issues and these preferences are represented as *utility functions*. Each player knows its own utility function but not that of the other. For this setting, we present polynomial time algorithms for computing a players optimal set of $g < m$ issues, and an optimal order for those g issues. The proposed methods have $\mathcal{O}(m)$ time complexity.

A naive approach for finding a player's optimal set of g issues and an ordering for them would be to exhaustively search all possible orderings of all possible subsets of size g (the number of all possible orderings of all possible subsets of size g being $m!/(m-g)!$). Clearly, this method will be computationally infeasible due to its exponential time complexity. Our work shows that such an exhaustive search is unnecessary, and that the above problem can, in fact, be solved in $\mathcal{O}(m)$ time.

Although the influence of the order in which sequential negotiations are held on the outcome of negotiations has been recognized, to date, there is no existing work on how to actually find a player's optimal order (in Sect. 5, we give a more detailed discussion of related literature). Hence, the main contributions of this work are as follows. We study the combined influence of first movers and the ordering of issues on the outcome of sequential negotiations and present computationally efficient methods for finding a player's optimal set of issues and an optimal ordering for them. The results of this research facilitate the design of software agents that can not only optimally negotiate over a given set of issues, but can also choose the right agenda before actual negotiation begins.

The remainder of the paper is structured as follows. In Sect. 2, we will describe the setting. In Sects. 3, and 4, we show how to compute optimal agendas for two different settings. In Sect. 5, we will place our work in the context of related literature, and conclude in Sect. 6.

2   The Negotiation Setting

There are two agents (a and b) and a set $I = (1, 2, \ldots, m)$ of issues available for negotiation. Each issue is a *divisible pie* of size one. Divisible means that a pie can be split in any way between the two agents. The agents want to negotiate about how to split each pie between themselves.

The negotiation procedure. The issues are negotiated using the *sequential procedure with independent implementation*. This procedure works as follows. The issues are negotiated one by one in *stages*, one stage for each issue. Thus, for m issues, there will be m stages.

Each stage is divided into discrete *time periods*. In each stage, the players are allowed to negotiate for at most n time periods. At time $t = 1$, negotiation begins with the first stage in which one of the m issues is negotiated. The deadline for this stage is $t = n$. If this negotiation ends in the time period $t \leq n$, then the second stage starts at time $t + 1$. In the second stage, one of the remaining $m - 1$ issues is negotiated. Since each stage is allowed n time periods, the deadline for this stage will be $t + n$. This process continues until all the m issues are negotiated in m stages.

Negotiation in each stage is conducted using Rubinstein's alternating offers protocol [10]. Each player is allowed to eat its share of a pie as soon as it is settled (i.e., without having to wait for negotiation on all the m pies to complete).

Time discounting. Each pie shrinks with time and this shrinkage is modeled with a discount factor. Let $0 < \delta < 1$ denote the discount factor for all the m pies. At the beginning of negotiation, all the m pies are of unit size. At time t each[1] pie shrinks to δ^{t-1} irrespective of whether negotiation on the pie has begun or not. Thus, if negotiation on a pie begins at time t, then the pie will have already shrunk to size δ^{t-1} by then.

---

[1] Another way of modeling time discounting is to let each pie be of size one when negotiation on it begins. A pie starts to shrink once negotiation on it has started but not before that. Thus, if negotiation on a pie starts are time t, the pie will have unit size at t and it will shrink in every subsequent time period. All our results can easily be extended to this situation.

Equilibrium for an individual issue. The players' equilibrium shares for any individual issue can be obtained using *backward induction.* Consider negotiation during the first stage. Assume that agent a is the first mover for this stage. Since the players take turns in making offers, a will be the proposing agent in all odd time periods and b in all even ones. Assume that n is odd (the case where n is even will be analogous) and look ahead to the time period $t = n$. At this time, the pie under negotiation will have shrunk to δ^{n-1} and the offering agent, i.e., a, will propose to keep a hundred percent of the shrunken pie. Since the deadline for the first stage is n, b will accept the offer. Now, look at the previous time period $t = n - 1$ when agent b will be the offering agent and the size of the pie will be δ^{n-2}. Agent b will propose to give a share of δ^{n-1} to a and keep the rest, i.e., $\delta^{n-2} - \delta^{n-1}$ for itself. We continue going back one time period at a time until we reach the first time period. At $t = 1$ the size of the pie will be 1 and agent a will propose to keep $\sum_{j=0}^{n-1}(-1)^j \delta^j$ for itself and give the rest of the pie, i.e., $1 - \sum_{j=0}^{n-1}(-1)^j \delta^j$ to b. Agent b will accept this offer and an agreement will occur at $t = 1$. Thus, negotiation during the first stage begins and ends in the first time period.

Equilibrium for multiple issues. Since negotiation for the first stage ends at time $t = 1$, stage 2 will begin at $t = 2$. As for the first stage, negotiation for the second stage will end at $t = 2$. In general, stage i ($1 \leq i \leq m$) will begin and end at time $t = i$. It will therefore take m time periods to complete negotiation on all the m issues. In Lemma 1, we characterize the offering agent's equilibrium share for the issue negotiated in stage $1 \leq i \leq m$.

Lemma 1. *For the sequential procedure with independent implementation, negotiation for the ith stage starts at time $\Gamma_i = i$ and has deadline $i + n - 1$. For the issue negotiated in this stage, the offering agent's equilibrium share for a time period $i + t - 1$ where $1 \leq t \leq n$ is as follows:*

$$\sum_{j=t-1}^{t+n-2}\left((-1)^{j+1} \times \delta^{i+j-1}\right) \quad for\, even\, t \tag{1}$$

$$\sum_{j=t-1}^{t+n-2}\left((-1)^{j} \times \delta^{i+j-1}\right) \quad for\, odd\, t \tag{2}$$

An agreement for stage i occurs at time $T_i = i$.

The second mover's share for a pie i will be the size of the pie at time i (i.e., δ^{i-1}) minus the first mover's share for it. Given this, the following example illustrates the fact that a player's equilibrium share for an individual issue depends on who the first mover is for the issue.

Example 1. Let there be two issues $I = (1, 2)$. Let the deadline for each issue be $n = 2$ time periods and the discount factor be $\delta = 1/4$. Then, assume that agent a is the first mover for both stages. For this case, a's equilibrium share for the first pie will be $3/4$ and that for the second will be $3/16$. Next, assume that a is

Table 1. The 4 possible 'first mover functions' for two stages.

i	First mover for Stage 1 $f_i(1)$	First mover for Stage 2 $f_i(2)$
1	a	a
2	b	b
3	b	a
4	a	b

the first mover for the first stage and b the first mover for the second. For this case, a's equilibrium share for the first pie will be 3/4 and that for the second will be 1/16.

In what follows, we will use the following notation. For a time t, let $\mathrm{XA}_i^a(t)$ $(\mathrm{XA}_i^b(t))$ denote player a's equilibrium share for the issue negotiated in the ith stage if a (b) is the first mover for that stage. For agent b, $\mathrm{XA}_i^a(t)$ and $\mathrm{XA}_i^b(t)$ will be analogous. And let T_i denote the equilibrium time of agreement for the ith stage.

Negotiation agenda. For the sequential procedure, the term *negotiation agenda* is defined as follows.

Definition 1. Given a set $I = (1, 2, \ldots, m)$ of m issues, an agenda $A^g \subset I$ of size $g < m$ is a set of g issues and an ordering on them.

In other words, an agenda of size g is a *permutation* or *sequence* of g issues from I. We will let AG^g denote the set of all possible agendas of size g. For an agenda $X \in AG^g$, the issue X_i will be negotiated in stage i.

First movers. For an agenda of size g, let there be a *first mover function* (FMF) that maps each stage to the first mover for that stage. Since there are two possibilities for the first mover for each stage, there will be $K = 2^g$ possible ways of defining this function. We will call these K functions $f_1, \ldots, f_K$ where, for $1 \le j \le K$, $f_j : \{1, \ldots, g\} \to \{a, b\}$. Table 1 illustrates the FMFs for two stages.

Utility functions. An agent has different preferences for different issues, and different agents have different preferences. An agent's preference for an issue is represented with a weight. Agent a's $(b$'s) weight for issue i is $w_i^a \in R_+$ $(w_i^b \in R_+)$. Given this, agent a's utility for an issue negotiated in the ith stage is defined as follows. During this stage, if, a receives a share of x_i at time t, then its utility will be:

$$U_i^a(x_i, t) = \begin{cases} w_i^a x_i \delta^{t-1} & \text{if } t \le \Gamma_i + n - 1 \\ 0 & \text{otherwise} \end{cases} \tag{3}$$

where Γ_i denotes the start time for the ith stage.

Then for multiple issues, we know that, each player is allowed to eat its share of a pie as soon as an agreement is reached on it. Thus, agent a's cumulative equilibrium utility from an agenda $X \in AG^g$ and first mover function f_j is defined as follows:

$$U^a(X, f_j) = \sum_{i=1}^{g} U_i^a(\text{XA}_i^{f_j(i)}(T_i), T_i). \tag{4}$$

Here $\text{XA}_i^{f_j(i)}(t)$ denotes a's equilibrium share for the time period t of the ith stage, T_i is the equilibrium agreement time for the ith stage, and $f_j(i)$ gives the first mover for stage i. Note that, in equilibrium, negotiation on the ith stage begins and ends at time i, i.e., $\Gamma_i = T_i = i$. Also, $\text{XA}_i^{f_j(i)}(t)$ and T_i can be obtained from Lemma 1. Here, it is important to note that the equilibrium time of agreement for a stage is independent of the first mover function. For agent b, U_i^b and U^b will be analogous.

Information. The players have *common knowledge* about n, m, g, δ, and I. In addition, each player has *private knowledge* about its own weights. Thus agent a knows w^a but not w^b, and b knows w^b but not w^a. With this common and private knowledge, we consider the following two information settings:

S_1 Before the first stage begins, both players know who the first mover for each individual stage will be. Thus, for example, the players know that first movers will be as defined by the function f_j for some $1 \le j \le K$.

S_2 Before the first stage begins, the players do not know who the first movers for the various stages will be. They only know that one of the functions $f_1, \ldots, f_K$ will be chosen randomly with each of the K functions having equal chance of occurrence.

3   Optimal Agendas for Setting S_1

For the setting S_1, an agent's *optimal agenda* is defined as follows.

Definition 2. Let $AA^g \in AG^g$ and, for a given j, let the first movers for the g stages be defined by the function f_j. Also, let T_i be the equilibrium time of agreement for the ith stage and $\text{XA}_i^{f_j(i)}$ be a's equilibrium share for the ith stage. Then, AA^g is agent a's optimal agenda if it satisfies the following condition:

$$AA^g = \underset{X \in AG^g}{argmax} \sum_{i=1}^{g} U_i^a(\text{XA}_i^{f_j(i)}(T_i), T_i) \tag{5}$$

Agent b's optimal agenda AB^g is defined analogously.

Given this definition, we will now show how to find an optimal agenda for agent a. That for agent b can be found analogously. From Definitions 1 and 2, it is clear that finding an agent's optimal agenda of size g will require finding the following: i/ a set $SA^g \subset I$ of g issues such that $SA^g \cap AA^g = SA^g$ (we will call this a's *optimal set* of size g) and ii/ an optimal order for the elements in SA^g. First, in Lemma 2, we will show how to find SA^g.

Table 2. Agent a's optimal sequence for two issues c and d with $w_c^a \geq w_d^a$.

Row	First mover for Stage 1	First mover for Stage 2	Agent a's optimal sequence	Condition
1	a	a	$\langle c, d \rangle$	$\times$
2	b	b	$\langle c, d \rangle$	$\times$
3	b	a	$\langle c, d \rangle$	even n
4			$\langle d, c \rangle$	odd n
5	a	b	$\langle d, c \rangle$	(even n) & ($\delta < \delta_c$)
6			$\langle c, d \rangle$	otherwise

Lemma 2. *For a given $2 \leq g \leq m$, agent a's optimal set of g issues is the set of the last g issues in I, i.e., $SA^g = (m - g + 1, \ldots, m)$.*

Now we will show how to find an optimal order for the issues in SA^g. We will do this in Theorems 1 and 2. Specifically, in Theorem 1, we will show how to find an optimal order for the issues in SA^g for the case $g = 2$. Then, in Theorem 2, we will extend the result of Theorem 1 and show how to find an optimal order for the issues in SA^g for the general case $2 \leq g \leq m$. In Lemmas 3 and 4, we will provide key results that will be used to prove Theorem 2.

Lemma 3. *For any integer $n \geq 1$ and any δ $(0 < \delta < 1)$, we have:*

$$\left(\sum_{j=0}^{n-1} (-1)^j \delta^j + \sum_{j=0}^{n-1} (-1)^j \delta^{j+1} \right) = 1 + (-1)^{n-1} \delta^n \tag{6}$$

Lemma 4. *For any integer $n \geq 1$ and any δ, if n is even, there will be a constant δ_c $(0 < \delta_c < 1)$ such that*

$$\left(\sum_{j=0}^{n-1} (-1)^j \delta^j + \sum_{j=0}^{n-1} (-1)^j \delta^{j+1} - \delta \right) \geq 0 \ if \delta < \delta_c \tag{7}$$

and

$$\left(\sum_{j=0}^{n-1} (-1)^j \delta^j + \sum_{j=0}^{n-1} (-1)^j \delta^{j+1} - \delta \right) < 0 \ if \delta \geq \delta_c \tag{8}$$

In what follows, we will denote a *sequence* by enclosing its elements in angle brackets. Thus, for example, $\langle 1, \ldots, g \rangle$ will denote a sequence of g issues.

Theorem 1. *Consider an agenda comprised of two issues: $c \in I$ and $d \in I$, and let $w_c^a \geq w_d^a$. Then, agent a's optimal sequence for the issues c and d is as given in Table 2.*

Proof. For two issues, we need two stages. For two stages, the FMF will be one of four possible functions (see Table 1). For a function f_k $(1 \leq k \leq 4)$, we will define $D^a(f_k)$ as follows:

$$D^a(f_k) = U^a(\langle c, d \rangle, f_k) - U^a(\langle d, c \rangle, f_k). \tag{9}$$

Then, as per Definition 2, if $D^a(f_k) \geq 0$, a's optimal sequence will be $\langle c, d \rangle$. Otherwise, it will be $\langle d, c \rangle$. Thus, to find a's optimal sequence, we must first find $U^a(\langle c, d \rangle, f_k)$ and $U^a(\langle d, c \rangle, f_k)$. Below, we will do this for $k = 1, \ldots, 4$:

1. *$k = 1$, i.e., the FMF is function f_1: Here, as per Table 1, agent a is the first mover for both stages. Consider the sequence $\langle c, d \rangle$ for which issue c is negotiated in the first stage and issue d in the second. Here, the time of agreement for the first stage will be $T_1 = 1$ and that for the second stage will be $T_2 = 2$. Also, a's equilibrium share for the first stage will be $\mathrm{XA}_1^a(1) = \sum_{j=0}^{n-1}(-1)^j \delta^j$. This is obtained by substituting $i = 1$ and $t = 1$ in Eq. 2. And a's equilibrium share for the second stage will be $\mathrm{XA}_2^a(2) = \sum_{j=0}^{n-1}(-1)^j \delta^{j+1}$. This is obtained by substituting $i = 2$ and $t = 1$ in Eq. 2. Thus, as per Eq. 4, agent a's cumulative utility for the sequence $\langle c, d \rangle$ will be:*

$$U^a(\langle c, d \rangle, f_1) = w_c^a \sum_{j=0}^{n-1}(-1)^j \delta^j + w_d^a \sum_{j=0}^{n-1}(-1)^j \delta^{j+1}.$$

Likewise, for the sequence $\langle d, c \rangle$, $U^a(\langle d, c \rangle, f_1)$ will be:

$$U^a(\langle d, c \rangle, f_1) = w_d^a \sum_{j=0}^{n-1}(-1)^j \delta^j + w_c^a \sum_{j=0}^{n-1}(-1)^j \delta^{j+1}$$

Substituting $U^a(\langle c, d \rangle, f_1)$ and $U^a(\langle d, c \rangle, f_1)$ in Eq. 9, and simplifying using Lemma 3 we get:

$$D^a(f_1) = (w_c^a - w_d^a) \times (1 + (-1)^{n-1}\delta^n) \tag{10}$$

Since $w_c^a \geq w_d^a$, $n \geq 1$, and $0 < \delta < 1$, we get $D^a(f_1) \geq 0$. Thus, a's optimal sequence will be $\langle c, d \rangle$.
The proof for $k = 2$, $k = 3$, and $k = 4$ will be analogous.

In the next theorem, we will combine the results of Lemma 2 and Theorem 1, and show how to find agent a's optimal agenda of size $2 \leq g \leq m$. For an agenda of size g, the ith issue will be negotiated in the ith stage. For a given j, let the first movers for the g issues on an agenda be defined by the function f_j. For ease of exposition, we will extract information about the first movers from f_j into two vectors called α and β. There are $|\alpha|$ elements in the vector α and $|\beta|$ elements in β with $|\alpha| + |\beta| = g$. The vector α (β) contains, in ascending order, those stages for which agent a (b) is the first mover. Thus, for $1 \leq i \leq |\alpha|$, agent a is the first mover for the stage $\alpha(i)$. And for $1 \leq i \leq |\beta|$, agent b is the first mover for the stage $\beta(i)$. In what follows, we will let the issues in $I = (1, \ldots, m)$ be in ascending order of a's weights and define a's optimal sequence in terms of α and β.

Theorem 2. *For the sequential procedure with independent implementation, agent a's optimal agenda OA^g of size g is as follows:*

(C_1) *If n is odd:*

$$OA^g(\alpha_i) = m - i + 1 \qquad \text{for } 1 \le i \le |\alpha|$$
$$OA^g(\beta_i) = m - |\alpha| - i + 1 \quad \text{for } 1 \le i \le |\beta|$$

(C_2) *If n is even and $\delta < \delta_c$:*

$$OA^g(\beta_i) = m - i + 1 \qquad \text{for } 1 \le i \le |\beta|$$
$$OA^g(\alpha_i) = m - |\beta| - i + 1 \quad \text{for } 1 \le i \le |\alpha|$$

(C_3) *If n is even and $\delta \ge \delta_c$:*

$$OA^g(i) = m - i + 1 \qquad \text{for } 1 \le i \le g$$

Proof. We will consider each of the three cases C_1, C_2, and C_3.

(C_1) *If n is odd:*

For this case, we will prove that OA^g as defined in the statement of the theorem is a's optimal agenda. To do so, we will first show that the issues in OA^g are a's optimal set of issues. Recall that the issues in $I = (1, \ldots, m)$ are in ascending order of a's weights. And, as per Lemma 2, a's optimal set is the set of g issues with the highest weights for a. Thus, OA^g must contain the issues $m - g + 1, \ldots, m$. The statement '$OA^g(\alpha_i) = m - i + 1$ for $1 \le i \le |\alpha|$' assigns, to OA^g, α issues (from I) with the highest weights for a. Specifically, these $|\alpha|$ issues are assigned in such a way that they will be negotiated in those $|\alpha|$ stages for which a will be the first mover. Then the statement '$OA^g(\beta_i) = m - |\alpha| - i + 1$ for $1 \le i \le |\beta|$' assigns to OA the issues $m - (|\alpha| + |\beta|) + 1, \ldots, m - |\alpha|$ to OA^g. Specifically, these $|\beta|$ issues are assigned in such a way that they will be negotiated in those $|\beta|$ stages for which b will be the first mover. Since $|\alpha| + |\beta| = g$, OA^g will contain the g issues with the highest weights for a, i.e., the optimal set of g issues.

Thus, after the above assignment of issues to OA^g, the following three conditions (R_1, R_2, and R_3) will be satisfied:

R_1 $w^a_{OA^g(\alpha_i)} \ge w^a_{OA^g(\alpha_j)}$ for $1 \le i \le |\alpha - 1|$ and $i < j$ (i.e., the issues in OA^g for which a will be the first mover are in descending order of a's weights).

R_2 $w^a_{OA^g(\beta_i)} \ge w^a_{OA^g(\beta_j)}$ for $1 \le i \le |\beta - 1|$ and $i < j$ (i.e., the issues in OA^g for which b will be the first mover are in descending order of a's weights.

R_3 $w^a_{OA^g(\alpha_i)} \ge w^a_{OA^g(\beta_j)}$ for $1 \le i \le |\alpha|$ and $1 \le i \le |\beta|$ (i.e., a's weight for every issue in OA^g for which a will be the first mover will be higher than the a's weight for every issue for which b will be the first mover).

Next, we will prove that the sequence in OA^g is a's optimal sequence. The main idea underlying this proof is as follows. We will prove that, every pair of issues in OA^g satisfies the optimal order prescribed by Theorem 1. Since every pair of issues in OA^g is sequenced optimally, the entire sequence OA^g will be optimal.

Consider any two issues from OA^g, say $OA^g(p)$ and $OA^g(q)$ and let $p < q$.

We know that $OA^g(p)$ will be negotiated in the pth stage and $OA^g(q)$ in the qth stage. For these two stages, there can be the following four possibilities for the first movers:

1. Agent a is the first mover for stage p and stage q: In other words, $p \in \alpha$ and $q \in \alpha$. Let $\alpha_i = p$ and $\alpha_j = q$. Since $p < q$, stage p will occur before stage q. And, since the elements in α are in ascending order, we get $i < j$. Then, from the condition R_1, we know that for any i and j such that $i < j$, $w^a_{OA^g(\alpha_i)} \geq w^a_{OA^g(\alpha_j)}$. Then, from Table 2 (Row 1), we know that, if a is the first mover for any two issues, then it is optimal for a to order the two issues in descending order of their weights. In other words, the issues $OA^g(p)$ and $OA^g(q)$ are in optimal order.

2. Agent b is the first mover for stage p and stage q: In other words, $p \in \beta$ and $q \in \beta$. Let $\beta_i = p$ and $\beta_j = q$. Since $p < q$, stage p will occur before stage q. And, since the elements in β are in ascending order, we get $i < j$. Then, from the condition R_2, we know that for any i and j such that $i < j$, $w^a_{OA^g(\beta_i)} \geq w^a_{OA^g(\beta_j)}$. Then, from Table 2 (Row 2), we know that, if b is the first mover for any two issues, then it is optimal for a to order the two issues in descending order of their weights. In other words, the issues $OA^g(p)$ and $OA^g(q)$ are in optimal order.

3. Agent b is the first mover for stage p and a for stage q: In other words, $p \in \beta$ and $q \in \alpha$. Let $\beta_i = p$ and $\alpha_j = q$. Since $p < q$, stage p will occur before stage q, i.e., $i < j$. Then, from the condition R_3, we know that for any i and j, $w^a_{OA^g(\alpha_j)} \geq w^a_{OA^g(\beta_i)}$. Then, from Table 2 (Row 4), we know that, for any two issues, if b is the first mover for the first stage and a that for the second, then it is optimal for a to order the two issues in ascending order of their weights. In other words, the issues $OA^g(p)$ and $OA^g(q)$ are in optimal order.

4. Agent a is the first mover for stage p and b for stage q: In other words, $p \in \alpha$ and $q \in \beta$. Let $\alpha_i = p$ and $\beta_j = q$. Since $p < q$, stage p will occur before stage q. Then, from the condition R_3, we know that for any i and j, $w^a_{OA^g(\alpha_i)} \geq w^a_{OA^g(\beta_j)}$. Then, from Table 2 (Row 6), we know that, for any two issues, if a is the first mover for the first stage and b that for the second, then it is optimal for a to order the two issues in descending order of their weights. In other words, the issues $OA^g(p)$ and $OA^g(q)$ are in optimal order.

Thus, every pair of issues in OA^g satisfies the optimal sequence prescribed by Theorem 1 for two issues. So the entire sequence of issues in OA^g will be the optimal sequence.

(C_2) If n is even and $\delta < \delta_c$: Analogous to the proof for the case C_1.
(C_3) If n is even and $\delta \geq \delta_c$: Analogous to the proof for the case C_1.

We have proved that OA^g contains a's optimal set of g issues, and also that the order of issues in OA^g is optimal. In other words, OA^g is a's optimal agenda.

The method for finding agent b's optimal agenda will be analogous. Based on Theorem 2, an algorithm for finding agent a's optimal agenda is given in

Algorithm 1. Since the maximum number of elements in α or β is m, the time complexity of this algorithm is $\mathcal{O}(m)$.

Algorithm 1. OptAgenda(I, w^a, w^b, δ, δ_c, n, g, m, α, β, $|\alpha|$, $|\beta|$)

Require: The elements in I, α, and β arranged in ascending order.
1: **if** odd(n) **then**
2:     **for** $i = 1$ to $|\alpha|$ **do**
3:         $OA(\alpha_i) \Leftarrow m - i + 1$;
4:     **end for**
5:     **for** $i = 1$ to $|\beta|$ **do**
6:         $OA(\beta_i) \Leftarrow m - |\alpha| - i + 1$;
7:     **end for**
8: **end if**
9: **if** even(n) and ($\delta < \delta_c$) **then**
10:     **for** $i = 1$ to $|\beta|$ **do**
11:         $OA(\beta_i) \Leftarrow m - i + 1$;
12:     **end for**
13:     **for** $i = 1$ to $|\alpha|$ **do**
14:         $OA(\alpha_i) \Leftarrow m - |\beta| - i + 1$;
15:     **end for**
16: **end if**
17: **if** even(n) and ($\delta \geq \delta_c$) **then**
18:     **for** $i = 1$ to g **do**
19:         $OA(i) \Leftarrow m - i + 1$;
20:     **end for**
21: **end if**

---

4 Optimal Agendas for Setting S_2

In Sect. 4, we showed how to find an optimal agenda of size g given the first mover for each of the g stages. But for the setting S_2, the players do not know who the first movers for the g stages will be. They only know that the first movers for the g stages will be given by one of the functions $f_1, \ldots, f_K$ chosen uniformly at random and that each of these $K = 2^g$ functions is equally probable. Because of this randomness, we can only find an agent's *expected equilibrium utility* from an agenda. Thus, agent a's expected equilibrium utility from an agenda $X \in AG^g$ ($EU^a(X, f)$) is defined as follows:

$$EU^a(X, f) = \frac{1}{K} \sum_{j=1}^{K} \left(U^a(X, f_j) \right) \tag{11}$$

$$= \frac{1}{K} \sum_{j=1}^{K} \left(\sum_{i=1}^{g} U_i^a(\mathrm{XA}_i^{f_j(i)}(T_i), T_i) \right) \tag{12}$$

Here, $\mathrm{XA}_i^{f_j(i)}(t)$ denotes a's equilibrium share for the time period t of the ith stage, T_i is the equilibrium agreement time for stage i, and $f_j(i)$ the first mover for stage i. Both $\mathrm{XA}_i^{f_j(i)}(t)$ and T_i can be obtained from Lemma 1. Given this, an agent's optimal agenda is defined as follows.

Definition 3. Let $AA^g \in AG^g$ and, let the first movers for the g stages be defined by the functions $f_1, \ldots, f_K$. Also, let $\mathrm{XA}_i^{f_j(i)}$ be a's equilibrium share for the ith stage for FMF f_j, and T_i be the equilibrium time of agreement for the ith stage and. Then, AA^g is agent a's optimal agenda if it satisfies the following condition:

$$
AA^g = \underset{X \in AG^g}{argmax}\, EU^a(X, f)
$$

$$
= \underset{X \in AG^g}{argmax}\, \frac{1}{K} \sum_{j=1}^{K} \left(\sum_{i=1}^{g} U_i^a (\mathrm{XA}_i^{f_j(i)}(T_i), T_i) \right) \tag{13}
$$

Agent b's optimal agenda AB^g is defined analogously.

Given this definition, we will now show how to find an optimal agenda for agent a. That for agent b can be found analogously.

As before, finding an agent's optimal agenda of size g will require finding an optimal set of g issues and an optimal order for them. From Eqs. 13 and 3, it is clear that Lemma 2 can be used for finding a's optimal set of g issues for the setting S_2 as well. Thus, we will show how to find an optimal order for the issues in SA^g. We will do this in Theorems 3 and 4. Specifically, in Theorem 3, we will show how to find an optimal order for the issues in SA^g for the case $g = 2$. Then, in Theorem 4, we will extend the result of Theorem 3 and show how to find an optimal order for the issues in SA^g for the general case $2 \le g \le m$.

Theorem 3. *Consider an agenda comprised of two issues: $c \in I$ and $d \in I$, and let $w_c^a \ge w_d^a$. Then, agent a's optimal sequence for the issues c and d is $\langle c, d \rangle$.*

Proof. Since we need two stages for negotiating two issues, there are $K = 2^2$ possible FMFs as listed in Table 1. For these functions, we will define $D^a(f)$ as follows:

$$
D^a(f) = EU^a(\langle c, d \rangle, f) - EU^a(\langle d, c \rangle, f). \tag{14}
$$

Then, as per Definition 3, if $D^a(f) \ge 0$, a's optimal sequence will be $\langle c, d \rangle$. Otherwise, it will be $\langle d, c \rangle$. Below, we will find $D^a(f)$. Substituting EU^a from Eq. 11 in Eq. 14 we get:

$$
D^a(f) = \frac{1}{K} \sum_{j=1}^{K} \left(U^a(\langle c, d \rangle, f_j) - U^a(\langle d, c \rangle, f_j) \right)
$$

$$
= \frac{1}{K} \sum_{j=1}^{K} D^a(f_j) \tag{15}
$$

Next, we will substitute $D^a(f_1)$ (from Eq. 10), $D^a(f_2)$, $D^a(f_3)$, and $D^a(f_4)$ in Eq. 15 to get the following:

$$D^a(f) = \frac{1}{2} \times (w_c^a - w_d^a) \times (1 - \delta) \tag{16}$$

Since $0 < \delta < 1$ and $w_c^a \geq w_d^a$, we get $D^a(f) \geq 0$. This implies that agent a's optimal sequence is $\langle c, d \rangle$ because it maximizes a's expected equilibrium utility.

In other words, if there are two issues to negotiate, it is optimal for a to negotiate the issue with higher weight in the first stage and the one with lower weight in the second.

In the next theorem, we will generalize the result of Theorem 3 to agendas of size $g \geq 2$. As before the issues in $I = (1, \ldots, m)$ will be assumed to be in ascending order of agent a's weights.

Theorem 4. *For the sequential procedure with independent implementation, agent a's optimal agenda OA^g of size g is as follows:*

$$OA^g(i) = m - i + 1 \qquad for\ 1 \leq i \leq g$$

Proof. We will first find a's optimal set of g issues, i.e., SA^g. As per Lemma 2, a's optimal set is the set of g issues with the highest weights for a. Since the issues in $I = (1, \ldots, m)$ are in ascending order of a's weights, $SA^g = (m-g+1, \ldots, m)$.

Next, we will find a's optimal sequence for the issues in the set SA^g. As per Theorem 3, a's optimal sequence for the case of two issues $c \in I$ and $d \in I$ with $w_c^a \geq w_d^a$ is $\langle c, d \rangle$. If we arrange the issues in OA^g in descending order of a's weights, we will get a's optimal sequence since every pair of issues from OA^g will form a's optimal sequence. In other words, $OA^g(i) = m - i + 1$ for $1 \leq i \leq g$.

In words, as per Theorem 4, a's optimal agenda of size g is the set of g issues with highest weights for a arranged in descending order of weights. Since the issues in I are in ascending order of a's weights, the time to compute OA^g will be $\mathcal{O}(m)$.

5 Related Research

The existing literature on sequential negotiations can broadly be divided into two types: those that treat the agenda as an *endogenous* variable, and those that treat it as an *exogenous* variable. The difference between these two is that, for the former, an agenda is selected during the process of negotiating over the issues. For the latter, an agenda is decided first, and then the parties negotiate over the issues on the agenda. Our research belongs to the latter category.

Research on endogenous agendas includes [1,2,5,6,8,9]. The work in [1,2] deals with two divisible issues in the context of an incomplete information setting where one of the two players is uncertain about the other's discount factor. Here, the authors study the properties of resulting equilibrium. While [1,2] deal with two divisible issues, [9] deals with multiple divisible issues and potentially infinite discrete time periods. Here, the parties are allowed to make an offer on any subset of a given set of issues but can only accept/ reject a complete offer. In this sense, an agenda is selected 'endogenously'. For this setting, the authors show *existence* and *uniqueness* conditions for equilibrium under the complete information assumption. A generalization of these results to a larger class of utility functions was given in [8], still under the complete information assumption. Then, for a negotiation model based on reservation prices, conditions for *existence* of equilibrium were determined in [6] for endogenous agendas. For a similar model based on reservation prices, [5] studied the problem of determining whether it is optimal for an agent to split a set of m issues into equal sized subsets of m/k ($k < m$) and negotiate them using a separate endogenous agenda for each subset, as compared to negotiating all the m issues with one endogenous agenda.

Research on exogenous agendas includes [7]. For the complete information setting, this work focuses on bargaining over two divisible pies using the sequential procedure. The authors take the set of issues as given, and show how the order in which the issues are negotiated, affects the outcome. Although this work recognizes the influence of the agenda on the outcome of a negotiation, it does not say anything about how to actually find an optimal agenda. Again, in the context of exogenous agendas and divisible issues, [4] dealt with how to find optimal agendas for the *package deal procedure*. In contrast, the focus of our work is on the sequential procedure.

In summary, we showed *how* to find an agent's optimal agenda for sequential negotiations with an exogenously defined agenda. In contrast, existing literature has merely recognized that the agenda can influence the outcome of a negotiation. To our knowledge, there is no previous work on methods for finding optimal agendas. Another key feature of our work is that our study shows the combined influence of the agenda and the first mover function on the outcome of a negotiation.

6   Conclusions

In this paper we presented computationally efficient methods for finding a player's optimal agenda for sequential negotiations. In such negotiations, there are m stages for negotiating over m issues; one stage for each issue. The players have time constraints in the form of *deadlines* and *discount factors*. Each player knows its own utility function but not that of the other. For such negotiations, we studied the combined influence of the agenda and the first mover on the outcome of a negotiation, and presented methods for computing a player's optimal agenda in two different settings. In one of the settings, the players know, in advance, who will be the first mover for each stage. In the other setting, the players do not have this information in advance; they only know that the first movers will be chosen randomly. For both settings, we showed how a player's optimal agenda can be determined in $\mathcal{O}(m)$ time.

There are several avenues for future research. These include extending the analysis to other incomplete information settings such as those where the agents are uncertain about the discount factor or the negotiation deadline, and developing methods for finding optimal agendas for other negotiation procedures such as the sequential procedure with simultaneous implementation and the simultaneous procedure.

References

1. Bac, M., Raff, H.: Issue-by-issue negotiations: The role of information and time preference. Games Econ. Behav. **13**, 125–134 (1996)
2. Busch, L.A., Horstman, I.J.: Bargaining frictions, bargaining procedures and implied costs in multiple-issue bargaining. Economica **64**, 669–680 (1997)
3. Busch, L.A., Horstman, I.J.: A comment on issue-by-issue negotiations. Games Econ. Behav. **19**, 144–148 (1997)
4. Fatima, S., Wooldridge, M., Jennings, N.: Optimal agendas for multi-issue negotiation. In: Proceedings of the Twelfth International Workshop on Agent Mediated Electronic Commerce (AMEC), pp. 155–168, Toronto, Cananda, May 2010
5. Fatima, S.S., Wooldridge, M., Jennings, N.R.: Optimal agendas for multi-issue negotiation. In: Proceedings of AAMAS, pp. 129–136, Melbourne, Australia, July 2003
6. Fatima, S.S., Wooldridge, M., Jennings, N.R.: An agenda based framework for multi-issue negotiation. Artif. Intell. J. **152**(1), 1–45 (2004)
7. Fershtman, C.: The importance of the agenda in bargaining. Games Econ. Behav. **2**, 224–238 (1990)
8. In, Y., Serrano, R.: Agenda restrictions in multi-issue bargaining (II): Unrestricted agendas. Econ. Lett. **79**, 325–331 (2003)
9. Inderst, R.: Multi-issue bargaining with endogenous agenda. Games Econ. Behav. **30**, 64–82 (2000)
10. Osborne, M.J., Rubinstein, A.: A Course in Game Theory. The MIT Press, Cambridge (1994)
11. Schelling, T.C.: The strategy of Conflict. Oxford University Press, New York (1960)
12. Sutton, J.: Non-cooperative bargaining theory: An introduction. Rev. Econ. Stud. **53**(5), 709–724 (1986)

An Empirical Analysis of QuiBids' Penny Auctions

Amy Greenwald[(✉)], Eric Sodomka, Eric Stix, Jeffrey Stix, and David Storch

Brown University, Providence, RI 02912, USA
amy_greenwald@brown.edu

Abstract. Given the string of bankruptcies of penny auction websites over the past two years, we use empirical data to investigate whether QuiBids remains profitable. Although profitable on an auction-by-auction basis, penny auction sites have problems retaining users. In order to alleviate this problem, QuiBids has implemented a Buy-Now system, in which losing bidders can contribute money they already lost in the auction towards the purchase of the item at a slightly inflated price. We find that QuiBids makes only limited profit after accounting for Buy-Now, but is able to remain profitable due voucher bid pack auctions. We also show that a large proportion of QuiBids' revenues come from experienced bidders, suggesting that rules designed to promote consumer retention may be working as intended.

1 Introduction

A *penny auction* is a form of an ascending auction in which, in addition to the winner paying its bid to acquire the good up for auction, each bidder pays a fixed cost for each bid it places in the auction. Penny auctions are so-called because each bid typically causes the good price to increase by at most a few pennies; bids themselves, however, can cost orders of magnitude more.

Past empirical studies of penny auctions (e.g., [1,4,7]) have established that penny auction bidders drastically overbid in aggregate. This excessive overbidding earned them the title "the evil stepchild of game theory and behavioral economics" in the Washington Post [3]. In other words, penny auctions are extremely costly for buyers. As such, one might expect them to be extremely profitable for sellers.

Past research estimates that Swoopo (formerly Telebid), a now defunct penny auction site, generated profits of just under $24 million from September 2005 to June 2009, and that each auction generated average revenues of in excess of 150 % of the good's value [1]. This means that Swoopo's profit margin was approximately 33 %. According to Fortune magazine, the most profitable sector of the retail economy in 2009 was department stores with an average profit margin of 3.2 %[1]. This profit margin pales in comparison to the order-of-magnitude larger margin estimated to have been captured by Swoopo.

---

[1] http://money.cnn.com/magazines/fortune/fortune500/2009/performers/industries/profits/

© Springer International Publishing Switzerland 2014
S. Ceppi et al. (Eds.): AMEC/TADA 2013 and 2014, LNBIP 187, pp. 56–69, 2014.
DOI: 10.1007/978-3-319-13218-1_5

The fact that penny auctions generate huge profits for sellers means that many buyers are taking huge losses; indeed, everyone but the winner is taking at least a small loss. Furthermore, Wang and Xu [7] observe that the penny auction model "offers immediate outcome (win or lose) feedback to bidders so that losing bidders can quickly learn to stop participating". Indeed, "the vast majorities of new bidders who join [BigDeal.com] on a given day play in only a few auctions, place a small number of bids, lose some money, and then permanently leave the site within a week or so". Augenblick further supports this observation with empirical data: 75 % of bidders leave [Swoopo] forever before placing 50 bids, and 86 % stop before placing 100 bids [1]. The majority of Swoopo's profits came from this "revolving door" of inexperienced bidders—a large number of new bidders who would soon leave the website never to return [7]. Consequently, if the supply of new, inexperienced bidders were to run out, a major source of income for these sites would evaporate.

To alleviate this problem, penny auction sites took measures to increase customer loyalty (i.e., to retain buyers), such as *win limits*, where the number of auctions a single bidder could win per month is limited to some small amount (e.g., 12 for QuiBids), and *beginner auctions*, in which all participants are bidders who have never before won an auction. These measures were designed to yield more unique winners, each of whom would be more likely than a loser to return to the site and bid in future auctions.

As of early 2009, many sites were still grappling with the issue of buyer retention, despite implementing these features. By late 2009, a new feature, *Buy-Now*, was adopted by numerous sites (Swoopo, BidHere, RockyBid, BigDeal, BidBlink, Bidazzled, PennyLord, Winno, and JungleCents to name a few [2,5]). Buy-Now allows bidders to contribute money spent in a lost auction towards the purchase price of that item, and buy a duplicate of the item post-auction for the amount of their shortfall. The purchase price of an item on a penny auction site is the retail value of that item marked up, usually by about 20 % (see Appendix A). Despite the inflated price, this feature still provides an extra sense of security to the bidder. The worst outcome for a bidder is now that she buys the item at an inflated price. This limits a bidder's loss to the difference between the site's marked-up purchase price of the item and its retail price. Because bidders could now choose to utilize the Buy-Now option and limit their losses, they were less likely to be discouraged from future participation.

As the Buy-Now feature limits a bidder's loss, it also limits a penny auction site's gain. To compensate for their losses, many penny auction sites sell voucher bids. Voucher bids are packets of bids that can be used to bid in other auctions. But voucher bids are not equivalent to purchased bids, because they do not contribute in full (or sometimes at all) to Buy-Now spending. That is, if a bidder places 200 bids, 100 with purchased bids, and 100 with voucher bids, at a cost of $.60 each for the purchased bids, it may only have contributed $60 towards its potential to Buy-Now. Voucher bids help offset the potential losses to sellers of the Buy-Now feature, since voucher bids are not fully incorporated into Buy-Now spending.

Between late 2009 and early 2011, almost 150 penny auction sites shut down inexplicably or went bankrupt [6]. This included such penny auction giants as Swoopo and BigDeal. Notably absent from the bankruptcy list is QuiBids, which has become one of the biggest penny auctioneers. In this paper, we set out to analyze QuiBids profits. We do so using empirical data scraped from the auction's web site. We analyze voucher bid auctions and non-voucher bid auctions separately, and we analyze profitability with and without buyers taking advantage of Buy-Now. We also determine the proportion of profits coming from inexperienced versus experienced bidders. These analyses allow us to identify the effects of QuiBids' auction rules on profitability. We find that despite the slew of penny auction bankruptcies, QuiBids appears to be turning profit margins on the order of 30 %, which is consistent with the margins achieved by Swoopo at its prime.

The rest of the paper is organized as follows. We first define penny auctions more formally, and outline some QuiBids-specific implementation details. We then describe the attributes of two QuiBids datasets we have collected. Using these datasets, we estimate QuiBids revenues, costs, and profits, first ignoring and then considering Buy-Now effects and voucher bid auctions. Finally, we present results on the makeup of inexperienced versus experienced bidders in QuiBids auctions and how each group contributes toward auctioneer revenues.

2   QuiBids' Penny Auction Rules

We first define our model of a standard penny auction. Let p be the current highest bid, let w be the identity of the current highest bidder, and let t be the amount of time remaining before the auction ends. Initially, $p := \underline{p}$, $w := \emptyset$, and $t := \overline{t}$. When the auction starts, the time t begins decreasing. While $t > 0$, any bidder b may place a bid. To do so, b must pay the auctioneer an immediate bid fee ϕ. After b places its bid, the new highest bid is $p := p + \delta$ (for some $\delta > 0$), the highest bidder is $w := b$, and the remaining time is reset to $t := \max(t, \underline{t})$, which ensures other bidders have at least time $\underline{t}$ to place an additional bid. When the auction ends (i.e., when $t = 0$), the current highest bidder w wins the item and pays the current highest bid p (in addition to any bid fees it paid along the way). *Note that even the losing bidders pay bid fees.*

QuiBids is a penny auction web site that hosts multiple simultaneous and sequential penny auctions. For each of its auctions, QuiBids follows with the above model with $\underline{p} = \$0$, $\phi = \$0.60$, $\delta = \$0.01$, and $\underline{t}$ in the range $\{20, 15, 10\}$ seconds and decreases as the time elapsed increases. The starting clock time $\overline{t}$ varies depending on the auction, but is on the order of hours. Additionally, QuiBids adds some variants to the standard penny auction, such as *Buy-Now*, *voucher bids*, and *BidOMatic*, and also imposes some winner restrictions. Each of these aspects is discussed below.

The *Buy-Now* feature allows any bidder who has lost an auction to buy a duplicate version of that good at a fixed price $\overline{m}$. As discussed in the Introduction, if a bidder uses Buy-Now, any bid fees the bidder incurred in the auction are subtracted from $\overline{m}$.

Voucher bids are a special type of good that are sold in penny auctions. When a bidder wins a pack of N voucher bids, it is able to place N subsequent bids in future auctions, each for a bid fee of \$0 instead of the usual fee ϕ. Of course, the bidder had to pay to purchase the voucher bids, but the bidder may be able to purchase them for less than the cost of placing standard bids. However, voucher bids do not usually contribute to Buy-Now in the same way as standard bids. Unlike standard bids, each of which reduces the Buy-Now price by ϕ, each voucher bid reduces the Buy-Now price by $\phi\rho$. For QuiBids, $\rho = 0$; that is, voucher bids do not contribute to Buy-Now at all.

For completeness, we mention one further feature of QuiBids auctions that we do not analyze in this paper but could be of interest to other researchers studying bidder and auctioneer behavior in penny auctions. The *BidOMatic* tool allows a bidder to specify a number of bids (between 3 and 25, for Quibids) to be automatically submitted on his behalf at a random time between $\underline{t}$ and zero seconds. Whether or not a bid is placed with a BidOMatic is public information.

Finally, QuiBids imposes the following win limits on each bidder:

- Each bidder may only win 12 items over a 28 day period.
- Each bidder may not win more than one of the same item valued over \$285 in a 28 day period.
- Each bidder may only win one item valued over \$999.99 in a 28 day period.
- Voucher bid auctions are not subject to any of the above restrictions and are only subject to a maximum of 12 wins per day limit.
- A subset of auctions, known as beginner auctions, only allow bidders who have never previously won an auction to bid.

3 Data Collection

Our analysis relies on two datasets scraped from QuiBids during the seven days following November 15th, 2011. We refer to these datasets as the auction end data A^{end} and full auction bid histories A^{hist}.

3.1 Auction End Data

The auction end data contains a single row of data for each of 37,233 auctions. For each auction, we recorded the following information:

- Auction ID - a unique auction number.
- Item Name - A brief item description.
- Auction End Price - The final price of the item.
- Date - Day the auction ended (EST).
- Time - Time the auction ended (EST).
- Purchase Price - The marked-up Buy-Now price.
- Winner - The bidder ID of the winning bidder.
- Bid-O-Winner - Whether or not the auction was won by a BidOMatic.
- Distinct Bidders - The number of distinct bidders in the last 10 bids.
- Distinct Bid-Os - The number of distinct bidders using BidOMatics in the last 10 bids.
- Last Ten Bidders - The bidder IDs of the last ten bidders.

3.2   Full Auction Bid Histories

Whereas the auction end data contains cursory information about many auctions, the full auction bid history auctions contains much more detailed information about a smaller set of auctions. The full auction bid histories record every bid placed in 50 different auctions. For each bid placed when the auction clock was at or below its reset time we recorded the following data:

- Auction ID - uniquely identifies each auction.
- Bidder ID - uniquely identifies each bidder.
- Bid Price - The new price of the item after this bid.
- BidOMatic? - Whether or not this bid was placed by a BidOMatic or placed manually.
- Bidders in Last 5 - The number of bidders in the last five minutes.
- Auction Clock - The time on the auction clock when this bid was placed.
- AC Reset - The time the auction clock resets to every time a new bid is placed.
- Date - The date on which this bid was placed (EST).
- Time - The time at which this bid was placed (EST).

4   QuiBids Profitability

We now estimate QuiBids' profitability from our datasets. Our interest is in the revenue and costs passing through the auctions, and we thus ignore other unknown operational and marketing costs, and assume that QuiBids receives zero net profit from its shipping fees.

Let A be some set of auctions and B_a be the set of bidders that placed at least one bid in auction $a \in A$. Let p_a be the winning price for auction a, w_a be the winning bidder for auction a, and $\overline{m}_a$ be the marked-up price for which the good sold in auction a can be purchased through Buy-Now. Let n_a^b be the total number of bids placed by bidder b in auction a and $y_a^b \in [0, 1]$ be the fraction of those bids that were voucher bids. Let $x_a^b \in \{0, 1\}$ indicate whether bidder b used Buy-Now in auction a.

QuiBids revenue r_a for auction a is equal to the winning price p_a paid by the winner plus, for each bidder, either the total price $\overline{m}_a$ the bidder paid to purchase through Buy-Now, or the total amount the bidder spent on bid fees:

$$r_a = p_a + \sum_{b \in B_a} \left[x_a^b \overline{m}_a + (1 - x_a^b)(1 - y_a^b) n_a^b \phi \right]. \tag{1}$$

QuiBids costs c_a for auction a are proportional to the number of goods it must procure and deliver to the auction winner and all bidders who used Buy-Now. We assume that QuiBids must pay a constant per-good price $\underline{m}_a$ for each good it procures for auction a:

$$c_a = \underline{m}_a + \sum_{b \in B_a} x_a^b \underline{m}_a. \tag{2}$$

Table 1. Glossary of symbols

Symbol	Description
A^{hist}	The set of auctions in the full auction bid histories
A^{end}	The set of auctions in the end auction data
A_n^{end}	The non-voucher auctions in the end auction data
A_v^{end}	The voucher bid pack auctions in the end auction data
a	An arbitrary auction
b	An arbitrary bidder
B_a	The set of bidders in auction a
w_a	The winning bidder for auction a
p_a	The winning price for auction a
x_a^b	Indicator for whether bidder b used Buy-Now in auction a
y_a^b	The fraction of bids that are not voucher bids
n_a^b	The number of bids placed by bidder b in auction a
$\underline{m}$	Per-good procurement cost
$\overline{m}_a$	Buy-Now price
ϕ	Bid fee
r	Revenue
c	Cost
π	Profit
ρ	Relative change in revenue under Buy-Now
κ	Relative change in cost under Buy-Now
f_{win}	The fraction of bids placed by auction winners

QuiBids profit π_a for auction a is simply its revenue minus its costs (Table 1):

$$\pi_a = r_a - c_a \tag{3}$$

There are some terms in Eqs. 1 and 2 that are private information and thus not available in either of our datasets. First, we do not observe whether any given bid was a standard or voucher bid, so we do not know what fraction y_a^b of bidder b's bids in auction a were voucher bids. Second, we do not know the price $\underline{m}_a$ that QuiBids pays to procure each good in auction a. Third, we have no information about whether or not each bidder used Buy-Now (i.e., x_a^b values).

To estimate the fraction y_a^b of bidder b's bids in auction a that were voucher bids, we simply assume that the fraction of voucher bids used was constant across all auctions and bidders: $y_a^b = \hat{y}$, for all $a \in A$ and $b \in B_a$. We then take $\hat{y}$ to be the ratio of voucher bids sold to total bids placed in the end data. This gives an estimate of $\hat{y} = 0.0704$.

In order to estimate QuiBids procurement cost $\underline{m}_a$ for the good sold in auction a, one approach would be to measure some statistic (e.g., mean or minimum) over sampled prices at which that good can be purchased from popular online retailers. While this approach may be a reasonable approximation, it doesn't scale well, since we would need retail pricing data for each good sold by QuiBids. As an alternative, we assume that QuiBids sets Buy-Now prices so that each good's Buy-Now price is a constant fraction h above its underlying purchase price. That is, $h = \overline{m}_a/\underline{m}_a$.

To approximate h, we take a subset of auction data $A' \subset A$ containing auctions for distinct goods. For each auction, we record the minimum price $\underline{m}'_a$ for which the corresponding good is available across a set of online retailers (see Appendix A). The estimated markup factor $\hat{h}$ is then computed as $\hat{h} = \frac{1}{|A'|} \sum_{a \in A'} \overline{m}_a/\underline{m}'_a$. Finally, for an auction $a \in A$, the QuiBids per-good procurement costs are estimated to be $\hat{\underline{m}}_a = \overline{m}_a/\hat{h}$. For our set A' of 25 distinct goods, we find that $\hat{h} = 1.21$. That is, the Buy-Now price is on average 21 % larger than the lowest discovered retail price.

5   The Effects of Buy-Now

Rather than estimate whether each bidder used Buy-Now in each auction (x_a^b), we computed possible profits under various assumptions about Buy-Now behavior. These various assumptions, and their ensuing implications, are discussed in turn in this section.

5.1   Ignoring Buy-Now Effects

We begin by looking at QuiBids' expected revenues, costs, and profits without accounting for additional revenue and costs that arise from bidders using the Buy-Now option. We also partition the set of auctions in the end data A^{end} into the set of voucher bid auctions A_v^{end} (i.e., the set of auctions in which a pack of voucher bids is the good being sold) and the set of non-voucher bid auctions A_n^{end}. For this analysis we will look only at A_n^{end}, but we will return to the analysis of voucher bid auctions in short order.

Note that, if no bidders used Buy-Now (i.e., $x_a^b = 0$, for all $a \in A_n$ and $b \in B_a$), QuiBids revenue for auction a simplifies to

$$r_a = p_a + \sum_{b \in B_a} (1 - y_a^b) n_a^b \phi \tag{4}$$

and QuiBids costs similarly simplify to $c_a = \underline{m}_a$.

Profit Breakdown. Summing across all auctions in A_n^{end}, we compute the total revenue $r(A_n^{end}) = \sum_{a \in A_n^{end}} r_a$, total cost $c(A_n^{end}) = \sum_{a \in A_n^{end}} c_a$, and total profit $\pi(A_n^{end}) = \sum_{a \in A_n^{end}} \pi_a$. We find that $r(A_n^{end}) = \$2.696\mathrm{M}$, $c(A_n^{end}) = \$1.428\mathrm{M}$, and $\pi(A_n^{end}) = \$1.268\mathrm{M}$. These numbers yield a profit margin of 47.0 % (see Fig. 4, Row 1).

Figures 1 and 2 summarize the distribution over profits π_a, for all $a \in A_n^{end}$. We find that the median profit is negative, meaning QuiBids loses money on more than half its auctions.

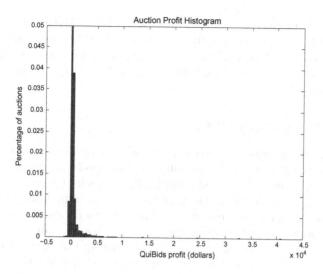

Fig. 1. A histogram that depicts the percentage of QuiBids' auctions in A_n^{end} which yielded various levels of profit.

Mean	$49.00
Median	−$9.67
Standard Deviation	$480.92
Range	$42.4K
Minimum	−$1.45K
Maximum	$40.9K
Sum	$1,268K
Count	25873

Fig. 2. Descriptive statistics for the distribution of profits across all QuiBids auctions for the week of November 15th, 011. Results were calculated using A_n^{end}.

Value Price Range	$0-$285	$285-$1,000	$1,000+
Count	24,943	881	49
Fraction of Auctions	0.964	0.034	0.002
Total Revenue	$1,539K	$890K	$267K
Total Cost	$1,043K	$320K	$65K
Total Profit	$496K	$570K	$202K
Margin	32.2%	64.0%	75.8%

Fig. 3. Descriptive statistics for the distribution of profits across QuiBids auctions split by value price for the week of November 15th, 2011. The bounds for each price range were determined based on QuiBids' win limit rules. (Profit) Margin is calculated as $100\pi/r\%$. Results were calculated using A_n^{end}.

However, there are also a significant number of auctions where QuiBids profits exceed $500. When we partition the profit data according to good price (Fig. 3), we see that QuiBids makes a disproportionately large share of its profit on a relatively small number of auctions. The top 0.132 % highest-priced auctions generated 11.1 % of Quibids' profits, and the top 2.50 % highest-priced auctions generated almost 43 % of Quibids' profits. In an extreme case, QuiBids made over \$40K in profit on a single auction for a MacBook Pro, in which over 75,000 bids were submitted.

5.2 Including Buy-Now Effects

The analysis in the previous section assumed that no bidders used Buy-Now. At the other extreme, we could compute QuiBids' profit assuming every losing bidder used Buy-Now. This would likely lead to a much higher QuiBids revenue than exists in reality, as it would assume that even a bidder who placed a single bid would use Buy-Now, whereas it would actually be cheaper for the bidder to purchase the good at retail without the QuiBids price markup.

In fact, it is not obvious *a priori* whether ignoring Buy-Now effects as done in the previous section artificially raises or lowers the estimate of QuiBids' profits. Whenever a bidder b uses Buy-Now, QuiBids must pay $\underline{m}_a$ to procure the good and receives revenue $\overline{m}_a$ from bidder b for a profit of $\overline{m}_a - \underline{m}_a$. If bidder b had already spent more than $\overline{m}_a - \underline{m}_a$ in the auction through bid fees, QuiBids would achieve greater short-term profit if b did not use Buy-Now. Similarly, if b spent less than $\overline{m}_a - \underline{m}_a$ in the auction through bid fees, QuiBids would achieve greater short-term profit if the bidder used Buy-Now.

Our analysis in this section gives an upper bound on costs, and thus a lower bound on profit, when bidders have a Buy-Now option. To provide this bound, we assume that any eligible bidder that could use Buy-Now to reduce QuiBids overall profits (i.e., any bidder who spent more than $\overline{m}_a - \underline{m}_a$ in bid fees) does use Buy-Now:

$$\hat{x}_a^b = \begin{cases} 1 & \text{if } b_a \neq w_a \text{ and } n_a^b y_a^b \phi \geq \overline{m}_a - \underline{m}_a \\ 0 & \text{otherwise} \end{cases} \tag{5}$$

In addition to giving a lower bound on QuiBids profits, this choice of function for $\hat{x}_a^b$ also has an economic interpretation: it assumes that bidders are utility maximizing, and that anyone willing to bid in the auction has an underlying value for the good that is greater than or equal to the good's retail price $\underline{m}_a$. After bidding in auction a and incurring bid fees Φ_a^b, each losing bidder b with underlying value v_a^b faces the option of using Buy-Now for utility $v_a^b - (\overline{m}_a - \Phi_a^b)$, not using Buy-Now and instead buying at retail for utility $v_a^b - \underline{m}_a$, or not using Buy-Now and not buying at retail for utility 0. The choice of using Buy-Now maximizes the bidder's utility when $\Phi_a^b \geq \overline{m}_a - \underline{m}_a$ (i.e., when the bidder's total bid fees exceed QuiBids' price markup).[2]

Determining whether a bidder uses Buy-Now requires knowledge of the fees the bidder accumulated in an auction. This information is not available in our dataset of auction end data A^{end}, and so we instead use the dataset with full

---

[2] We are assuming the Quibids' procurement price equals the retail price here, which was usually the case in the early days of penny auctions.

auction bid histories A^{hist}. From A^{hist}, we estimate the relative change in revenues ρ and costs κ when bidders use Buy-Now according to $\hat{x}_a^b$ as opposed to never using Buy-Now. More formally, let $r(A|x_a^b = g)$ be the total revenue from auctions in A when each bidder in each auction uses Buy-Now according to g, we compute $\rho = r(A^{hist}|x_a^b = \hat{x}_a^b)/r(A^{hist}|x_a^b = 0)$. Assuming that the auctions in A^{hist} provide a representative sample of the auctions in A^{end}, we apply the same revenue change to the end data in order to account for Buy-Now: $r(A_n^{end}|x_a^b = \hat{x}_a^b) = r(A_n^{end}|x_a^b = 0)\rho$. The term on the left-hand side cannot be directly computed from auction end data, but the terms on the right-hand side are all known. The terms $\kappa = c(A^{hist}|x_a^b = \hat{x}_a^b)/c(A^{hist}|x_a^b = 0)$ and $c(A_n^{end}|x_a^b = \hat{x}_a^b)$ are computed similarly.

Profit Breakdown. From the full auction histories A^{hist}, we compute $\rho = 1.47$ and $\kappa = 2.85$. Applying these estimates to A^{end} we find we find $r(A_n^{end}|x_a^b = \hat{x}_a^b) = \$3.965$M, $c(A_n^{end}|x_a^b = \hat{x}_a^b) = \$4.068$M, and $\pi(A_n^{end}|x_a^b = \hat{x}_a^b) = -\$0.102$M. The corresponding profit margin is $\pi(A_n^{end}|x_a^b = \hat{x}_a^b)/r(A_n^{end}|x_a^b = \hat{x}_a^b) = -2.6\%$ (see Fig. 4, Row 2). In contrast to our estimate of QuiBids' profit margin without Buy-Now (47.0 %), these results suggest that Quibids might actually experience a small loss on non-voucher auctions if all bidders were to use Buy-Now rationally (i.e., maximize their utility) to minimize their loss.

5.3   Voucher Bid Auctions

We now seek to analyze the profitability of the voucher bid partition of our dataset, A_v^{end}. An auction a for a voucher bid pack containing n_{bids} bids will have a Buy-Now price of $\overline{m}_a = n_{bids}\phi$, where the bid cost is $\phi = \$0.60$. Since voucher bids cannot be used towards Buy-Now purchases, voucher bid packs are not actually worth $n_{bids}\phi$. If a bidder places a voucher bid and wins the auction, the voucher bid was worth its full $0.60 cents. But if the bidder loses, the voucher bid is worth nothing, since it cannot be applied towards Buy-Now.

This begs the question: how much are voucher bids really worth? We tackle this question in two ways. First, we assume that the reduced value of voucher bid packs is given by the average markup rate h, so that $\underline{m}_a = \overline{m}_a/h$. We will refer to this valuation of voucher bid packs as "Valuation 1". Using Valuation 1, we estimate the profits of A_v^{end} both ignoring Buy-Now (Fig. 4, Row 3), and assuming full rational utilization of Buy-Now as described in the previous section (Fig. 4, Row 4). When bidders ignore Buy-Now, the profit margin is estimated to be a whopping 63.8 %; but when bidders are rational, that margin drops to 29.9 %.

We can improve upon Valuation 1 using the fraction f_{win} of bids that are spent by winners. The complete bid histories A^{hist} show that only $f_{win} = 4.438\%$ of bids are spent by winners. Assuming that voucher bids are evenly distributed among winners and losers, this implies that we should value voucher bid packs by $\underline{m}_a = f_{win}\overline{m}_a$, and individual voucher bids at only $f_{win}\phi = 0.04438 \times \$0.60 = \$0.0266$. We refer this valuation of voucher bid packs as "Valuation 2." Under Valuation 2, voucher bids are nearly worthless, implying that QuiBids' costs in voucher bid auctions are minimal.

	Count	Revenue	Cost	Profit	Margin	PPA
1	A_n^{end} without Buy-Now	25,873	$2,696K	$1,428K	$1,268K	47.0%	$49.00
2	A_n^{end} with Buy-Now	25,873	$3,965K	$4,068K	−$102K	−2.6%	-$3.96
3	A_v^{end} without Buy-Now, Valuation 1	11,360	$698K	$253K	$445K	63.8%	$39.19
4	A_v^{end} with Buy-Now, Valuation 1	11,360	$1,027K	$720K	$307K	29.9%	$27.01
5	A_v^{end} with Buy-Now, Valuation 2	11,360	$1,027K	$32K	$995K	96.9%	$87.55
6	A^{end} without Buy-Now, Valuation 1	37,233	$3,394K	$1,681K	$1,713K	50.5%	$46.00
7	A^{end} with Buy-Now, Valuation 1	37,233	$4,992K	$4,788K	$204K	4.1%	$5.49
8	A^{end} with Buy-Now, Valuation 2	37,233	$4,992K	$4,010K	$892K	17.9%	$23.96

Fig. 4. Profit statistics for non-voucher auctions and voucher auctions, separately and combined. We also include results either ignoring Buy-Now or assuming rational utilization of Buy-Now by all bidders, as well as results for both Valuation 1 and Valuation 2 of voucher bid packs. The final column, labeled "PPA", reports profit per auction.

Figure 4, Row 4 shows profits for A_v^{end} using Valuation 2 and accounting for Buy-Now. The extremely high profit margin of 96.9 % is explained by the fact that Valuation 2 estimates the worth of voucher bids at somewhere between 2 and 3 cents. It seems that QuiBids boosts its profitability by exploiting its users' dramatic overbidding for voucher bids.

5.4   Combining Voucher and Non-voucher Auctions

We now investigate QuiBids' overall profitability for the complete set of auctions A by summing revenues, costs, and profits for the two partitions of the dataset. Total revenue is computed as $r(A^{end}) = r(A_n^{end}) + r(A_v^{end})$, with equivalent calculations for cost and profit. As before, we consider three scenarios:

- No use of Buy-Now, with Valuation 1 for voucher bid packs (Fig. 4, Row 6).
- Full rational use of Buy-Now, with Valuation 1 for voucher bid packs (Fig. 4, Row 7).
- Full rational use of Buy-Now, with Valuation 2 for voucher bid packs (Fig. 4, Row 8).

Comparing Fig. 4, Rows 7 and 8, we see that the profit-limiting effects of Buy-Now are offset by accounting for the value of voucher bids. Although voucher bids auctions comprise only 30.5 % of the total auctions in our end data set, they account for the entirety of QuiBids profit (in the non-voucher auctions A_n^{end}, with Buy-Now, QuiBids took a small loss). Indeed voucher bid auctions allow QuiBids to be profitable despite Buy-Now.

6   Bidder Experience

We have already characterized Buy-Now as a strategy designed to limit profitability in the short term in exchange for greater consumer retention, and hence greater profitability in the long term. One proxy for user retention that we can use to evaluate QuiBids' success in this regard is bidder experience. Namely, we investigate what fraction of revenue comes from experienced bidders compared to the fraction from novice bidders.

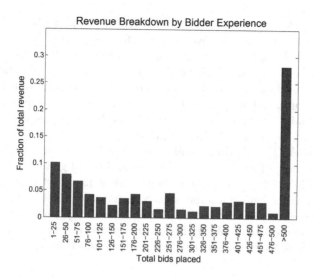

Fig. 5. Revenues derived from bidders with varying degrees of experience, as measured by the total number of bids placed over the course of all recorded auctions.

We define an experienced bidder as any bidder that has placed strictly more than 50 bids, based on Augenblick's assessment that the vast majority of inexperienced bidders (75 %) were discouraged before placing 50 bids [1].

New QuiBids users are required to purchase a starter bid pack consisting of 100 bids, so we also investigate the definition of an experienced bidder as a bidder who has placed strictly more than 100 bids. QuiBids has, at the very least, convinced such users to buy a second bid pack.

Using the threshold of 50, we find that of the approximately 135,000 bids placed in the complete auction histories, 73.5 % are placed by experienced bidders and 26.5 % are placed by inexperienced bidders. With a threshold of 100, 57.5 % of bids are placed by experienced bidders.

Assuming full rational utilization of Buy-Now and using a threshold of 100, this corresponds to 71.1 % of revenues coming from experienced bidders. In other words, nearly three-quarters of QuiBids' revenue comes from bidders who have purchased at least two bid packs.

Figure 5 gives a more detailed breakdown of revenue based on bidder experience. This figure shows that although QuiBids does garner a significant amount of revenue from inexperienced bidders, much of its revenue also comes from experienced bidders. These data are consistent with the notion that QuiBids' use of Buy-Now has been effective at ensuring long-term profitability by combating the "revolving door" effect.

7   Conclusion

In light of the recent slew of penny auctioneer bankruptcies, we have sought to determine whether QuiBids auctions remain profitable. Our conclusion is a qualified "yes". Although at first blush QuiBids appears to be achieving large profit margins comparable to Swoopo's, we find that Buy-Now sharply limits this profitability. In order to remain profitable after the limitations imposed by Buy-Now, QuiBids appears to rely on voucher bid auctions. We find that users overvalue voucher bids, and that by overbidding on arguably valueless voucher bid packs, such users allow QuiBids to extort large profit margins on voucher bid auctions. QuiBids' non-voucher auctions may not be profitable under Buy-Now, but voucher bid auctions make up for this deficiency.

We posit that QuiBids purposefully uses Buy-Now to limit short-term profitability in exchange for consumer retention, and hence greater long-term profitability. Voucher bids are a mechanism for enhancing short-term profitability, presumably without having a large negative impact on consumer retention.

Finally, we examine whether rules designed to keep users coming back to the site have been effective. We find that large proportions of QuiBids' revenues come from experienced bidders. This is a positive signal for QuiBids' long-term prospects.

A   Appendix

(See Fig. 6)

Item Name	Value Price	Retail Price	Markup
Samsung-PN51D6500-51-1080P-3D-HDTV	$1,100.00	$952.84	15.44%
The-New-Apple-iPad-16GB-WiFi	$530.00	$499.00	6.21%
Jamo-S426HCS3-51-Home-Theater-system	$430.00	$300.00	43.33%
Palm-Harbor-Outdoor-Wicker-Chair	$220.00	$219.00	0.46%
Nambe-MT0254-Swoop-Bowl	$212.00	$190.00	11.58%
Universal-Remote-MX450-2-LCD	$200.00	$179.00	11.73%
Yamaha-YPT-230-61-Key-Portable-Keyboard	$144.00	$111.64	28.99%
10K-Gold-Onyx-Diamond-Butterfly-Pendant	$137.00	$99.95	37.07%
Garmin-Nuvi-2250LT-GPS	$99.00	$86.50	14.45%
Ogio-METRO-II-Backpack	$82.00	$60.72	35.05%
Adidas-ClimaLite-Navy-and-Gulf-Polos	$74.00	$60.00	23.33%
Burberry-Brit-for-Women-34-oz-Tester	$68.00	$34.00	100.00%
50-Kohls-Gift-Card	$51.00	$50.00	2.00%
50-Department-Store-You-Choose-It	$51.00	$50.00	2.00%
Kalorik-Carnival-Popcorn-Popper	$51.00	$40.00	27.50%
Fox-Racing-Soleed-Digi-Camo-Boardshort	$44.00	$35.00	25.71%
Jensen-JCR-275-Alarm-Clock-Radio	$35.00	$35.00	0.00%
50-Bids-Voucher	$31.00	$30.00	3.33%
WMF-10-in-PP-Flat-Silicone-Ball-Whisk	$30.00	$15.00	100.00%
Kalorik-Jug-Kettle	$27.50	$24.95	10.22%
25-Bass-Pro-Shops-Gift-Card	$26.00	$25.00	4.00%
Slap-Watch-Regular	$20.00	$20.00	0.00%
Axis-GK-310-Multimedia-Keyboard	$16.00	$15.00	6.67%
10-Walmart-Gift-Card	$11.00	$10.00	10.00%
15-Bids-Voucher	$10.00	$9.00	11.11%
		Average Markup:	21.21%

Fig. 6. The 25 items we used to estimate the average value price markup. These data were collected in April of 2012, mostly from Amazon, but when unavailable, from the good's primary retailer.

References

1. Augenblick, N..: Consumer and producer behavior in the market for penny auctions: a theoretical and empirical analysis. Unpublished manuscript (2012). http://faculty.haas.berkeley.edu/ned/Penny_Auction.pdf
2. Fance, C.: Unique auction site Swoopo expands to Canada, testing "Buy It Now" (2010). http://tomuse.com/penny-auctions-entertainment-shopping-sites-review-compare/ixzz2Ogx2HoLI
3. Gimein, M.: The big money: the pennies add up at swoopo.com, July 2009. http://www.washingtonpost.com/wp-dyn/content/article/2009/07/11/AR2009071100684.html
4. Hinnosaar, T..: Penny auctions are unpredictable, January 2010. Unpublished manuscript. http://toomas.hinnosaar.net/pennyauctions.pdf
5. Kincaid, J.: Unique auction site Swoopo expands to Canada, testing "Buy It Now", June 2009. http://techcrunch.com/2009/06/26/unique-auction-site-swoopo-expands-to-canada-testing-buy-it-now/
6. Lee, A.: Over 150 closed penny auction sites: is the model sustainable? (2011). http://www.pennyauctionwatch.com/2011/04/over-150-closed-penny-auction-sites-is-the-model-sustainable/
7. Wang, Z., Xu, M.: Learning and strategic sophistication in games: evidence from penny auctions on the internet (2012)

Analysis of Fairness and Incentives of Profit Sharing Schemes in Group Buying

Feyza Merve Hafızoğlu[✉] and Sandip Sen

Department of Computer Science, University of Tulsa, Tulsa, OK 74104, USA
{feyza-hafizoglu,sandip}@utulsa.edu

Abstract. Payoff distribution within coalitions in group-buying environments, where a group of buyers pool their demands to benefit from volume discounts, is a well-studied problem. However, the general assumption in literature is unit demand, where every buyer needs one item. In the case of varying volume demands, both the valuation and the contribution of buyers will change. In this paper, we introduce the *variable demand group-buying game* with implied values, where the valuation of one item for the buyer is equal to the unit price, which the buyer can obtain by itself. Buyers with higher volumes of demand have lower valuation per unit. We consider scenarios where volume discounts kick in at multiple volume thresholds and investigate the effect of different profit sharing mechanisms in coalitions of buyers: proportional cost sharing based on volume demand and valuation, proportional profit sharing based on volume and contribution, and adjusted Clarke mechanism. All these mechanisms are efficient, budget-balanced, and individual rational. We evaluated these five payoff mechanisms on the following criteria: stability, incentive compatibility, and fairness. We introduce a fairness criteria that correlates with marginal contribution. Experimental results show that fairness and stability are difficult to satisfy simultaneously.

Keywords: Group-buying · Variable demand · Fairness · Payoff distribution

1 Introduction

Electronic marketplaces offer great opportunities for sellers of products and services to reach out to and attract new prospective buyers. On the other hand, such markets also allow prospective buyers to search for opportunities to seek and find better products under possibly more advantageous contractual obligations. Interestingly, win-win situations can arise in such environments where sellers offer volume discounts to facilitate selling of larger quantities of products with resultant increase in total profits, and buyers forming "buying groups" by pooling their individual demands.

Forming "buying groups" can lower their per unit costs for both the sellers and buyers. From the perspective of the sellers, the order processing, shipping, manufacturing, and inventory costs decrease, the customers tend to buy more

© Springer International Publishing Switzerland 2014
S. Ceppi et al. (Eds.): AMEC/TADA 2013 and 2014, LNBIP 187, pp. 70–83, 2014.
DOI: 10.1007/978-3-319-13218-1_6

since some money will be left after volume discount, and the vendor can access to the revenue earlier than when it has sell to individual customers. From the perspective of the buyers, they save money by taking advantage of volume discounts.

Group-buying problem is well-studied in theory [1–6] and practice [7–9]. The most popular cost distribution in real group-buying markets is equity: every buyer will pay the same amount per unit item. The cost distribution problem can also be determined by using auctions [1–4]. The buyers can combine their demands in a bundle [3]. The common assumption in most studies that adopt a game-theoretical approach [1,2,4,6] is unit demand. However, there are real-life group buying environments where the buyers need multiple items.

The purpose of this study is to understand the behavior of the profit sharing mechanisms for the buyers with varying demand sizes. When the number of items purchased by each buyer is different from each other, the contribution of each buyer will change dramatically with comparison to domains with unit demand. Hence a critical question arises: Who will pay how much? Should buyers make their payment based on the same price per unit? If not, why and what should price per unit for each buyer be? What are the desirable features of an ideal profit sharing mechanism? Do they differ from the desirable features of mechanisms designed for unit demand?

We study the resultant *variable demand group-buying game* scenarios, formally identifying novel aspects of the problem. In particular, the buyers are only required to express their volume demands and not their true valuation per item. From the volume demand expressed by a buyer, one can infer its minimal valuation per item, which is the price per unit item it had to pay if it was the lone buyer. Then, we identify desirable features of profit distribution schemes for buying groups: stability, incentive compatibility, and fairness. We find that the concept of fairness (the correlation between the marginal contribution of a buyer to the group and its profit) becomes more important, because of varying buyer demands. Although stability is a desirable criterion, a stable mechanism might not be attractive to buyers because it might be unfair in these kind of games of implicit valuation. For instance, if a buyer contributes more than the other buyers in a coalition, and gets zero profit, this buyer probably loses its faith in this mechanism. Another aspect of the comparison between stability and fairness is that in real life it is not easy to detect the stability of a mechanism (they need to try at all possible coalitions). On the other hand, a group of buyers who participate in a coalition can easily see the unfairness. In fact, humans strongly care about fairness in real life [10].

Section 2 introduces the variable demand group-buying game; Sect. 3 addresses the evaluation criteria of the mechanisms that are presented in Sect. 4. In Sect. 5, the mechanisms adapted to the variable demand group-buying game are discussed based on the criteria. Finally Sect. 7 concludes.

2 Group Buying Game

We introduce the *Variable Demand Group Buying Game* to represent and reason about scenarios where buyers who need multiple items of one type or different amounts of some particular service. For instance, in group travel domain, e.g. travel deals in GroupOn[1], a group of people who are interested in travelling to the same destinations can combine their travel demands and benefit from group discounts. The unit price is the price per person for the travel and determined by the travel agency: the unit price monotonically decreases as the total demand increases. The number of travelers for each buyer will vary: some buyers might be couples, while others travel with their families or friends.

The unit price for two buyers, one traveling with a spouse and another travelling with a group of friends, is same in practice. However, the contribution of the second buyer travelling with a group of friends, in reducing per person cost is more than the couple. If this crowded friend group would not attend the travel, the couple and the rest of the buyers might not benefit from such a high discount and end up paying more for their trip. Furthermore, the expected discount for the buyers might differ based on their demand size. Buyers with lower demands, e.g. a couple, is ready to pay for higher unit prices than the unit price for the buyer traveling with a group of friends, because the couple cannot get better deals by themselves. On the other hand, the buyer travelling with a friend group will expect a more discounted rate per group member.

Since our primary goal is to describe the features of ideal profit sharing mechanisms for group-buying markets with multiple demands, we make some simplifying assumptions about the market. We are interested in the buyers' benefits assuming that sellers decided their price schedules to maximize their own profit. We do not address the issue of competition between the sellers. The price schedule of the seller is assumed to be public information.

2.1 Variable Demand Group-Buying Game

Variable demand group-buying game is a non-convex game (see Appendix for proof) consisting of buyers, price schedule, profit sharing scheme, and the utility function.

Variable Demand Group-buying Game: The group-buying game is a tuple $\langle G = (N, \mathbf{n}, p) \rangle$

- $N = \{b_i\}$, $i = [1 \ldots l]$ is a set of l buyers;
- $\mathbf{n}$ is the vector of agent demands, where n_i is the demand volume of the ith buyer.
- $p : \mathbb{N} \mapsto \mathbb{R}$ is the price schedule of the seller;

In addition, we consider different *payment schemes* which determine the payment to be made by each buyer given a game G: $S : \mathbf{n} \times p \mapsto \mathbb{R}$. A given payment

---

[1] http://www.groupon.com/

scheme, in turn, decides the profit of each of the buyers from this particular purchase.

Sellers and price schedules: We consider one type of item and the profit distribution of one seller. The profit sharing scheme is considered to be generic to be used for any price schedule of volume discounts. There are two constraints for a price schedule, $p(n)$, given n, the total number of items required by the buyers (also referred to as the total demand): when $n_1 \geq n_2$ we require (1) $p(n_1) \leq p(n_2)$, i.e., the price schedule is monotonically non-increasing, and (2) $n_1 \, p(n_1) \geq n_2 \, p(n_2)$, i.e., increasing demand will not lower the total cost or business volume.

Buyers: The population of buyers is denoted as $N = \{b_1, \ldots, b_l\}$. The buyer i, denoted as b_i, only reports its volume demand, n_i, where $n_i \geq 1$. Although the true valuation of b_i, i.e., $p(n_i^*)$, is unknown, the minimum valuation of a unit item for the buyer is implied as the unit price that it can obtain by itself, i.e., $p(n_i)$. Hence, the implied valuation of b_i's demand is $n_i p(n_i)$.

Coalition: Let's say N is a set buyers, $\{b_1, \ldots, b_l\}$, in a coalition, denoted as C_N. The profit of the coalition becomes the total valuation minus the total cost of the coalition

$$u(C_N) = \sum_{i \in C_N} n_i p(n_i) - n_T p(n_T) \tag{1}$$

where n_T is the total volume, i.e., $\sum_{i \in C_N} n_i$. b_i's profit becomes its valuation minus what it pays, i.e., $n_i \, p(n_i) - \text{pay}_i$.

Coalition Formation: In this game, the grand coalition is the optimal coalition because the buyers are ready to make a payment based on their valuation. Considering the first constraint of the price schedule, the price per unit item that existing members of the coalition will pay cannot increase by including other buyers. That means the profit of the coalition never decreases by adding another buyer. Furthermore, the utility of the coalition increases as we keep adding buyers into it, i.e., $u(C_S) \leq u(C_N)$ given that $S \subseteq N$. The contribution of b_i is defined as the difference in the utilities of the coalitions with, C_N, and without, $C_{N/\{i\}}$, b_i:

$$con_i(C_N) = u(C_N) - u(C_{N/\{i\}}) = n_i p(n_i) + (n_T - n_i) p(n_T - n_i) - n_T p(n_T). \tag{2}$$

Figure 1 shows a coalition with three buyers: $\{b_1, b_2, b_3\}$ for the given price schedule. Each bar represents one buyer, where the width of the bar shows the expressed demand volume, n_i, and the height is the buyer's valuation per unit, $p(n_i)$. Thus, the area of the bar is the total valuation of b_i for its demand, i.e., $n_i p(n_i)$. Buyers are sorted in descending order based on their value per unit to better visualize the big picture (this is not key for the working of the system as all buyers are finally included in the grand coalition, the order of inclusion does not matter).

Total value of the coalition, i.e., $\sum_{i \in N} n_i \, p(n_i)$, is the area consisting of three bars. According to the price schedule, the unit price is 6 (specified by the dashed line) for demand volume 6, and the cost of the coalition is the area under the dashed line. Thus the area above the dashed line is the profit of the coalition. Our goal is to understand the desirability of different mechanisms for sharing this profit between buyers based on their expressed demands. Which buyer desires more profit? For Fig. 1, should it be b_3, because of its contribution in reducing the per unit cost, or should it be b_1, with its higher value per unit item?

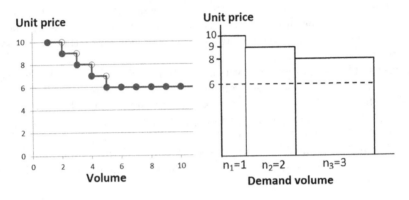

Fig. 1. Price schedule and a coalition with three buyers

3   Evaluation Criteria

We use the following criteria for evaluating profit sharing mechanisms:

Individual Rationality: The net utility of participants should be nonnegative, i.e., $\forall i \in C_N$, $u_i(C_N) \geq 0$.

Budget-balanced: The coalition should get exactly what it pays for, i.e., $\sum_{i \in C_N} pay_i = n_T p(n_T)$, where pay_i is the payment of b_i.

Incentive Compatibility: Participants cannot gain more utility by misrepresenting their valuations or, as in this case, their demands. The valuation of b_i is implicitly determined based on n_i and the price schedule. A profit sharing mechanism will be incentive compatible if b_i cannot increase its utility by speculating on n_i, i.e., $n_i = n_i^*$, where n_i^* is the true demand of agent b_i.

Efficiency: The social welfare, the sum of the utility of the participants, should be maximized, i.e., $\sum_{i \in C_N} u_i(C_N) + u_s$ where u_s is the utility of the seller.

Stability/Core: None of the subgroups of the coalition can gain more utility by leaving the current coalition and forming a new coalition, i.e., $\forall S \subseteq N$, $\sum_{i \in C_S} u_i(C_N) \geq u(C_S)$.

Fairness: In this game, fairness is measured in terms of the correlation between the contribution of a buyer and its profit. The idea is that b_i should receive a share of the profit proportional to its (non-negative) contribution to the coalition. The rationale for this fairness measure is that if b_i is not compensated for its contribution then it is being "underpaid" or not recognized. Also, such an "unfair" compensation may incentivize b_i to leave the coalition, in which case the value or profit of the entire coalition may decrease.

Furthermore, people may be able to recognize unfair treatment and avoid such environments in real life. In our domain of group-buying, given the public price schedule in a market, a buyer can approximately compute its contribution by estimating total demand (the individual demands of other buyers are not needed). In case of an unfair profit distribution, this buyer will lose its trust in the process and refuse further participation. We use two different fairness metrics:

1. *Pearson correlation coefficient* between the contribution and the profit of a buyer in a coalition
2. The deviation in the profit distributions of mechanisms from the fairest mechanism, *profit sharing proportional to contribution.*

4 Mechanisms

We introduce five mechanisms with different characteristics to understand their behavior in this setting. Even though they distribute profit (or cost) based on simple heuristics, their approaches are diverse enough to highlight the desirable features of mechanisms in the presence of varying demands.

1. **Cost Sharing Proportional to Volume:** The total cost is distributed proportional to demand volumes, i.e., $pay_i = n_i p(n_T)$. b_i's utility (share of profit) is

$$u_i(C_N) = n_i p(n_i) - n_i p(n_T) = n_i(p(n_i) - p(n_T)) \qquad (3)$$

by paying $n_i p(n_T)$. Everybody obtains the same per unit price regardless of their demand volume. It is extremely advantageous for the buyers with lower demands because of their higher valuations. The profit of buyers only depends on their valuation and the per unit price for the coalition. This mechanism is quite popular in real group-buying markets.
2. **Cost Sharing Proportional to Valuation:** The cost is distributed proportional to the valuation of b_i. This mechanism is not explicitly favoring any buyer type. b_i's utility is

$$u_i(C_N) = n_i p(n_i) - \frac{n_i p(n_i)}{\sum_{i \in C_N} n_i p(n_i)} n_T p(n_T). \qquad (4)$$

3. **Profit Sharing Proportional to Volume:** The profit of the coalition, i.e. $u(C_N) = \sum_{i \in C_N} n_i p(n_i) - n_T p(n_T)$, is distributed proportional to volume. b_i's utility is

$$u_i(C_N) = u(C_N) \frac{n_i}{\sum_{i \in C_N} n_i}. \qquad (5)$$

This mechanism is more advantageous to buyers with larger demands. Although it guarantees that the buyers with smaller demands will obtain a non-negative profit, their share of profits will be smaller.

4. **Profit Sharing Proportional to Contribution:** Contributions of buyers fairly determine their profits:

$$u_i(C_N) = \frac{\text{con}_i(C_N)}{\sum_{i \in C_N} \text{con}_i(C_N)} u(C_N). \tag{6}$$

5. **Adjusted Clarke Mechanism [2]:** This mechanism, similar to the profit sharing proportional to contribution mechanism, shares the utility based on the marginal contribution of buyers, but the actual payment is derived through a two-stage calculation. First a tentative payment of a coalition member is determined by reducing its valuation by its contribution. At this point the total sum of the buyer payments falls below the total cost of the coalition, $n_T p(n_T)$. Then the shortfall, i.e., the rest of the cost, is equally divided between the buyers to achieve budget balance. Hence,

$$\text{pay}_i = \begin{cases} n_i \, p(n_i) & \tau_i + \mu > n_i \, p(n_i) \\ \tau_i + \mu & \text{otherwise} \end{cases} \tag{7}$$

where $\tau_i = n_i p(n_i) - \text{con}_i(C_N)$ and μ is a positive constant number which makes the solution budget balance.

Using Shapley value [11] is an ideal approach to assess the marginal contribution, we did not examine this mechanism because of its exponential computational complexity. In addition to that using Shapley value for profit sharing is advantageous in the case of convex games because the solution is guaranteed to be in the core. Since variable demand group-Buying game is a non-convex game, we cannot take advantage of this mechanism in terms of stability.

5   Analysis

Budget-balanced: Three of five mechanisms, cost sharing proportional to volume and valuation, and adjusted Clarke mechanism, distribute the total cost of the coalition among the buyers. The others, namely profit sharing proportional to volume and contribution, compute the profit by subtracting the total cost from the total valuation to make sure that total cost is allocated to pay the seller. Hence, the coalition pays exactly what it gets from the buyers. The other relevant fact is that in the game there is no external agency that transfers utility to buyers or sellers. Therefore, all mechanisms are budget-balanced by definition.

Individual Rationality: Profit sharing proportional to volume and contribution mechanisms distribute the non-negative profit among buyers and are individual rational by definition. Cost sharing proportional to volume and valuation mechanisms compute what percentage of the total valuation of each buyer will be paid. In other words, the per unit price assigned to buyers is always lower than their valuation of the unit item. That is why these four methods are individually rational. Finally, adjusted Clarke mechanism is explicitly designed to be individually rational as $\text{pay}_i \leq n_i p(n_i)$, i.e., payment is less than or equal to valuation.

Efficiency: Since the grand coalition is optimal yielding a maximum profit in the game to the entire set of buyers and the seller, as all buyers are included and profit is monotonically non-decreasing in the group of buyers; all mechanisms are efficient because of this nature of the game.

Stability: The core of the game is not empty and out of five mechanisms only the cost sharing proportional to volume mechanism is in the core (see Appendix for proof). During the test runs with other mechanisms and while varying price schedules and demand volumes, subcoalitions rarely stand to gain by leaving the grand coalition, and even then the gain is very small and may not warrant deviation in practice because of knowledge requirements and other contributing factors like the cost of forming subcoalitions, etc. The rareness of instability is largely due to the fact that grand coalitions typically get the minimum price per unit and hence by far the higher total profit or social welfare.

Incentive Compatibility: None of five mechanisms is incentive compatible.

5.1 Fairness Analysis

Before discussing fairness, we show an example scenario where the cost sharing proportional to volume mechanism, which satisfies the stability, produces an unfair profit distribution. Figure 2 shows a coalition of buyers $\{b_1, b_2, b_3\}$ given the price schedule: $p(n) = 10$ when $n < 4$, and $p(n) = 9$ for $n \geq 4$. The demand volumes are 1, 2, and 4, respectively. The implied per unit valuations of buyers, i.e. $p(n_i)$, are 10, 10, and 9, respectively. The discounted per unit price for the coalition is 9 (dashed line). In this case, the total valuation of the coalition is 66, the total cost of the coalition (the total area under the dashed line) is 63, and the total profit is 3 (the area above the dashed line). Finally, the contributions of buyers are 1, 2, and 3, respectively.

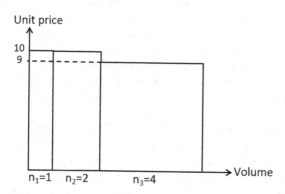

Fig. 2. A critical scenario for fairness

Cost sharing proportional to volume mechanism distributes the profits as 1, 2, and 0, respectively. Although b_1 and b_2 cannot reduce the price without b_3, b_3 has no share from the profit in return for having larger contribution. Furthermore, b_3 does not need to participate in a coalition unless the per unit price drops below its implied value. Hence, b_3 has no motivation to stay in the coalition and can be unhappy if it can infer or estimate this unfair profit distribution. The natural expectation of such buyers would be to gain nonzero profit in return for their contribution to the profits of others.

Table 1. Profit distributions for the coalition in Fig. 2

Mechanism	$u(b_1)$	$u(b_2)$	$u(b_3)$
Cost Sharing Prop. to Volume	1	2	0
Cost Sharing Prop. to Valuation	0.45	0.91	1.64
Profit Sharing Prop. to Volume	0.43	0.86	1.71
Profit Sharing Prop. to Contribution	0.5	1	1.5
Adjusted Clarke	0	1	2

Table 1 presents the profit distributions for this scenario. It can give an idea about how mechanisms treat buyers with different demands. Cost sharing proportional to volume mechanism produces a less than fair share of profits for buyers with larger demands and having a significant contribution. The positions of three mechanisms, namely, cost sharing proportional to valuation, profit sharing proportional to volume, and contribution, are somewhat similar: every buyer gets a share from the profit somewhat proportional to their contributions. Interestingly, the adjusted Clarke tax mechanism too yields an unfair profit distribution, though the under-rewarding is less conspicuous. When using the adjusted Clarke tax, b_1 suffers from the unfairness. Interestingly, the two sufferers for the two mechanisms, b_1 and b_3, are buyers at two extreme demands: one with a relatively large demand volume and the other with a relatively small demand.

From the representative example, we conclude that in such critical coalitions, adjusted Clarke mechanism is advantageous for buyers like b_3 while it severely deprives buyers like b_1 of the profit. Precisely the opposite happens with cost sharing proportional to volume mechanism where buyers with high marginal contributions are not rewarded enough.

Experimental evaluation of fairness: To gauge the fairness of different mechanisms over a large set of scenarios, we implemented a simple group-buying market. The number of buyers is fixed in a run to understand the behavior of the mechanisms. However, the demand volumes are uniformly distributed within the range between 1 and 10, i.e., $n_i \in U[1, 10]$. 100 price schedules are randomly generated: each price schedule is tested with 100 randomly generated volume demands for a group of buyers. Therefore $100 \times 100 = 10000$ different coalition settings (a unique combination of demand volumes of buyers and the price schedule) are tested with a fixed number of buyers to report the averages.

Correlation coefficient: Initially, Pearson correlation coefficients of each mechanism's profit distribution is computed for each coalition and then the average coefficients are calculated within each mechanism. This process is repeated for different numbers of buyers.

Figure 3 shows the correlation coefficients of mechanisms for varying coalition sizes. The closer the correlation coefficient is to 1, the fairer is the mechanism. We observe that the correlation coefficients of all mechanisms gradually increases up to coalition size of 15 and then stabilize with small oscillations. This result illustrates how the impact of one buyer is more remarkable in a small coalition. The unfairness of mechanisms is ameliorated in larger groups.

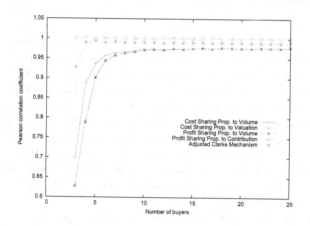

Fig. 3. Correlation between contribution and profit

Apart from the profit sharing proportional to contribution (fairest by definition) the next fairest mechanism is the adjusted Clarke mechanism. For lower coalition sizes (up to 10), the cost sharing proportional to volume mechanism surprisingly produces fairer profit sharing than those produced by the cost sharing proportional to valuation and profit sharing proportional to volume mechanisms. For coalition sizes larger than 10, these three mechanisms have the same fairness attitude. One final point is that the correlation coefficients of these mechanisms do not converge to the same value, i.e. the relative order of fairness is preserved in larger groups even if the lack of fairness is mostly eliminated.

Deviation from fairness: The second metric measures how much mechanisms deviate from a fair distribution. Profit sharing proportional to contribution mechanism is again, therefore, the standard against which other mechanisms are evaluated. Let the fair profit for b_i be u_i^f and the profit distributed by mechanism m to b_i be u_i^m, then the relative deviation of mechanism m for b_i's profit is calculated $\frac{u_i^f - u_i^m}{u_i^f}$.

Figure 4 depicts the deviation of mechanisms from fairness for varying contribution levels in coalitions of seven buyers. We do not include the plot for the

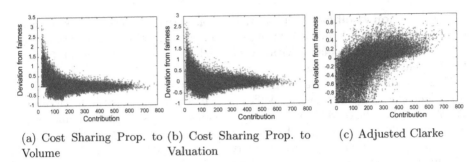

(a) Cost Sharing Prop. to Volume
(b) Cost Sharing Prop. to Valuation
(c) Adjusted Clarke

Fig. 4. Contribution vs. deviation from fairness in coalitions consist of seven buyers

profit sharing proportional to volume mechanism because its behavior is very similar to cost sharing proportional to valuation mechanism. Figure 4 confirms the observations from using the Pearson correlation coefficient but more clearly depicts in which cases they deviate from being fair. The general trend is that the magnitude of the deviation reduces as the contribution increases. Cost sharing proportional to volume (Fig. 4(a)) and valuation (Fig. 4(b)) mechanisms frequently reward lower contributors at a disproportionately high rate and deviate both negative and positive for different contribution levels. However, adjusted Clarke mechanism (Fig. 4(c)) tends to provide gradually higher rewards to higher contributors. In addition to this, the absolute sum of magnitude of the deviation is clearly higher in adjusted Clarke's case.

The fairness metrics indicate that cost sharing proportional to volume and adjusted Clarke mechanisms diverge most from the fair distribution. Comparatively, the other mechanisms are more balanced for varying coalition sizes and contribution levels. One can argue that the fairness metrics we proposed are not powerful enough to demonstrate that cost sharing proportional to volume and

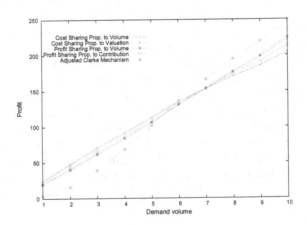

Fig. 5. Profit distributions in coalitions of seven buyers

adjusted Clarke mechanisms favoring two opposite buyer types. To demonstrate this claim, we compare the profits for varying volume demands.

Figure 5 shows the average profit distribution for varying demand volumes in coalitions of 7 buyers. Adjusted Clarke mechanism is advantageous for buyers with larger demands and less profitable for buyers with smaller demands. Contrarily, cost sharing proportional to volume mechanism produces relatively higher profits for buyers with smaller demands and lower profits for buyers with larger demands. The other mechanisms produce profit distributions between these two. However, the order of being advantageous for buyers with larger demands between mechanisms is preserved for increasing demand volumes.

6 Prior Work

Our study differs from prior work based on two dimensions: unit demand and auctions. Unit demand is the common assumption in group-buy auction games [1,2,4,6], where buyers report their bids in auctions. We believe that implied value better corresponds to the true valuation of the buyer with comparison to bids in group-buy auctions because a buyer can only slightly increase its utility by deviating from its true valuation by reporting higher demand volumes (it will pay more for more items which cause a decrease in utility) or lower demand volumes (smaller demand volumes cause a decrease in the total value obtained from items) based on simulations. It is also practical way to infer valuations in case of lack of an auction mechanism. To the best of our knowledge, variable demand group-buying game is the first study that is specifically designed for the settings where buyers have varying demand volumes and does not require a bid. Furthermore, this study addresses the significance of fairness in particular for real-life group-buying environments. Since, humans are not purely self-interested [10] and fairness is an important criterion for them.

Group-buying markets are studied from social and economic perspectives. Lu and Boutilier [12] studied the problem of matching of buyers and sellers where a group of buyers with varying preferences over sellers to benefit volume discounts and investigate the computation of buyer-welfare maximizing matchings. Walter [5] studied trust in group-buy environment, where trust is used to model the similarity in preferences. Erdoğmuş and Çiçek [8] empirically investigate the behavior of buyers in group-buying markets by conducting interviews. Their results show that buyers are mostly attracted by the price advantage and discount amount and have complaints about the discriminatory and dishonest behavior of the service providers, which can be considered unfair. Liao et al. [7] analyze the customer behavior in online group-markets by using clustering analysis and rule generation. Kaufmann and Wang [9] analyze the number of orders in group-buy auctions over time for Mobshop.com products list. They characterize three different effects in the auction: positive participation externality effect (the number existing orders has a positive effect on prospective orders placed), price-drop effect (orders increase more when current price drops), auction-ending effect (more orders have been placed during the final period). The results of these social studies can be helpful for sellers to provide better service to customers and increase their profit.

7 Conclusion

We seek an answer for the question "How the profit should be distributed?" in the presence of buyers with varying demand sizes. As seen in the group-buy travel example, there is a critical issue that should be investigated to empower both sellers and buyers and increase social welfare. We introduce the variable demand group-buying game and define the implied value per item as the per unit price which can be obtained by the buyer itself. We identify several desirable features of payoff distribution schemes in the group-buy situation. In particular, we highlight the importance of the fairness issue by analyzing representative critical scenarios.

We propose and evaluate five profit distribution mechanisms in terms of the identified criteria. We observe that even though cost sharing proportional to volume is the only mechanism that is stable, it poorly distributes profit in terms of fairness by under-rewarding buyers having higher implied values. This indicates that satisfying stability and incentive compatibility criteria does not guarantee desirable coalitions in the eyes of buyers. On the other extreme, adjusted Clarke mechanism charges relatively higher payments to the buyers with lower contributions to subsidize the budget deficiency that arises from decreasing the payments of buyers with higher contributions.

Our findings suggest that the profit sharing should be carefully managed in the group buying markets with varying demand volumes. To avoid unfair situations, which will cause losing customers, an ideal profit sharing mechanism should not have a position which is explicitly advantageous for certain type of buyers, e.g. having higher implied value for per unit in cost sharing proportional to volume mechanism, and having high contributions in adjusted Clarke mechanism. Rather, a mild manner should be adopted to achieve fairer profit distributions based on the diversity of the buyers' attributes, e.g. implied value per unit, contribution, and demand volume.

Appendix

Proof 1. Variable demand group-buying game is a non-convex game: A game is convex when $\forall_{S,T}\ u(C_{S\cup T}) \geq u(C_S) + u(C_T) - u(C_{S\cap T})$ is satisfied. We will prove that variable demand group-buying game is not convex by giving a counter example. Let's say $S = \{b_1, b_2, b_3, b_4\}$ and $T = \{b_1, b_2, b_3, b_5, b_6\}$ are two sets of buyers and every b_i has a demand of 1. $S \cap T = \{b_1, b_2, b_3\}$ and $S \cup T = \{b_1, b_2, b_3, b_4, b_5, b_6\}$.

$$p(n) = \begin{cases} 10 & n < 4 \\ 9 & n = 4 \\ 8 & n > 4 \end{cases} \tag{8}$$

Given the price schedule $p(n)$, the utilities become: $u(C_S) = 4$, $u(C_T) = 10$, $u(C_{S \cup T}) = 12$, and $u(C_{S \cap T}) = 0$. When we set these values into the convex game criteria $12 \geq 4 + 10 - 0$, the condition is not satisfied. Hence, variable demand group-buying game is a non-convex game.

Proof 2. Cost sharing proportional to volume mechanism is in the core:

$$\forall S \subseteq N, \sum_{i \in C_S} u_i(C_N) \geq u(C_S)$$

$$\sum_{i \in C_S} [p(n_i) - p(n_T)] \geq \sum_{i \in C_S} [p(n_i) - p(n_S)]$$

$$p(n_S) \geq p(n_T)$$

$$(9)$$

References

1. Chen, J., Chen, X., Kauffman, R., Song, X.: Cooperation in group-buying auctions. In: Proceedings of the 39th Annual Hawaii International Conference on System Sciences, 2006. HICSS '06. Vol. 6 (January 2006) 121c
2. Li, C., Rajan, U., Chawla, S., Sycara, K.: Mechanisms for coalition formation and cost sharing in an electronic marketplace. In: Proceedings of the 5th International Conference on Electronic Commerce. ICEC 2003, pp. 68–77. ACM, New York (2003)
3. Li, C., Sycara, K., Scheller-Wolf, A.: Combinatorial coalition formation for multi-item group-buying with heterogeneous customers. Decis. Support Syst. 49(1), 1–13 (2010)
4. Matsuo, T., Ito, T., Shintani, T.: A volume discount-based allocation mechanism in group buying. In: Proceedings International Workshop on Data Engineering Issues in E-Commerce, 2005, pp. 59–67 (april 2005)
5. Walter, F.E.: Trust as the basis of coalition formation in electronic marketplaces. Adv. Complex Syst. (ACS) 14(02), 111–131 (2011)
6. Yamamoto, J., Sycara, K.: A stable and efficient buyer coalition formation scheme for e-marketplaces. In: Proceedings of the Fifth International Conference on Autonomous Agents. AGENTS '01. ACM, New York, pp. 576–583 (2001)
7. Liao, S., Chu, P., Chen, Y., Chang, C.C.: Mining customer knowledge for exploring online group buying behavior. Expert Syst. Appl. 39(3), 3708–3716 (2012)
8. Erdoğmuş, İ.E., Çiçek, M.: Online group buying: What is there for the consumers? Procedia - Soc. Behav. Sci. 24, 308–316 (2011)
9. Kauffman, R.J., Lai, H., Ho, C.T.: Incentive mechanisms, fairness and participation in online group-buying auctions. Electron. Commer. Res. Appl. 9(3), 249–262 (2010)
10. Jong, S.d., Tuyls, K., Verbeeck, K.: Artificial agents learning human fairness. In: Proceedings of the 7th International Joint Conference on Autonomous Agents and Multiagent Systems, pp. 863–870 (2008)
11. Shapley, L.S.: A value for n-person games. Contrib. Theory of Games 2, 307–317 (1953)
12. Lu, T., Boutilier, C.E.: Matching models for preference-sensitive group purchasing. In: Proceedings of the 13th ACM Conference on Electronic Commerce. EC '12. ACM, New York, pp. 723–740 (2012)

Distributed Prediction Markets Modeled by Weighted Bayesian Graphical Games

Janyl Jumadinova[✉] and Prithviraj Dasgupta

Computer Science Department, University of Nebraska at Omaha,
Omaha, NE, USA
{jjumadinova,pdasgupta}@unomaha.edu

Abstract. We consider a novel, yet practical setting of prediction markets called distributed prediction markets, where the aggregated price of a security of an event in one prediction market is affected dynamically by the prices of securities of similar events in other, simultaneously running prediction markets. We focus on the problem of decision making facing a market maker to determine the price of a security within such a setting. We propose a formal framework based on graphical games called a weighted Bayesian graphical game (WBGG) to model the distributed prediction market setting and to capture the local interactions between multiple market makers. We then describe a distributed message passing algorithm based on NashProp algorithm to calculate the Bayes-Nash equilibrium in a WBGG. We provide analytical results including convergence and incentivizing truthful revelation among market makers. Our experimental results show that market makers that consider the influence of other market makers in a distributed prediction market setting while using our proposed WBGG-based algorithm obtain higher utilities and set prices more accurately in comparison to market makers using a greedy strategy to set prices or those that do not consider the influence of other market makers. We also observe that extreme sizes of the neighborhood of a market maker have an adverse impact on its utilities.

Keywords: Prediction market · Distributed · Bayes-Nash · Graphical games

1 Introduction

Over the past decade prediction markets have shown ample success as a tool for aggregating information and predicting the outcome of events that are going to happen in the future. A prediction market operates by aggregating the opinions or beliefs on the outcome of a future, real-world event from the market's participants, called traders, and forecasts the event's possible outcome based on their aggregated opinion. A trader's belief about an event's possible outcome is usually represented as a price for a security related to the event and a trader can buy or sell securities according to its belief. Traders' beliefs or prices are aggregated by an entity called the market maker that implements rules to deter

© Springer International Publishing Switzerland 2014
S. Ceppi et al. (Eds.): AMEC/TADA 2013 and 2014, LNBIP 187, pp. 84–98, 2014.
DOI: 10.1007/978-3-319-13218-1_7

misreporting of prices by traders, limits trading quantity, etc., using an aggregation mechanism. In general, existing research on prediction markets mainly focusses on the operation of a single prediction market, and considers that the aggregated price of a security in a prediction market is determined by prices of traders only within that prediction market.

Contrary to single prediction markets with confined traders, there are several real-life instances where multiple prediction markets running simultaneously have similar events. For example, both Intrade and Iowa Electronic Market ran prediction markets on several events related to the 2012 U.S. Presidential elections. With such similar events across markets, it is very likely that the expected outcomes (prices) of an event in one market will influence the price of the same or similar event in a different market. Based on this insight, our main hypothesis in this paper is that the predicted outcome of events in one prediction market is dynamically affected not only by the market's traders but also by the expected outcome of similar events in other prediction markets. Such inter-market influence is frequently observed in financial markets, which operate very similarly to prediction markets. For example, after analyzing the data from the retail online brokerage, called eToro, Pan *et al.* reported that the prices of securities in one market affect the prices of similar securities in other markets and that social trading (when traders can see each others' trades) results in higher profits to the traders [11]. Therefore, it makes sense to investigate the effects of events across multiple prediction markets and analyze how prices evolve due to such inter-market effects. The main contributions made by our paper towards studying this problem are the following: we describe a model of a distributed prediction market that comprises multiple, parallel running prediction markets and uses a graphical structure between the market makers of the different markets to represent inter-market influence. We then propose a formal framework based on graphical games [7] called a Weighted Bayesian Graphical Game (WBGG) to capture the interaction between multiple market makers and describe an algorithm based on NashProp [9] to calculate an approximate Bayes-Nash equilibrium efficiently for an n-player WBGG. Finally, we conduct a number of experiments with two types of market makers and with two possible actions for each market makers to analyze the effect of different parameters in distributed prediction markets. We find that when the size of the neighborhood is too small or too large, market makers' utilities decrease, and, that market makers using our algorithm in a distributed prediction market setting can outperform the market makers using a greedy strategy or the market makers in the setting where prediction markets are disjoint. To the best of our knowledge, this work represents the first attempt at studying inter-market influences between similar events across multiple prediction markets through strategic decision making by market makers.

2   Related Work

Prediction Markets. A prediction market is a market-based aggregation mechanism that is predominantly used to combine the opinions on the outcome of a future, real-world event from different people, called the market's *traders* and forecast the event's possible outcome based on their aggregated opinion. The basic operation rules of a prediction market are similar to those of a continuous double auction, with the role of the auctioneer being taken up by an entity called the *market maker* that runs the prediction market. The seminal work on prediction market analysis [14] has shown that the mean belief values of individual traders about the outcome of a future event corresponds to the event's market price. Since then researchers have studied the traders' behavior in prediction markets [2,3], rules that a market maker can use to combine the opinions (beliefs) from different traders [5], and the properties of prediction markets used for decision making [1,10]. In contrast to these previous works, we consider a setting with multiple prediction markets where the inter-market influence on market prices is incorporated through decision-making (price selection) by the market-makers.

Graphical Games. The original work by Kearns et al. [7] considered acyclic graphical games of complete information in which the underlying graph is a tree and presented a message-passing algorithm, known as TreeProp or KLS algorithm, for computing approximate Nash equilibria (NE) efficiently. Consequently, in [9] the authors generalized the TreeProp algorithm to an arbitrary graph structure by proposing a message-passing NashProp algorithm for complete information games which involves an approach analogous to loopy belief propagation in graphical games. In other work, Vickrey and Koller [13] presented multi-agent algorithms for solving graphical games including hill-climbing, constraint satisfaction, and hybrid approaches. In [12] the authors studied the graphical games with incomplete information with discrete and continuous types and propose an extension to KLS algorithm to find Bayes-Nash equilibrium efficiently in a tree structured graphical game. In our work we build upon [9,12] and propose a form of *weighted* graphical games *with incomplete information* and *an arbitrary graph structure*. We extend NashProp algorithm to find BNE in such games with an arbitrary graph structure and apply this algorithm to the distributed prediction market setting.

3   Distributed Prediction Markets

In this section we define and characterize distributed prediction markets. We consider n prediction markets with each prediction market having one market maker that is responsible for aggregating traders' beliefs and setting the market price for its market. Let $N = \{1, ..., n\}$ denote the set of market makers with i being the market maker for the i-th prediction market. Let $\Gamma = \{\Gamma_1, ..., \Gamma_n\}$ denote a set of trading agents representing human traders, with Γ_i being the set of trading agents in the i-th prediction market. Note that trading agents can participate in multiple prediction markets simultaneously. Also let $E = \{E_1, ..., E_n\}$ denote the set of events across all the prediction markets with E_i

representing the set of events in the i-th prediction market[1]. Finally, let P denote the trader population.

Next, we present two axioms that outline the behavior of market makers in the distributed prediction market setting. Consider two market makers i and j running events e_{f_i} and e_{g_j} in their respective prediction markets. Let d_{f_i, g_j} be a metric that measures the similarity between the definitions of the two events e_{f_i} and e_{g_j}[2].

Definition 1. Related Event. *An event e_{f_i} is related to event e_{g_j} if $d_{f_i, g_j} > \epsilon_{sim}$, where ϵ_{sim} is a constant.*

We denote the number of market makers that market maker i interacts with by η_i and the influence of the market maker i on market maker j by ϖ_{ij}.

Axiom 1. *Local interaction, Influence, Competition: If events e_{f_i} and e_{g_j} run by market makers i and j correspondingly are related, then (1) market maker i interacts with market maker j for determining the price of event e_{f_i}, (2) $0 < \varpi_{i,j} < 1$, and (3) market makers i and j are competitive.*

The first part of Axiom 1 determines the criterion for interaction between two market makers. Market maker i interacts with another market maker j for updating event e_{f_i}'s price, only if j's market has an event that is related to event e_{f_i}. The second part of Axiom 1 states that two market makers that have a pair of related events in their market have a non-zero, positive influence on each other. Influence values are normalized to a range of 0 and 1. In a prediction market a market maker needs to be able to calculate the market price (aggregate) and to stimulate the trading by always allowing traders to buy or sell securities. If there are prediction markets with similar events, the traders may choose one prediction market over the other, and market makers may end up competing over the traders just like in financial markets [6]. The third part of Axiom 1 summarizes this competitive behavior between market makers.

Axiom 2. *Incentives: Let θ_i be the private information of market maker i denoted as i's type. Let $u_i(a_i, \theta_i, t)$ be the utility that the market maker i gets for interacting with other market makers when its type is θ_i. If $d_{f_i, g_j} > \epsilon_{sim}$, for any i, j, e_{f_i}, e_{g_j}, then $\exists\, \theta_i'$ such that $u_i(a_i, \theta_i', t) > u_i(a_i, \theta_i, t)$.*

Finally, because market makers are competing with each other to attract traders on related events, a market maker may have incentives to misreport its inside information about aggregated prices when interacting with other market makers. In other words, market-makers have preferences over their types to improve their utility as mentioned in Axiom 2.

---

[1] For legibility, we refer to the security corresponding to an event as the event itself.

[2] We assume that d_{f_i, g_j} is based on the similarity between the written description of the events e_{f_i} and e_{g_i} and is provided externally to the market makers either by a human expert or by an automated program.

Definition 2. Distributed prediction market. *A distributed prediction market is specified by the tuple* $\mathcal{M} = \langle N, P, E, \mathcal{W} \rangle$ *where* N, P, E *are as defined before and* $\mathcal{W} = \{\varpi_{ij} : i, j \in N\}$.

For simplicity of analysis in the rest of the paper we assume the setting where multiple market makers interact over one related event; but the results are valid for multiple events. Since the decision making for inter-market influence is done mainly by market makers, we abstract the operation of the trading agents and assume that the intra-market price of each prediction market is updated by the market maker's actions in the locality of the current market price. Nevertheless, our proposed technique can be combined easily with any other intra-market price update method such market scoring rules. Since we are not focussing on the interactions of trading agents, we refer to market maker agents as agents in the rest of the paper.

3.1 Weighted Bayesian Graphical Games for Distributed Prediction Markets

We propose a form of graphical games [7,9,12] as a formal model for the interaction between market makers in a distributed prediction market. *Graphical games* are a compact representation of complete information, one-shot, normal-form games that use graphical models to represent the set of agents whose actions influence each others' payoffs. A graphical game representation is appropriate for modeling distributed prediction markets because they can capture the interactions and influences between agents that are within a certain local neighborhood of each other, unlike for example conventional Bayesian games. A graphical game is described by an undirected graph G in which agents are identified with nodes, and the edge between two nodes implies that the payoff of each of the two agents is dependent on the other agent's actions.

We present an augmented form of the conventional graphical game to represent distributed prediction markets, called a Weighted Bayesian Graphical Game (WBGG). Unlike previous works on graphical games, WBGG incorporates incomplete information, the influence of agents on each other as a pair of *directed* edges, and an arbitrary graphical structure in one representation. We assume that a set of similar events in a distributed prediction market have a duration of T periods with t denoting the current time period. The agents that are able to interact and therefore influence each other's utilities define a neighborhood $\mathcal{N}$, where $\mathcal{N}_{-i} = \{j | j \in N_{-i}, \xi_{ij} \in \Xi_i\}$ and $\mathcal{N}_i = \mathcal{N}_{-i} \cup \{i\}$. We also assume that each agent can be one of two possible types, i.e. if Θ_i is the type space of market maker agent i then $\Theta_i = \{\theta_{iopt}, \theta_{ipes}\}$ with θ_{iopt} implying that agent i is an *optimistic* market maker agent and θ_{ipes} implying that it is a *pessimistic* market maker agent. Specifically, we define a WBGG as follows:

Definition 3. *A WBGG is a tuple* $(N, \Theta, p, \Xi, \mathcal{W}, A, u)$, *where*

- $N = \{1, ..., n\}$ - *set of market maker agents.*
- $\Theta = \Theta_1 \times ... \times \Theta_n$, *where* Θ_i *is the type space of agent* i.

- $p : \Theta \to [0,1]$ *is the common prior over types.*
- $\Xi = \{\Xi_1, ..., \Xi_n\}$ - *set of directed edges, where* $\Xi_i = \{\xi_{ij} | \xi_{ij} = (i,j), i, j \in N\}$ *with ξ_{ij} being an edge between agents i and j that are able to interact.*
- $\mathcal{W}$ - *set of edge weights, where* $\varpi_{ij} \in \mathcal{W}$ *is the weight of the edge ξ_{ij} between agents i and j. ϖ_{ij} is determined by agent i and indicates the influence of agent i on agent j. Given agent i's type is θ_{iopt}, ϖ_{ij} is calculated as:*

$$\varpi_{ij} = \alpha p(\theta_{jopt} | \theta_{iopt}) + (1 - \alpha) p(\theta_{jpes} | \theta_{iopt}), \tag{1}$$

where $\theta_{iopt} \in \Theta_i$, $\theta_{jopt}, \theta_{jpes} \in \Theta_j$ and α is a confidence parameter representing i's belief that j is of the same type as itself.
- $A = A_1 \times ... \times A_n$, *where A_i is a finite set of actions available to agent i.*
- $u_i : \Theta_{i \in N} \times A_{i \in N} \times T \to R$ *is the utility of agent i.*

Following Bayesian games [8] we use $s_i(\theta_{iopt})$ to denote agent i's mixed strategy over A_i given its type is θ_{iopt}. S_i is the set of all i's mixed strategies. We use notation s_i for unconditional mixed strategy of agent i. We use $A_{\mathcal{N}_i}, \bar{s}_{\mathcal{N}_i}, \bar{\theta}_{\mathcal{N}_i}$ to denote the vector of actions, strategies and types of all agents in the neighborhood of agent i, $\bar{\varpi}_{\mathcal{N}_{-i}}$ denote the vector of weights between agent i and all agents in the neighborhood of agent i, a_i, s_i, θ_i to denote the action, strategy and type of agent i, and $A_{\mathcal{N}_{-i}}, \bar{s}_{\mathcal{N}_{-i}}, \bar{\theta}_{\mathcal{N}_{-i}}$ to denote actions, strategies and types of all agents in the neighborhood of agent i except agent i itself.

Agent action set and utility function. For specifying the actions in agent i's action set A_i, we assume that agent i can have two possible actions in A_i - to raise the current market price or to lower it by a certain amount that is specified by a *jump* parameter λ_i^t, i.e., $A_i = \{\lambda_i^t, -\lambda_i^t\}$. To prevent arbitrary values of λ_i^t, we make λ_i^t inversely proportional to the market price π_i^t, i.e. $\lambda_i^t = \frac{\delta_i^t}{\pi_i^t}$, where $\pi_i^t \in (\zeta, 1]$ is the market price at time step t, with ζ being a small positive constant corresponding to a very nominal price change, and δ_i^t is a constant that determines the direction (up or down) of the price change[3]. The value of δ_i^t is determined by agent i depending on its type and by observing the direction of the market prices changes among its neighbors, as given by the following equations:

$$\delta_{i|\theta_i=opt}^t = \begin{cases} +\zeta & \text{if } \frac{\sum_{j \in \mathcal{N}_{-i}} \pi_j^t - \pi_j^{t-1}}{|\mathcal{N}_{-i}|} \geq 0, \\ -\zeta & \text{otherwise} \end{cases}$$

$$\delta_{i|\theta_i=pes}^t = \begin{cases} +\zeta & \text{if } \forall j \in \mathcal{N}_{-i}, \pi_j^t - \pi_j^{t-1} \geq 0, \\ -\zeta & \text{if } \exists j \text{ s.t. } \pi_j^t - \pi_j^{t-1} < 0 \end{cases}$$

If agent i is optimistic, it sets $\delta_i^t = +\zeta$ if the average change in the market price of its neighbors in the last time step has been non-negative, otherwise it sets $\delta_i^t = -\zeta_i$. Similarly, if agent i is pessimistic, it sets $\delta_i^t = +\zeta_i$ only if all of

---

[3] If π_i crosses either its lower or upper bound due to action A_i, we set it back to its lower or upper bound correspondingly.

its neighbors increased their prices in the last time step but sets $\delta_i^t = -\zeta_i$ if at least one of its neighbors decreased its prices in the last time step.[4]

The utility of agent i is calculated as:

$$u_i(a_i, \theta_i, t) = (T - t)e^{-a_i(\theta_i)(T-t)}, \tag{2}$$

where t is the current time period ($t = 0$ at the start of the market). The above utility equation guarantees that the utility of changing the market price (by taking an action in the WBGG) is proportional to the remaining duration of the event in the market, and, more exploration (large price changes) gives higher utility towards the beginning of the event, but as the event nears its end and its price converges, large explorations are punished with lower utility.

Next, we define the agent's expected utility in a weighted Bayesian graphical game as

$$EU_i(s_i, \bar{s}_{\mathcal{N}_{-i}}, \theta_i) = \sum_{a_{\mathcal{N}_i} \in A_{\mathcal{N}_i}} \bar{\varpi}_{\mathcal{N}_{-i}} \times \left(s_i \bar{s}_{\mathcal{N}_{-i}} u_i(A_{\mathcal{N}_i}, \bar{\theta}_{\mathcal{N}_{-i}}, \theta_i) \right),$$

where $\bar{\varpi}_{\mathcal{N}_{-i}} = \prod_{j \in \mathcal{N}_{-i}} \varpi_j$. Note that agent i has to consider every assignment of types to the other agents in its neighborhood $\theta_{\mathcal{N}_{-i}}$ and every action profile $\bar{a}_{\mathcal{N}_i}$ in order to calculate the utility $u_i(\bar{a}_{\mathcal{N}_i}, \bar{\theta}_{\mathcal{N}_{-i}}, \theta_i)$.

Definition 4. *For agent i a strategy s_i is said to be **best response (BR)** in a WBGG for type θ_i to $\bar{\theta}_{\mathcal{N}_i}$, if*

$$\forall s', EU(s_i, \bar{s}_{\mathcal{N}_{-i}}, \theta_i) \geq EU(s', \bar{s}_{\mathcal{N}_{-i}}, \theta_i) \tag{3}$$

Definition 5. *A strategy vector $\bar{s}$ is a **Bayes-Nash Equilibrium (BNE)** in a WBGG if and only if every agent i is playing a best response to the others.*

3.2   Computing Bayes-Nash Equilibrium

In this section we first present an abstract algorithm for computing BNE in a weighted Bayesian graphical game of an arbitrary graphical structure. This algorithm is similar to NashProp algorithm [9] that has been extended to incomplete games with an arbitrary graphical structure, thus the definition of the expected utility and the best response have been modified.

For now, we will not purposefully specify a certain representation and a certain implementation. After proving the correctness of the abstract algorithm, we will fill in the unspecified gaps. The abstract algorithm is basically a two-stage message passing algorithm. In the first step, local optimal response is found for each agent, where each agent calculates the optimal strategy given its neighbor's strategies and sends it to its neighbors. In the second step, global solution is constructed by eliminating inconsistent local optimal response.

---

[4] We drop superscript t from λ_i^t, δ_i^t, and π_i^t henceforth, assuming it to be understood from the context.

Let $D_{i,j}$ be the binary table indexed by all possible strategies of agent i and agent j that is sent from agent j to agent i. $D_{i,j}$ indicates player j's belief that there is a global Nash equilibrium when players i and j choose s_i, s_j respectively. Let $\mathcal{N}^j_{-i} = (1, ..., m - 1)$ denote the neighbors of agent j besides agent i. And let $\overline{s}_{\mathcal{N}^j_{-i}} = (s_1, ..., s_{m-1})$ be the vector of mixed strategies of agents in $\mathcal{N}^j_{-i}$, called the *witness* to $D_{i,j}$. Also let P_j be the projection set of agent j that is used just to consolidate the information sent to agent j by all of its neighbors.

Theorem 1. *Algorithm 1 computes BNE for an arbitrary graphical game and the tables and witnesses calculated by it contain all possible BNE of the game.*

Proof. The proof is a constructive argument of the workings of the algorithm. The stage 1 starts with an arbitrary node. Each node(agent) i sends each of its neighbors j a binary-valued table $D_{j,i}$ indexed by all possible strategies of agents j and i. For any pair of strategies (s_j, s_i) a table $D_{j,i}$ is 1 if and only if there exists a BNE in which agent i plays s_i when its neighboring agent j plays s_j.

Consider a node i with neighbors j and $\mathcal{N}^j_{-i} = \{1, ..., m - 1\}$. For induction, assume that each h sends node i table $D_{i,h}$. For any pair of strategies (s_j, s_i) a table $D_{j,i}$ is 1 if and only if there exists a vector of strategies $\overline{s}_{\mathcal{N}^j_{-i}} = \{s_1, ..., s_{m-1}\}$ (witness) for $\mathcal{N}^j_{-i}$ such that:
1. $D_{i,h}(s_i, s_h) = 1 \ \forall 1 \leq h \leq m$, and
2. s_i is the best-response to $\overline{s}_h$ and s_j.

There maybe more than one witness for $D_{j,i}(s_j, s_i) = 1$. In addition to computing the binary-valued tables (i.e. $D_{j,i}$), stage 1 of the algorithm also saves a list of witnesses for each pair of strategies (s_j, s_i) for which the table $(D_{j,i})$ is 1.

Now assume that $D_{j,i} = 1$ for some node i with neighbors j and $\mathcal{N}^j_{-i}$ for some witness $\overline{s}_{\mathcal{N}^j_{-i}}$. By construction, $D_{i,h}(s_i, s_h) = 1 \ \forall h$, and therefore by induction it must be that there exists BNE in which h plays s_h given that node i plays s_i and by construction of $D_{j,i}$ s_i is a best response of agent i and must be a part of BNE given that agent j plays s_j.

Stage 1 converges because all tables begin filled with 1 entries and entries can only change from 0 to 1, [9].

Stage 2 is a backtracking local assignment passing stage. It starts at an arbitrary node j which can chose any s_j for which $P(s_j) = 1$ and any witness $\overline{s}_{\mathcal{N}^j_{-i}}$ from the associated witness list. The node j then passes (s_j, s_h) to each its neighbors h telling h to play s_h. From the semantics of this message passing and backtracking step if s_j turns out to not be the best response when all of j's neighbors are assigned strategies, it must be true that s_j is the best response to its neighbors for any node j.

3.3 Computing Approximate Bayes-Nash Equilibrium

Algorithm 1 is incompletely specified because the representation and computation of the step of passing tables in stage 1 is not completely specified. Since the strategy for an agent is a mapping from types to the simplex of probability

findBNE( )
Input: Game specification, duration T
Output: BNE of the game
Set $t = 0$; // initialize the prediction market's time period
Set $r = 0$; // initialize the round for the first stage
Set $D_{j,i}^0(s_i, s_j) = 1 \ \forall s_i, s_j, \ \forall i, j$; // initialize the table, where agent i and agent j are the neighbors
foreach *time period* $t \leq T$ **do**
    Stage 1 : Local Optima
    while *not converged* **do**
        foreach *agent pair* i, j **do**
            foreach s_i, s_j **do**
                if $D^r(s_j, s_h) = 1 \ \forall h$ *AND* s_j *is Best Response to* $\overline{s}_{\mathcal{N}_{-i}^j}$ *and* s_i
                then
                    $D^{r+1}(s_i, s_j) = 1$;
                    save $\overline{s}_{\mathcal{N}_{-i}^j}$ as a witness to $D^{r+1}(s_i, s_j) = 1$;
                end
                else
                  $D^r(s_j, s_h) = 0 \ \forall h$;
                end
            end
            send D^{r+1} to all of its neighbors;
        end
        $r = r + 1$;
    end
    Stage 2 : Global Optima
    foreach *agent* j **do**
        if $\exists \ \overline{s}_{\mathcal{N}_{-i}^j} \ s.t. \ D(s_j, s_h) = 1 \ \forall h \in \mathcal{N}_{-i}^j$ **then**
            $P_j(s_j) = 1$;
        end
        else
            $P_j(s_j) = 0$;
        end
        // construct BNE - local search
        1. Pick any agent j and any s_j s.t. $P(s_j) = 1$ with witness $\overline{s}_{\mathcal{N}_{-i}^j}$;
        2. Agent j assigns itself s_j and each of its neighbors h it assigns s_h;
        3. Pick next node and assign of all its unassigned neighbors with its witness;
        4. Backtrack if s_j is not the Best Response when all of the agent j's neighbors are assigned;
    end
    t++;
end

Algorithm 1. Algorithm to find BNE in a WBGG.

distributions over actions, it may not be possible to represent tables D compactly or finitely for an arbitrary graphical game. We now present an algorithm

Approximate-findBNE( )

Input: Game specification and ϵ approximation parameter Output: ϵ-BNE of the game

Run Algorithm 1 with two changes:

1. Only consider type-conditional discretized strategies
2. Change the requirement of best response to ϵ-best response.

Algorithm 2. Approximation algorithm to find BNE in a weighted graphical game.

for computing approximate BNE in incomplete information general structured graphical games with discrete types.

We adopt our abstract algorithm to compute ϵ-BNE in graphical games of an arbitrary structure with discrete types. Our updated algorithm takes parameter ϵ as input, that specifies how close of an approximation to BNE we want to get. The strategy space is discretized analogous to [7], such that any agent can only choose actions with probabilities that are multiples of τ, for some τ, instead of playing an arbitrary mixed strategy in $[0, 1]$. For a graphical games that contains l actions the probability that each action will be selected is a multiple of τ with the sum of all probabilities being 1. Then any agent i will have $O(\frac{1}{\tau^{2(l-1)}})$ different strategies.

Theorem 2. *For any $\epsilon > 0$, $k = max_i \eta_i \ll n$, and the discretization parameter $\tau \le \frac{\epsilon}{l^k(4k log(k))}$ Algorithm 2 computes ϵ-BNE for an arbitrarily structured graphical game with incomplete information.*

Proof. In [12] it was shown that if the mixed strategy space for every type is restricted to multiples of τ, then for any ϵ and $\tau \le \frac{\epsilon}{l^k(4k log(k))}$ there exists ϵ-BNE in tree structured graphical games. Their result however does not depend on the underlying graph being a tree, and therefore holds for arbitrary graphs also. The witness lists and tables of Algorithm 2 represent all ϵ-BNE. Therefore, Algorithm 2 is guaranteed to converge to an ϵ-BNE.

Theorem 3. *For arbitrary structured graphical games with discrete types stage 1 in Algorithm 2 converges in at most $\frac{nk}{\tau^{4(l-1)}}$ rounds.*

Proof. The total number of entries in each table D is $O(\frac{1}{\tau^{2*2(l-1)}})$ since the number of entries is determined by the number of joint strategies of two agents with two possible types. Every round r before the algorithm converges has to change at least one entry in one table. Therefore, stage 1 of the Algorithm 2 has to converge in at most $\frac{nk}{\tau^{4(l-1)}}$ rounds, where k is the maximum degree of any node in the graph.

Since our work in this chapter extends the existing NashProp algorithm, we don't expect scalability and complexity to be significantly different from [9]. Instead we report the dynamics in market-maker prices and utilities which demonstrate the behavior, important features and successful operation of our model in a distributed prediction markets setting.

Proposition 1. *Algorithm 2 applied to a distributed prediction market problem that uses utility function given in Eq. 2 encourages truthful revelation.*

Proof. For the simplicity of notation we show the proof for two agents i and j, with two possible types θ_{iopt} and θ_{ipes}, but the proof is extendable to multiple agents with several possible types. We want to show that the expected utility that the agent i gets when choosing action A_i^{true} truthfully is greater or equal to the expected utility it gets when it chooses action A_i^{false}, i.e. $EU_i^{true} \geq EU_i^{false}$. Since there are only two possible actions $A_i = \{\lambda_i, -\lambda_i\}$, misreporting would mean that when Algorithm 1 recommends agent i to take action $A_i = \lambda_i$, it takes action $-\lambda_i$ instead; i.e. $A_i^{false} = -A_i^{true}$. From definition of utility given in Eq. 2 we can express the utility as $u_i(\lambda_i) = (T-t)e^{-|A_i|(T-t)}$. Now,

$$EU_i^{true} = \alpha p(\theta_{jopt}|\theta_{iopt})(T-t)\left(e^{-|A_i^{true}|(T-t)}\right)$$
$$+ (1-\alpha)p(\theta_{jpes}|\theta_{iopt})(T-t)\left(e^{-|A_i^{true}|(T-t)}\right)$$
$$\text{and } EU_i^{false} = \alpha p(\theta_{jopt}|\theta_{iopt})(T-t)\left(e^{-|-A_i^{true}|(T-t)}\right)$$
$$+ (1-\alpha)p(\theta_{jpes}|\theta_{iopt})(T-t)\left(e^{-|-A_i^{true}|(T-t)}\right).$$

Since $|A_i^{true}| = |-A_i^{true}|$, we get $EU_i^{true} = EU_i^{false}$. Therefore, agent i does not have any incentive to reveal its action untruthfully.

4   Experimental Results

We have conducted several simulations using our algorithm for a distributed prediction market setting to observe and verify the effect of different parameters on the evolution of market maker utilities and prices in the markets. To make it easier to analyze the effect of different parameters, in all of our simulations we assume that the number of neighbors is fixed for each market maker. For each experiment we vary one set of parameters as specified in each set of experiments and we hold the other parameters fixed at their default values given in Table 1.

Table 1. Parameters used for our simulation experiments.

Name	Symbol	Value
Number of market makers	N	20
Market price's jump scaling parm	ζ	0.01
Confidence that other market maker is of the same type	α	0.5
Prob. distr. over types	p	$U[0,1]$
Discretization parameter	τ	0.3
Approximation value	ϵ	0.05
Number of actions	$l_i \forall i$	2
Number of neighbors	$\eta_i \forall i$	8

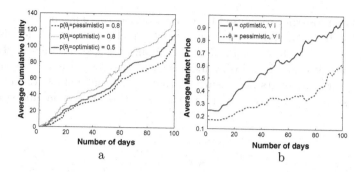

Fig. 1. The average cumulative utility(a) and the average market price(b) for different types of market makers

For our first set of experiments, we vary p, the probability distribution over types. We allow for three types of market maker populations: mostly pessimistic, equal number of optimistic and pessimistic, and optimistic. Figure 1(a) shows the cumulative utility averaged over all 20 market makers, where the market maker population is either 80 % pessimistic, 50 % pessimistic and 50 % optimistic, and 80 % optimistic. The type of each market maker is determined at the beginning of the prediction market and it does not change over time. We observe that when the majority of market makers is pessimistic the average utility is 23 % less than when the majority of market makers is optimistic. This is because optimistic market makers' strategy selection is affected by the average strategies of their neighbors, whereas pessimistic market makers' strategy selection is affected by just one other market maker choosing a pessimistic strategy. In Fig. 1(b) we continue analyzing the effect of different market makers' types by looking at the average market price produced by the optimistic and the pessimistic market makers for the outcome of the event that happens (market price = 1). We note that optimistic market makers are able to predict a more accurate market price as opposed to the pessimistic ones. Again, this is due to the optimistic market makers taking into account the average strategies of all the market makers in their neighborhood. However, in real prediction market, there may be a mix of different types of market makers. Therefore, for the default setting for the type distribution we assume that there is about the same number of optimistic market makers as pessimistic ones.

Next, we compare our Algorithm 2 to two other strategies:

- **Greedy strategy:** In this setting, each agent i chooses λ_i that maximizes immediate utility given in Eq. 2. This strategy does not consider the types of the market makers.
- **Influence-less markets**: In this setting, we consider conventional single, isolated markets where the market price is determined by the market maker based on that market's traders' decisions only. This setting is the completely opposite scenario of a distributed prediction market and it captures the effect of inter-market influences on the market makers' utilities and prices.

These two strategies were used for comparison as there are no other existing strategies for distributed prediction market setting. To abstract the details of the traders' decisions, we have assumed that each agent i uses a derivative follower (DF) [4] strategy where it keeps on increasing its market price π_i by δ_i until its immediate utility u_i starts decreasing, at that time agent i starts decreasing π_i by δ_i. This strategy does not consider the types or the interaction among market makers.

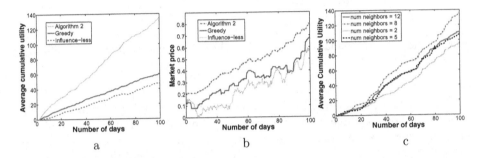

        a   b   c

Fig. 2. The average cumulative utility(a) and the market price(b) of one market maker using Algorithm 2, Greedy, or Influence-less markets strategies, the cumulative utility averaged over all neighbors for different number of neighbors, i.e. $2, 5, 8,$ and 12(c)

Figures 2 (a) and (b) show the utilities and market prices for the market makers using our proposed algorithm, greedy strategy, or influence-less markets strategy correspondingly. We observe that market makers using our Algorithm 2 obtain 56 % more utility than the market makers following the next best greedy strategy. We also note that market prices fluctuate more when market makers use a greedy strategy or are in influence-less markets than when they use WBGG because greedy and influence-less market strategies are myopic and do not consider market makers' types. Finally, this result provides an important justification of our work - that, as compared to influence-less markets with isolated market makers, interacting market makers in a distributed prediction market are able to improve their utilities and predict prices with less fluctuations.

Finally, we report the results for different number of market makers and different number of neighbors of each market maker. Figure 2(c) shows the cumulative utility averaged over neighboring market makers for a setting with 20 market makers. We can see that when market makers have a small number of neighbors then they get less utility than when the number of neighbors is larger, up to a certain point. For example, market makers with 2 neighbors (10 % of the total number of market makers) get 29 % less utility than when market makers have 8 neighbors (40 % of the total number of market makers). However, this relationship is not linear, i.e. when market makers have 12 neighbors (60 % of the total number of market makers) they get 19 % less utility than when market makers have 8 neighbors. We posit that increasing the number of neighbors up to a point translates to an increased utility because the market maker can improve its decision based on the information of its neighbors, but having too many neighbors may end up creating more noisy information for the market maker.

We also conduct experiments showing the scalability of our Algorithm 2 with respect to the number of market makers, and our results show that our algorithm scales linearly with the number of market makers and that the running time increases with the increased number of neighbors.

5   Conclusion

In this paper we proposed a novel distributed prediction market setting where the aggregated (market) price of a security of an event in one prediction market is affected dynamically by the prices of securities of similar events in other, simultaneously running prediction markets. Our proposed formal framework, called a weighted Bayesian graphical game (WBGG), is able to capture the local interactions between multiple market makers and uses the Bayes-Nash equilibrium concept to find a suitable action for each market maker in a WBGG. Our experimental results showed that our algorithm results in higher utilities and more accurate prices in comparison to a greedy strategy or a disjoint prediction markets.

In the future, we plan to extend our current distributed prediction market model to include direct influences between traders across multiple prediction markets. We also want to extend our algorithm to study stochastic graphical games to model uncertainty in repeated games. We also plan to extend our algorithm to make it strategy-proof for graphical games in general. In summary, the novel framework for distributed prediction markets that we introduced in this paper can lead to several challenging and important directions that can help to gain a better understanding of the distributed information aggregation problem.

References

1. Chen, Y., Kash, I.: Information elicitation for decision making. In: Proceedings of 10th International Conference on Autonomous Agents and Multiagent Systems (AAMAS 2011), pp. 175–182 (2011)
2. Chen, Y., Mullen, T., Chu, C.: An in-depth analysis of information markets with aggregate uncertainty. Electron. Commer. Res. 6(2), 201–222 (2006)
3. Feigenbaum, J., Fortnow, L., Pennock, D., Sami, R.: Computation in a distributed information market. Theor. Comput. Sci. 343(1–2), 114–132 (2005)
4. Greenwald, A., Kephart, J.: Shopbots and pricebots. In: Sixteenth International Joint Conference on Artificial Intelligence, Stockholm, pp. 506–511 (1999)
5. Hanson, R.: Logarithmic market scoring rules for modular combinatorial information aggregation. J. Predict. Markets 1(1), 3–15 (2007)
6. Jrgen, D.: Price competition between market makers. Rev. Econ. Stud. 60(3), 735–751 (1993)

7. Kearns, M., Littman, M., Singh, S.: Graphical models for game theory. In: Proceedings of the 17th Conference in Uncertainty in Artificial Intelligence, pp. 253–260 (2001)
8. Myerson, B.: Bayesian equilibrium and incentive-compatibility: an introduction. In: Hurwicz, L., Schmeidler, D., Sonnenschein, H. (eds.) Social Goals and Social Organization Essays in Memory of Elisha Pazner, pp. 229–259. Cambridge University Press, Cambridge (1985)
9. Ortiz, L., Kearns, M.: Nash propagation for loopy graphical games. In: Neural Information Processing Systems, pp. 793–800 (2003)
10. Othman, A., Sandholm, T.: Automated market making in the large: the gates hillman prediction market. In: Proceedings of the 11th ACM Conference on Electronic Commerce (EC 2010), pp. 367–376 (2010)
11. Pan, W., Altshuler, Y., Pentland, A.: Decoding social influence and the wisdom of the crowd in financial trading network. In: IEEE Social Computing (2012)
12. Singh, S., Soni, V., Wellman, M.: Computing approximate Bayes-Nash equilibria in tree-games of incomplete information. In: Proceedings of the 6th ACM Conference on Electronic Commerce (EC 2005), pp. 81–90 (2004)
13. Vickrey, D.: Multi-agent algorithms for solving graphical games. In: Proceedings of the National Conference on Artificial Intelligence, pp. 345–351 (2002)
14. Wolfers, J., Zitzewitz, E.: Prediction markets. J. Econ. Perspect. **18**(2), 107–126 (2004)

A Successful Broker Agent for Power TAC

Bart Liefers$^{(\boxtimes)}$, Jasper Hoogland, and Han La Poutré

Centrum Wiskunde and Informatica (CWI), P.O. Box 94079,
1090 GB Amsterdam, The Netherlands
liefers@cwi.nl

Abstract. The Power TAC simulates a smart grid energy market. In this simulation, broker agents compete for customers on a tariff market and trade energy on a wholesale market. It provides a platform for testing strategies of broker agents against other strategies. In this paper we describe the strategies of our broker agent. Amongst others, due to a beneficial trading technique related to equilibria in continuous auctions on the wholesale market and a strategy inspired by Tit-for-Tat in the Iterated Prisoner's Dilemma game on the tariff market, our broker ended second in the 2013 Power TAC.

1   Introduction

Variable prices for electrical energy are seen as an important prerequisite for the development of smart grids [1]. These prices can provide an economical motivation for consumers to shift part of their loads from peak times to times where energy is more abundant. Various mechanisms for setting prices for electricity in the retail market are proposed [2]. The performance of these mechanisms depends on the behaviour of self-interested actors, and they should therefore be tested in a competitive setting.

The Power Trading Agent Competition (Power TAC) is a platform in which agent strategies for trading energy in a smart grid setting can be tested. Competing researchers create agents (referred to as 'brokers') that act in the retail market for electricity. They try to maximize their profit by publishing tariffs to attract customers and by trading on a wholesale market. After a pilot and a demonstration in 2011 and 2012, the inaugural Power TAC was held in 2013 [3].

In this paper we present cwiBroker, a broker that was created for this competition. It utilized an adaptive strategy in order to achieve the most profitable setting for itself. Thus, the actions our broker takes depend on the actions of other brokers. In the tariff market, we took into account the number of competitors, which yielded strategies suitable for either a duopoly or an oligopoly setting. In duopoly games, our broker uses an adaptive strategy inspired by Tit-for-Tat in the Iterated Prisoner's Dilemma [4] game. In oligopoly games, our broker aims to find the optimal tariff by estimating the profit for a set of candidate tariffs. Furthermore, we used regression analysis to accurately make predictions about energy prosumption. Finally, for wholesale energy we used a beneficial

© Springer International Publishing Switzerland 2014
S. Ceppi et al. (Eds.): AMEC/TADA 2013 and 2014, LNBIP 187, pp. 99–113, 2014.
DOI: 10.1007/978-3-319-13218-1_8

trading technique, related to equilibria in continuous auctions. The combined set of strategies of cwiBroker resulted in a second place in the competition.

This document is organised as follows. In Sect. 2 we describe our broker's basic architecture and the setting in which it has to act. Next, each of the components of our broker will be described in more detail (Sect. 3 for the tariff market, Sect. 4 for the wholesale market, and Sect. 5 for the prosumption estimator). In Sect. 6 we will analyse the performance of each component, based on results of the 2013 Power TAC.

2   The 2013 Power Trading Agent Competition

In the Power TAC [3], a central server simulates several entities that act in a smart grid environment. Among those entities are large generation companies (gencos), consumers (e.g. households, offices, hospitals), small producers (e.g. owners of solar panels and wind farms), a distribution utility (DU), and a wholesale market. Brokers that trade in this environment are created by competing researchers. The brokers are tested against each other in various settings (differing in e.g. number of players, weather conditions or customer behavior).

In the simulations, time is divided into 1-h intervals, referred to as timeslots. Within each timeslot, demand and supply must be balanced. This means the net amount of energy bought and sold on different markets must be zero. Three different markets are present: a tariff market, a wholesale market and a balancing market. On the tariff market brokers trade energy with consumers and small producers by publishing consumption and production tariffs respectively. Potential customers evaluate the tariffs and subscribe to the one they prefer. On the wholesale market energy is traded in a periodic double-sided auction, in which the brokers can trade energy ahead with each other and with the gencos. If a broker has a real-time net imbalance, then the DU will buy or sell energy for the broker in order to match demand and supply on the balancing market. The rewards or penalties for imbalances depend on the imbalance of the broker, but also on the total imbalance of all brokers. In addition to the competing brokers, in every game there is a default broker, to which all customers are initially subscribed. For a detailed description of Power TAC we refer to [3].

In the 2013 Power TAC, there were 7 participants. Each broker played six 2-player games (one against each competitor) and 20 4-player games (one for each combination of three out of the six other players). Four games with all 7 participants were held. Each game consists of at least 1320 timeslots. After that, there is a fixed probability that the game will end in each timeslot.

The cwiBroker. Participation in the Power TAC requires brokers to make complex decisions. Roughly speaking, brokers have to operate on two different markets: the tariff market and the wholesale market. The balancing market could theoretically also be used strategically, but this is hard, and penalties for under supply are generally higher than rewards for over supply [5]. Our broker, called cwiBroker, therefore aims to balance its own demand and supply.

In order to achieve this, we created a component that estimates the production or consumption of each type of customer. Furthermore, we created separate components for the tariff market and the wholesale market.

Although the task for each component is quite complex, their interaction is rather straightforward. The prosumption estimator requires as input the historical data (energy usage of each type of customer and weather data). Given a weather forecast, it predicts the production or consumption for a future timeslot for each type of customer. This is used as input for the wholesale market component. The latter trades on the wholesale market in order to balance the estimated prosumption for cwiBroker and maintains, for each quantity, an expected unit price for wholesale energy (based on historical results). This expected unit price is used as input for the tariff market component, which uses this information to decide which tariffs will be most profitable.

3   Tariff Market Strategy

In this section we will describe the tariff market component, which manages the set of published tariffs. It can publish new tariffs, modify existing tariffs, or revoke old tariffs. A tariff consists of rates, which specify a retail price that may depend on the time of the day, day of the week, or the quantity that is consumed or produced. A tariff may also contain features such as a periodic fee, a sign up bonus or fee, or an early-exit fee. The number of customers that a tariff attracts, depends on its exact specification and the alternative tariffs that are available.

The optimal strategy for trading on the tariff market depends on the behavior of other brokers, in particular the tariffs they publish. Therefore, our broker compares its tariffs with the tariffs of opponents. The structure of our broker's tariffs is kept relatively simple. It publishes at most one tariff at a time, with a fixed-price, single-rate, no sign-up bonuses or fee's, no early-exit bonuses, and no periodic payments. It can therefore be represented by a single price p. We will make some simplifications when considering the tariffs of opponents. When opponents publish multiple tariffs, we will only consider their cheapest tariff. This tariff is expected to be the most relevant one, since it attracts the most customers. Furthermore, we take for any tariff only a single price, equal to the lowest rate in the tariff. The more complex features of a tariff are ignored.

We argue that, in order to obtain high revenues, brokers should cooperate with each other. This can be achieved if all brokers publish tariffs that are very profitable to them, but unfavourable for customers. In this case, the brokers each obtain a similar share of customers, and may make large revenues. However, if one broker does not cooperate, by publishing more competitive tariffs, it will attract more customers than other brokers, which may trigger competition between them. This competition may lead to a price war, in which tariff prices ultimately approach the cost price for brokers. In this case it will be very hard for brokers to make a profit. It is possible to avoid this situation if all brokers cooperate. However, if one broker does not cooperate, this can be sufficient to make cooperation of other brokers fail. For this reason, cooperation is more likely to succeed in games with fewer brokers. Therefore, we implemented different tariff market strategies for duopoly games (games with two players) and oligopoly games (with three or more players).

3.1 The Duopoly Tariff Market Strategy

In duopoly games, our broker is initially competitive, i.e. it first tries to obtain a reasonable number of customers. However, we do not always want to price cut our opponent, if this leads to unprofitable tariffs. Therefore, after we published a number of competitive tariffs, we switch to a strategy in which we copy the tariffs of the opponent. In case our opponent also no longer competes with us, we can achieve a tacit collusion. If our opponent reacts by increasing its prices, we also copy the higher prices. In this case both brokers may make large revenues.

In more detail, our broker publishes an initial tariff with a relatively low price p_{min}, which is chosen to be higher than the estimated cost price. After that, whenever the opponent publishes a tariff with price p', our agent responds by replacing its current tariff with a new tariff with price $p = p' - \Delta$, within bounds $[p_{min}, p_{max}]$. First we choose $\Delta > 0$, but after two times we use $\Delta = 0$.

Intuitively, our strategy has some analogies with Tit-for-Tat (TFT) in the Iterated Prisoner's Dilemma (IPD) [4]. The duopoly game is somewhat similar to IPD, in the sense that brokers have an incentive to compete with their opponent (the 'Defect' action in IPD), but their profits would be higher if both published high-priced tariffs (the 'Cooperate' action in IPD). After the first few competitive actions, our broker will copy the last action from the opponent in the rest of the game. This is analogous to TFT.

3.2 The Oligopoly Tariff Market Strategy

We will now describe our broker's tariff market strategy in oligopoly games. In oligopoly games, a cooperative strategy is less likely to succeed than in duopoly games, so in these games our broker plays a more competitive strategy. Our broker considers a set of tariff prices and estimates for each price p in this set how much profit it would make if it published a tariff this price. It then publishes the most profitable one. Our broker computes an estimation $\hat{TP}(p)$ of the profit it would make if it published a tariff with retail price p:

$$\hat{TP}(p) = (p - \hat{p}_{cost}) \sum_{c \in C} \hat{N}_c(p) \hat{q}_c \tag{1}$$

where C is the set of customer types and $\hat{p}_{cost}$ is the estimated cost price of energy. $\hat{q}_c$ is the estimated prosumption per customer of type c, computed by the prosumption estimator (see Sect. 5). $\hat{N}_c(p)$ is the estimated number of customers of type c that subscribe to a tariff with price p. It is modelled as:

$$\hat{N}_c(p) = N_c^{total} \frac{e^{bp}}{a + e^{bp}} \tag{2}$$

The total number of consumers N_c^{total} of type c in the game is public information. The parameters a and b are estimated during the game. This is done by
sequentially publishing two test tariffs with different prices p_1, p_2. The broker
keeps each tariff for a number of timeslots and records the number of customers
$N_{c,1}$ and $N_{c,2}$ respectively, for each customer type c. The parameters a, b are
then computed from the pairs $\langle p_1, N_{c,1}\rangle, \langle p_2, N_{c,2}\rangle$. Finally, our broker computes
$\hat{TP}(p)$ for several p, and publishes a tariff with the price p that maximizes $\hat{TP}(p)$.

In order to successfully estimate $\hat{N}_c(p)$, the other brokers must not publish
tariffs while $N_{c,1}, N_{c,2}$ are being measured. Furthermore, even if $\hat{N}_c(p)$ has been
successfully determined, the computed optimal tariff price only remains optimal
as long as other brokers publish no new tariffs. Thus, this approach only works
if the set of published tariffs remains stable. Due to the fierce competition in
oligopoly games, we expect tariff prices to reach an equilibrium quickly. Therefore, our broker waits a period of time before it starts estimating the subscription
models. After a predetermined number of timeslots K_1, it publishes a competitive tariff with a price p_{init} equal to the lowest observed price of competitors.
Then, after K_2 more timeslots, it will publish both test tariffs sequentially, each
for K_3 timeslots. Finally, it publishes the estimated optimal tariff.

If the subscription models are inaccurate, or if the environment changes
because other brokers have published new tariffs, then the estimated optimal
tariff may not be correct (anymore). In order to escape from such situations,
our broker aims for a number of customers N of the type $CentervilleHomes$
within a manually chosen interval $[N_{min}, N_{max}]$. If $N < N_{min}$, then our broker's current tariff (with price p) is too expensive and it will be replaced by a
new tariff with a lower price $p' = p - \delta$. If $N > N_{max}$, then our broker's tariff
(with price p) is too cheap and it will be replaced by a new tariff with a higher
price $p' = p + \delta$. δ is chosen manually. Our broker keeps replacing tariffs as
long as $N \notin [N_{min}, N_{max}]$. We expect that if a tariff attracts customers for type
$CentervilleHomes$, it is likely to attract customers of other types too.

4   The Wholesale Market Strategy

In this section we will describe the strategy played by cwiBroker on the wholesale market. We will first introduce the market rules and properties of other
players (in particular the gencos) and analyse the particularities of the Power
TAC wholesale market design. Next, we explain the strategies cwiBroker used
to obtain the desired amount of energy at a unit price that is most profitable.

4.1   Power TAC Wholesale Market Properties

On the Power TAC wholesale market, energy for a particular timeslot can be
traded in 24 sequential auctions (between one and 24 timeslots ahead). Brokers
can place both bids (orders to buy energy) and asks (orders to sell energy),
represented by a quantity and an optional limit price. This limit price represents
a maximum price to buy or a minimum price to sell. There is no official limit on

the number of orders a broker is allowed to submit for a single auction (although there is a practical limit due to overhead for the server).

The market is cleared as follows. Bids are sorted in descending order of limit price, and asks in ascending order. The orders will be cleared iteratively, as long as the limit price of the first bid is higher than the limit price of the first ask. If the quantities q of the cleared orders are not equal, the quantity $min(q_{bid}, q_{ask})$ will be cleared, and the remainder of either the bid or the ask will be kept for the next iteration. If the ask price exceeds the bid price, or if there are no more bids or asks left, this process will terminate. The market clearing price is set at the mean of the last cleared ask price and the last cleared bid price.

Besides the orders of the brokers, the gencos send in asks for their capacity (which is variable, determined by a mean reverting random walk around their nominal capacity) for a fixed limit price. If a genco has already sold a part of its capacity in previous auctions for a specific timeslot, it will send in an ask for the remainder in the next auction, at the same limit price (which is constant for a single genco, but varies between them).

4.2   Strategy

The particular market design chosen to represent the wholesale market in Power TAC can be regarded as a mix between a call market and a continuous market. Each individual market clearing is a call market, because orders of all brokers are gathered and cleared once per timeslot. However, this process is repeated 24 times for each timeslot. Traders are thus flexible in choosing when to place their orders, like in a continuous market.

It is not uncommon for continuous auctions to open the trading with a call market [6]. The opening call market will yield an equilibrium price and quantity for the specific commodity that is traded. Any possible future deviations will be traded in the subsequent continuous auction. In the Power TAC wholesale market, brokers should therefore try to trade their desired amounts of energy in the first auction for each timeslot. The subsequent auctions facilitate trading of fluctuations in demand or supply due to e.g. changes in predicted number of customers or weather forecasts.

In contrast to this analysis, it may be tempting for brokers to start bidding at relatively low prices in early auctions, aiming for the asks of the cheapest gencos, instead of bidding at the equilibrium price. Our broker anticipated that this strategy, or similar variants, would be dominant among competitors. However, such strategies expose an opportunity for other brokers to make a profit by reselling energy, as we will explain below.

The Wholesale Bidding Strategy of cwiBroker. As a reference to the clearing process in the first auction for a specific timeslot we include Fig. 1a. Here the green lines (with open diamonds) indicate asks, sent in by the gencos, and the red lines (with closed circles) represent bids. The market clears at the intersection, where the limit prices of the asks and bids meet.

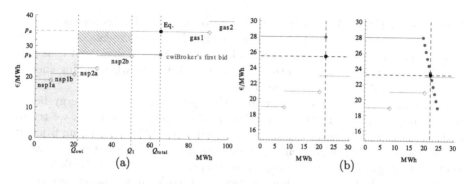

Fig. 1. (a) Our main bidding strategy. The green lines (with open diamonds) represent the asks of the gencos (subscripted with their names). In the first auction, we place a bid (cwiBroker's first bid) for a quantity Q_{total}. The limit price of our bid, p_b, is chosen just above the limit price of the last genco that has to operate fully to meet this demand (in this case nsp2b). When selling energy in future auctions, we ask a limit price, p_a, just below the next cheapest genco (gas1). The net price we pay is represented by the red area minus the green area. (b) Sending in multiple bids (red lines with circles). Compare the left situation (ordinary), to the right (including multiple bids). Due to the additional bids, the clearing price will be lower without otherwise influencing the outcome of the auction (Color figure online).

The first step in our bidding strategy is to estimate the equilibrium price and equilibrium quantity for the particular timeslot. Therefore, we estimate how much energy is going to be needed to fulfil the needs of all customers present in the tariff market (irrespective of their subscriptions). For this quantity, denoted Q_{total}, we depend on the prosumption estimator (see Sect. 5). If all wholesale energy were to be traded in a single auction, then the equilibrium would be set at Q_{total}, at the price level of the genco's ask that intersects with this quantity (the point labelled 'Eq' in Fig. 1a). We expect that any energy that can be obtained below this price, can be resold in future auctions at a higher price.

Therefore, in the first auction our broker makes a bid for Q_{total}. However, the limit price will not be chosen at the equilibrium price, but below it. We choose our limit price (p_b) just above the limit price of the second last genco that sells energy at the equilibrium. This is the last genco that has to operate fully to meet the demand of Q_{total}. In the situation in Fig. 1a, this is genco 'nsp2b'.

The actual energy obtained in the first auction is denoted Q_1. It is possible that Q_1 is larger than the energy needed to meet the total demand of the customers of cwiBroker (denoted Q_{cwi}). In this case, the difference ($Q_1 - Q_{cwi}$) can be sold again in the 23 remaining auctions for this timeslot. For these auctions, the gencos from whom we have bought power in the first auction will no longer submit asks. Therefore, if we set the limit price of our asks, p_a, to just below the limit price of the next cheapest genco (at the estimated equilibrium price), this will be the lowest ask price. It will however be higher than the price we paid for it ourselves ($p_a > p_b$). If other brokers then want to buy wholesale power, they will have to bid at a limit price of at least p_a. The difference in unit price ($p_a - p_b$), multiplied by $(Q_1 - Q_{cwi})$ is the revenue for our broker. This is represented by the green (hatched) area in Fig. 1a. The red (filled) area represents our costs. In some cases, the green area may become larger than the red area, and thus it is possible to make a net profit on the wholesale market, even when buying energy. This is indicated by a negative unit price.

Summarizing, we derive benefit from the opportunity to buy energy below the equilibrium price in the first auction. In the remaining auctions, we try to earn back some of our investments by sending in asks at the equilibrium price. If we do not succeed in buying enough energy in the first auction, we fall back to another strategy. This other strategy is to simply look at the orderbook (the set of uncleared orders of the previous auction) and bid for more energy just above the limit price of the last uncleared ask.

Our main strategy, described above, can easily be countered by other brokers. The other brokers could for example mimic our strategy. If they also bid on large quantities in the first auction, but at a slightly higher limit price, their bids will get cleared, and ours rejected. To solve this, we could, in turn, raise our limit price slightly above the competitor's price. However, at a certain point we will reach the price level of the next cheapest genco. Above this price level, our broker risks buying more energy than it can ultimately sell again, because now both our bid and the competitor's bid may be accepted. In fact, at this point we will have reached the equilibrium price and quantity. We conclude that our strategy can only fare well in the absence of competition in the first auction.

Multiple Orders per Auction. We note that there is no limit on the number of orders brokers can submit for a single auction. It can be advantageous to send in multiple orders, as we will explain below. If we send in bids, we want the market clearing price to be as low as possible, and if we send in asks, we want it to be as high as possible. Suppose we want to buy an amount q, at limit price p. We then send in the usual bid (q, p), but now we also send in a few other bids, with a very small quantity, and each with a slightly lower unit price. So we send in the following bids as well:

$$\{(q_\epsilon, p - i\Delta_p) \mid i \in \{1, ..., N\}\} \tag{3}$$

where $q_\epsilon = 2^{-1074}$ (the lowest possible value for a double in Java), for some Δ_p and some N. We used $N = 8$, not too high in order to limit overhead for the server. Δ_p was calculated from p and N such that it would yield reasonable step sizes. If our original bid is cleared, it is likely that some of these additional bids will get cleared too, up to the last one with a limit price much closer to the highest ask price (see Fig. 1b). Effectively, we make sure the clearing price is as close as possible to the limit price of the last cleared ask. Note that this only works if the intersection of asks and bids occurs such that the last cleared ask (rather than the last cleared bid) is partially executed. Similarly, when selling energy, it can be advantageous to send in multiple asks, in order to raise the clearing price to a value as close as possible to the last cleared bid.

5   Prosumption Estimator

In order to make optimal decisions broker agents must be able to predict the total portfolio prosumption of a timeslot. This is the portfolio production minus the portfolio consumption. Our broker computes the estimation $\hat{Q}_t$ of the portfolio prosumption in timeslot t in the following way:

$$\hat{Q}_t = \sum_{c \in C} \sum_{\tau \in T} n(c, \tau) \hat{q}_{c, h(t)}(temp(t)) \tag{4}$$

C is the set of customer types, T is the set of tariffs published by our broker, $n(c, \tau)$ is the number of customers of type c subscribed to tariff τ, and $temp(t)$ is the predicted temperature in timeslot t. $h(t)$ is the hour of the week of timeslot t, which is composed of the hour of the day (0–23) and the day of the week (weekday, saturday, sunday). The predicted prosumption $\hat{q}_{c,h}(x)$ per customer of type c, for hour of the week h, and temperature x is given by

$$\hat{q}_{c,h}(x) = a_{c,h} + b_{c,h} x \tag{5}$$

After every timeslot t, the parameters $a_{c,h}, b_{c,h}$ for hour of the week $h = h(t)$ and all customer types c are updated using the data observed so far. First, the observed prosumption per customer for each type c and the observed temperature are added to the data. Then, a least squares fit is performed on the data to compute $a_{c,h}$ and $b_{c,h}$. In the Power TAC in 2013 the prosumption estimator only used temperature as a predictor, but in future versions we will incorporate other weather conditions as well.

6   Tournament 2013 Results

Our broker ended second out of seven participants in the competition. It obtained the highest score in each of the 7-player games and in five of the six 2-player games it played. In the 4-player games, cwiBroker always had a decent score (six times 1st, 11 times 2nd, three times 3rd). Furthermore, cwiBroker had a positive score in all games except one (the 4-player game with game number 120, where all players had a negative score). See Table 1 for the scores of all brokers in each setting.

6.1   Tariff Market

In duopoly games we played a strategy that copied the opponent's tariffs. A nice example of where it was profitable to do this, is the game against INAOEBroker02. This broker did not obtain large market shares in games against other brokers (see Table 2), because its tariffs were not very competitive. Although our broker obtained a market share of only 0.47, our profit against INAOEBroker02 was much larger than any other broker, even though they obtained market shares of at least 0.89.

Table 1. Total scores per category per broker. The normalized values represent the z-scores. The total normalized scores define the competition results.

Broker	Score			Normalized			
	7-player	4-player	2-player	7-player	4-player	2-player	total
TacTex	−705, 248	13,493,825	17,853,189	0.386	0.449	0.691	1.526
cwiBroker	647,400	12,197,772	13,476,434	0.437	0.442	0.536	1.415
MLLBroker	8,533	3,305,131	12,796,064	0.413	0.391	0.395	1.199
CrocodileAgent	−361, 939	1,592,764	8,336,061	0.399	0.381	0.311	1.091
AstonTAC	345,300	5,977,354	5,484,780	0.425	0.406	0.254	1.086
Mertacor	−621, 040	1,279,380	4,919,087	0.389	0.380	0.234	1.003
INAOEBroker02	−76, 112, 159	−497, 131, 383	−70, 255, 037	−2.449	−2.449	−2.421	−7.319

Table 2. The market share of each broker in duopoly games. Market share is calculated as the normalised net consumption of a broker's portfolio (negative numbers indicate net production of a brokers customers). The final column represents the mean (± standard-deviation) of the market share of a broker.

	Aston	Croc	cwi	INAOE	Mert	MLL	Tex	$\mu \pm \sigma$
AstonTAC	-	0.95	0.98	0.89	1.03	0.99	0.66	0.78±0.37
CrocodileAgent	0.24	-	0.54	1.18	0.77	0.00	0.26	0.43±0.43
cwiBroker	0.02	0.46	-	0.47	0.89	0.71	0.00	0.36±0.36
INAOEBroker02	0.11	-0.18	0.53	-	0.01	0.10	-0.15	0.06±0.24
Mertacor	0.18	0.36	0.11	0.98	-	0.77	0.09	0.36±0.38
MLLBroker	0.01	1.00	0.29	0.90	0.23	-	0.00	0.35±0.43
TacTex	0.52	0.95	1.00	1.15	1.09	1.00	-	0.82±0.41

In the games against AstonTAC and TacTex, our broker did not attract many customers, because their strategies were too competitive. TacTex was able to benefit from this. AstonTAC however, was unable to make a profit, although it had almost all customers.

In oligopoly games, our broker attempted to estimate the optimal tariff price using subscription models. In most games, however, our broker overestimated the number of subscriptions of its tariffs. As a result, the estimated optimal tariffs were too expensive. Fortunately, the back-up strategy (decreasing the tariff price, until customers subscribed to the tariff) ensured we still had some customers in these games.

6.2   Wholesale Market

We analysed the results of the Power TAC wholesale market, to validate whether our strategy was successful. We investigated how much energy every broker bought or sold, and how much money it paid or received for this. In this section, we will represent the aggregated outcomes of the 24 relevant auctions, for each timeslot t and each broker b, as a total quantity $Q_{t,b}$ and a total cost $C_{t,b}$.

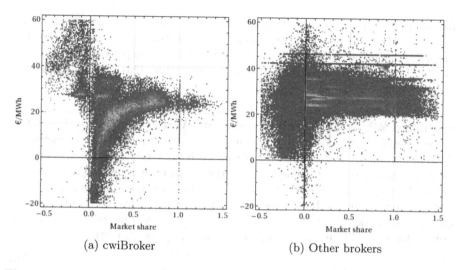

Fig. 2. Results of the wholesale market for cwiBroker and other brokers (all brokers except cwiBroker) combined. The yellow and red colors represent higher densities of points (Color figure online).

Figure 2 shows the results for all timeslots for all games that were played in the competition as a heat map for cwiBroker and, for comparison, also for the other brokers. The vertical axis represents the unit price ($C_{t,b}/Q_{t,b}$) and the horizontal axis a market share ($Q_{t,b}/\sum_{i\in B} Q_{t,i}$, where B is the set of all brokers). The market share is a normalised measure for the net amount of energy a broker bought or sold, relative to the total of all brokers. The market share may be negative (indicating the broker has sold energy and the combined market share of the other brokers was positive) or larger than 1 (indicating the broker bought energy and the combined market share of the other brokers was negative).

From the results in Fig. 2, it becomes clear that for market shares between 0 and 0.5, cwiBroker often obtained a much lower unit price than its competitors. The unit prices for cwiBroker are generally below 20€/MWh, while for other brokers this is the lower limit. Negative unit prices are also present, which effectively means money was earned even when we had to buy energy. Furthermore, for negative market shares, the unit prices for cwiBroker are much higher than those of other brokers. This means our broker earns more money by selling energy than other brokers. From this we conclude that our strategy was very successful for market shares below 0.5. This is the case when the total energy needed by other brokers is larger than that of cwiBroker. Our resaling strategy ensured that the other brokers had to buy part of the energy they needed from our broker. For market shares above 0.5, there is less opportunity to make a profit by trading in a smart way, but our broker still obtained energy at unit prices comparable to, or lower than other brokers.

The results of the wholesale trading in the 7-player setting are of particular interest, since in this setting all brokers compete directly with each other.

We aggregated the outcomes of all auctions for all timeslots. This yields a total quantity and a total cost of energy on the wholesale market, per game per broker, which can again be converted to a unit price. The net unit price for wholesale energy of our broker ranges from 12.2 to 18.5€/MWh. This is much lower than all other brokers, who pay at least 25.7€/MWh.

Estimated Wholesale Earnings Indicator. We are interested in the relative importance of the wholesale market, compared to other incomes and expenses in the competition. Therefore, we estimate for each game how much money brokers spent on wholesale energy compared to others. For each game, we made a least squares linear fit through the data $(Q_{t,b}, C_{t,b})$ of all timeslots in this game, for all brokers except one (the broker for which we built the model to compare with). This yields coefficients a (in €/MWh) and b (in €) in a model of the average costs C for a specific amount of wholesale energy Q for competitors:

$$C = aQ + b \tag{6}$$

The difference between the costs according to the model and the actual costs then indicates how much money a broker saved (or spent excessively) compared to competitors in this game:

$$E_b = \sum_{t \in T} (aQ_{t,b} + b - C_{t,b}) \tag{7}$$

where E_b is an indication for the wholesale earnings (in €) of the broker compared to its competitors. T is the set of all timeslots in a game. The total values (summed over all games in a category) for each broker for each type of game can be found in Table 3. If we compare these values with the competition results in Table 1, we can see that a significant part of our total profit is due to our wholesale strategy. For the 7-player games, the relative earnings in the wholesale market are even larger than our total profit in these games.

Table 3. An indicator for the performance of each broker in wholesale trading. The values represent the amount of money (in €) a broker saved (or spent excessively, in case of negative numbers) on wholesale energy, compared to competitors. The scores represent the total amount of money for a broker for all games in a category.

Broker	2-player	4-player	7-player
AstonTAC	924,200	770,100	1,100
CrocodileAgent	−1,302,000	−2,001,900	−101,200
cwiBroker	2,456,000	4,332,600	835,700
INAOEBroker02	−3,926,700	−2,176,500	−318,700
Mertacor	−3,675,800	−519,300	−20,000
MLLBroker	−1,700,300	−848,100	−110,400
TacTex	1,011,200	420,000	−1,177,400

We also checked the relative advantages of sending in multiple orders for an auction. In order to estimate how much money brokers could have saved, we analysed the wholesale result for every auction in the competition. If the orders in each auction are augmented with additional orders with infinitesimal small quantities, as described in Sect. 4, the clearing price will be either higher or lower, but the cleared quantities will remain the same. In case all submitted wholesale orders were augmented, cwiBroker would have made less money (€502,771 less over the entire competition), because the price at which we sold energy would have been lower. Other brokers could have saved on average €363,494 per broker, summed over all games. The potential benefits of this strategy are therefore not that large, compared to the total income and expenses of brokers. It should however be noted that this strategy is completely free of risks.

6.3 Prosumption Estimator

The prosumption estimator must predict the total portfolio prosumption as accurately as possible. In order to measure its performance we define a performance measure for the relative absolute error $err_{g,t}^{rel}$ in game g for timeslot t:

$$err_{g,t}^{rel} = \frac{|Q_{g,t} - \hat{Q}_{g,t}|}{Q_{g,t}^{prod} + Q_{g,t}^{cons}} \tag{8}$$

$Q_{g,t}$ represents the actual prosumption and $\hat{Q}_{g,t}$ the estimated value, one timeslot ahead. $Q_{g,t}^{prod}$ and $Q_{g,t}^{cons}$ represent respectively the production and the consumption of cwiBroker's customers (such that $Q_{g,t} = Q_{g,t}^{prod} - Q_{g,t}^{cons}$). We divide by the sum of production and consumption, rather than their difference, because we are interested in the error relative to the size of our total portfolio, rather than to the net consumption. Additionally, in case $Q_{g,t}^{prod}$ and $Q_{g,t}^{cons}$ have similar values, we would otherwise risk dividing by zero.

Note that $err_{g,t}^{rel}$ for a single timeslot t typically decreases during a game, because the prosumption estimator improves its model by learning from the game data. We are not only interested in its performance at the end of the game, though, as a prosumption estimator must perform well during the entire game. Therefore, we computed err_g^{rel} for an entire game g as the mean of the relative prosumption errors $err_{g,t}^{rel}$ over all timeslots in game g. Over the entire competition, the mean of err_g^{rel} ($\pm$ standard-deviation) is 0.131 ± 0.053.

Our prosumption estimator used temperature as a predictor. However, production depends on cloud cover, wind speed, and wind direction, rather than temperature. We had not yet implemented this in the 2013 competition, but we expect that it could have improved our prosumption estimator even further. In order to analyse this, we also tested our prosumption estimator offline. In this experiment we ran 30 simulations, in which we applied three different prosumption estimators to the same portfolio. As a benchmark we used the prosumption estimator of the sample broker [7], which is delivered as part of the Power TAC platform. Furthermore, we used the prosumption estimator from the 2013 competition, and an improved version, which used cloud cover and wind speed instead of temperature as predictors for solar and wind energy respectively.

We computed the relative prosumption estimation error err_g^{rel} for each prosumption estimator. The means ($\pm$ sd) are 0.151 ± 0.037 for the sample broker, 0.107 ± 0.029 for the 2013 version, and 0.089 ± 0.021 for the improved version. In each simulation, the 2013 prosumption estimator was better than the sample broker's, and the improved version was never worse than the 2013 version.

7   Conclusion

We developed cwiBroker for the 2013 Power TAC.

The duopoly tariff market strategy was inspired by TFT in the IPD game, which generally resulted in good performance. Unfortunately, the oligopoly tariff-market strategy was often not able to reliably predict the optimal tariff to publish, and resulted in tariffs that were too expensive to attract any customers. However, the back-up strategy of decreasing our tariff price until a satisfactory number of customers was obtained solved this issue to some degree.

On the wholesale market, cwiBroker was able to buy energy for bargain prices in the first auction for each timeslot. In most cases, it was able to sell the surplus of energy in later auctions for a higher price. The result was that our broker was able to make significant profits, by trading on the wholesale market. From the 7-player games we can conclude that, when competition on the tariff market is fierce, it is essential to have a good wholesale strategy. We achieved the highest scores in each of the 7-player games, where it was very hard to earn money on the tariff market. Our wholesale strategy ensured we still made a net profit.

Finally, our broker was able to accurately predict the prosumption of its customers. This was essential input for our wholesale strategy, and in the estimation of the profitability of tariffs that our broker considered. The combined set of strategies resulted in a versatile and robust broker, that performed very well in all settings that were tested, and ended second overall in the competition.

References

1. Schweppe, F.C., Caramanis, M.C., Tabors, R.D., Bohn, R.E.: Spot Pricing of Elecricity. Kluwer Academic Press, Boston (1988)
2. Stoft, S.: Power System Economics: Designing Markets for Electricity. Wiley-IEEE Press, Hoboken (2002)
3. Ketter, W., Collins, J., Reddy, P., de Weerdt, M.: The 2013 Power Trading Agent Competition, ERIM report Series Reference No. ERS-2013-006-LIS (2013)
4. Axelrod, R., Hamilton, W.D.: The evolution of cooperation. Science **211**(4489), 1390–1396 (1981)
5. Ketter, W., Peters, M., Collins, J.: Autonomous agents in future energy markets: the 2012 power trading agent competition. In: Association for the Advancement of Artificial Intelligence (AAAI) Conference, Bellevue (2013)

6. Harris, L.: Trading & Exchanges: Market Microstructure for Practitioners. Oxford Press, Oxford (2003)
7. Ketter, W., Collins, J., Reddy, P.: Power TAC: a competitive economic simulation of the smart grid. Energy Econ. **39**, 262–270 (2013)

Online Double Auction for Perishable Goods

Kazuo Miyashita[✉]

Center for Service Research, AIST, 1-1-1 Umezono,
Tsukuba, Ibaraki 305-8568, Japan
k.miyashita@aist.go.jp

Abstract. One-sided auctions are used in the spot markets for perishable goods because production cost is already "sunk." Moreover, the promptness and simplicity of one-sided auctions are beneficial for trading in perishable goods. However, sellers cannot participate in the price-making process in these auctions. A standard double auction market collects bids from traders and matches them to find the most efficient allocation, assuming that the value of unsold items remains unchanged. Nevertheless, in the market for perishable goods, sellers suffer a loss when they fail to sell their goods, because their salvage values are lost when the goods perish. To solve this problem, we investigate the design of an online double auction for perishable goods, where bids arrive dynamically with their time limits. Our market mechanism aims at improving the profitability of traders by reducing trade failures in the face of uncertainty of incoming/departing bids. We develop a heuristic market mechanism with an allocation policy that prioritizes bids based on their time-criticality, and evaluate its performance empirically using multi-agent simulation. We find out that our market mechanism realizes efficient and fair allocations among traders with truthful behavior in different market situations.

Keywords: Market design · Online double auction · Perishable goods

1 Introduction

Perishable goods such as fishes are traded mainly in the spot market because their yield and quality are unsteady and unpredictable. In the spot markets, the variable production costs of the goods are typically *sunk costs* and these costs are *irretrievable*[1] when the goods remain unsold and perish. Therefore, sellers of perishable goods may suffer large losses if the trade fails in the markets [1].

In traditional markets for perishable goods, one-sided auctions such as a *Dutch auction* are widely practiced because their simplicity and promptness are vital for smoothly consummating large volume transactions of perishable goods with many participating buyers. In the one-sided auction, a seller can influence price-making only subsidiarily by limiting the quantity of goods to be traded. Nevertheless, sellers cannot always maximize their profit by selling the optimum

---

[1] In other words, their *salvage value* reduces to zero.

© Springer International Publishing Switzerland 2014
S. Ceppi et al. (Eds.): AMEC/TADA 2013 and 2014, LNBIP 187, pp. 114–128, 2014.
DOI: 10.1007/978-3-319-13218-1_9

amount of goods because finding the optimal quantity is difficult for sellers in real auctions where precise demands are unknown. Moreover, the markets make a loss in *social surplus* (called *deadweight loss*) when sellers try to make profits by manipulating quantities of goods to be traded.

To solve the problems by realizing fair price-making among traders while reducing allocation failures, we develop a prototypical market for the perishable goods, which adopts online *double auction* (DA) as a market mechanism. In the online DA, multiple buyers and sellers arrive dynamically over time with their time limits. Both buyers and sellers tender their bids for trading commodities. The bid expresses a trader's offer for valuation and quantity of the commodity to be traded. The arrival time, time limit, and bid for a trade are all private information to a trader. Therefore, the online DA is uncertain about future trade. It collects bids over a specified interval of time, and clears the market on expiration of the bidding interval by application of pre-determined rules.

The online DA market for perishable commodities should decide the bids with different prices and time limits that should be matched to increase the utility of traders and reduce trade failures in the face of uncertainty about future trade. The online market also presents the tradeoff for clearing all possible matches as they arise versus waiting for additional buy/sell bids[2] before matching. Although waiting could engender better matching, it can also hurt matching opportunities because the time limit of some existing bids might expire.

1.1 Related Works

Double auction mechanism in the spot market has been investigated in the fields of agricultural economics [2] and experimental economics [3]. They observed the behavior of human subjects in the experimental periodic market and found that their decisions are influenced by the inability to carry unsold goods from one trading period to the next period.

Until recently, few works of research have addressed online double auction mechanisms [4–7]. They examine several important aspects of the problem: design of matching algorithms with good worst-case performance within the framework of competitive analysis [4], construction of a general framework that facilitates truthful dynamic double auction by extending static double auction rules [5], and development of computationally efficient matching algorithms using weighted bipartite matching in graph theory [6]. Gerding applied the online double auction mechanism to an imaginary market for advance reservation of electric vehicle charging facilities [7]. Although their research results are theoretically significant, we cannot readily apply their mechanisms to our online DA problem because their models incorporate the assumption that trade failures never cause a loss to traders, which is not true in markets for perishable goods.

In this paper, we advocate a heuristic online DA mechanism for the spot markets of perishable goods, which improves revenue of the traders by reducing

---

[2] When we must distinguish between claims made by buyers and claims made by sellers, we refer to the *bid* from a buyer and the *ask* from a seller.

allocation failures. The remainder of the paper is organized as follows. Section 2 introduces our market model and presents desiderata and objectives of the market. Section 3 proposes the allocation policy to prevent trading failures in the online DA market. Section 4 explains the settings of multi-agent simulations used to evaluate the developed market mechanism. Section 5 analyzes the performance of various types of agents in the markets and investigates the market equilibria. Section 6 concludes the paper and discusses future research directions.

2   Preliminaries

In our market model, we consider discrete time rounds, $T = \{1, 2, \cdots \}$, indexed by t. For simplicity, we assume the market is for a single commodity. Agents are either sellers (S) or buyers (B), who arrive dynamically over time and depart according to their time limit. In each round, the agents trade multiple units of goods. The market is cleared at the end of every round to find new allocations.

Each agent i has a private information called *type*, $\theta_i = (v_i, q_i, a_i, d_i)$, where v_i, q_i, a_i, d_i are non-negative real numbers, v_i is agent i's valuation of a single unit of the good, q_i is the quantity of the goods that agent i wants to trade, a_i is the arrival time, and d_i denotes the departure time. The duration between the arrival time and the departure time defines the agent's trading period $[a_i, d_i]$ indexed by p, and agents can repeatedly participate in the auction over several trading periods.

We model our market as a wholesale market for B2B transactions. In the market, seller i brings her goods by the arrival time a_i. Therefore, seller i incurs production cost before the trade starts and considers the production cost together with its associated opportunity cost as the valuation v_i of the goods. Furthermore, at the departure time d_i of seller i, the salvage value of the goods evaporates because of its perishability unless it is traded successfully. Because of advance production and perishability, sellers face the distinct risk of failing to recoup the production cost in the trade. Buyers in our market procure the goods to resell them in retail markets. For buyer j, valuation v_j represents the maximum budget for procuring the goods. The arrival time a_j is the first time when buyer j values the item. Furthermore, buyer j is assumed to gain some profit by retailing the goods if she succeeds to procure them before the departure time d_j. In other words, d_j denotes the due time for the buyer to procure the goods for a coming retail opportunity.

Agents are self-interested and their types are private information. At the beginning of a trading period, agent i submits a bid by making a claim about its type $\hat{\theta}_i = (\hat{v}_i, \hat{q}_i, \hat{a}_i, \hat{d}_i) \neq \theta_i$ to the auctioneer. In succeeding rounds in the trading period, the agent can modify the value of its unmatched bid.

2.1   Misreports by Agents

An agent's self-interest is exhibited in its willingness to misrepresent its type when this will improve the outcome of the auction in its favor. Misrepresenting its type is not always beneficial or feasible for agents. As for quantity, it is impossible for a seller to report a larger quantity $\hat{q}_i > q_i$ because the sold goods must be delivered immediately after trade in a spot market. Moreover, it is unreasonable for a buyer to report a larger quantity $\hat{q}_j > q_j$ because excess orders may produce dead stocks. Reporting an earlier arrival time is infeasible for a seller and buyer because the arrival time is the earliest timing that they decide to participate in the market. Reporting a later arrival time or an earlier departure time can only reduce the chance of successful trade for the agents. For a seller, it is impossible to report a later departure time $\hat{d}_i > d_i$ since her goods perish by the time d_i. For a buyer, misreporting a later departure time $\hat{d}_j > d_j$ may delay retailing the procured goods.

Additionally, a seller can misreport a smaller quantity $\hat{q}_i < q_i$ with the intention of raising the market price, but in that case, she needs to throw out some of her goods before she arrives at the market. If a buyer misrepresents a smaller quantity $\hat{q}_j < q_j$ to lower the market price, she loses a chance of retailing more goods. Therefore, we assume that the agents do not like to misrepresent a quantity value in their type. On the other hand, we suppose that an agent has incentives to misreport its valuation for increasing its profit because it is the most instinctive way for the agent to influence market prices. In ordinary markets, a seller has an incentive to report a higher valuation and a buyer reports a lower valuation. However, in a market for perishable goods, a seller may report a lower valuation $\hat{v}_i < v_i$ when she desperately wants to sell the goods before they perish.

2.2 Desiderata and Objectives

Let $\hat{\theta}^t$ denote the set of all the agent's types reported in round t; $\hat{\theta} = (\hat{\theta}^1, \hat{\theta}^2, \ldots, \hat{\theta}^t, \ldots)$ denote a complete reported type profile; and $\hat{\theta}^{\leq t}$ denote the reported type profile restricted to the agents with reported arrival no later than round t. Report $\hat{\theta}_i^t = (\hat{v}_i^t, q_i^t, a_i^p, d_i^p)$ is a bid made by agent i in round t within trading period p (i.e., $t \in [a_i^p, d_i^p]$). The report represents a commitment to trade at most q_i^t units[3] of goods at a limit price of $\hat{v}_i^t$ in round t within trading period p. As discussed previously, we assume agent i reports truthful values about quantity q_i, arrival time a_i, and departure time d_i at any round t.

In the market, a seller's ask and a buyer's bid can be matched when they satisfy the following condition.

Definition 1 (Matching condition). *Seller i's ask $\hat{\theta}_i^t = (\hat{v}_i^t, q_i^t, a_i^p, d_i^p)$ and buyer j's bid $\hat{\theta}_j^t = (\hat{v}_j^t, q_j^t, a_j^p, d_j^p)$ are matchable when*

$$(\hat{v}_i^t \leq \hat{v}_j^t) \wedge ([a_i^p, d_i^p] \cap [a_j^p, d_j^p] \neq \emptyset) \wedge (q_i^t > 0) \wedge (q_j^t > 0). \tag{1}$$

An online DA mechanism, $M = (\pi, x)$, is composed of an allocation policy π and a pricing policy x. The allocation policy π is defined as $\{\pi^t\}^{t \in T}$, where $\pi_{i,j}^t(\hat{\theta}^{\leq t}) \in \mathbb{I}_{\geq 0}$ represents the quantity traded by agents i and j in round t,

---

[3] Successful trade in previous rounds of period p make the current quantity of goods reduce to $q_i^t \leq q_i^p$.

given reports $\hat{\theta}^{\leq t}$. The pricing policy x is defined as $\{x^t\}^{t \in T}, x^t = (s^t, b^t)$, where $s_{i,j}^t(\hat{\theta}^{\leq t}) \in \mathbb{R}_{\geq 0}$ represents the payment seller i receives from buyer j as a result of the trade in round t, given reports $\hat{\theta}^{\leq t}$. Furthermore, $b_{i,j}^t(\hat{\theta}^{\leq t}) \in \mathbb{R}_{>0}$ represents a payment made by buyer j as a result of the trade with seller i in round t, given reports $\hat{\theta}^{\leq t}$. In this paper, an auctioneer is supposed to make neither profit nor loss in the trade, so that $b_{i,j}^t(\hat{\theta}^{\leq t}) = s_{i,j}^t(\hat{\theta}^{\leq t})$.

Most studies on DA mechanisms assume agents with simple quasi-linear utility, $\sum_j (s_{i,j} - \pi_{i,j} v_i)$, for seller i and $\sum_i (\pi_{i,j} v_j - b_{i,j})$ for buyer j. However, in order to represent idiosyncratic motivation of agents in a wholesale spot market for perishable goods, we define the utility for sellers and buyers as follows.

Definition 2 (Seller's utility). *Seller i's utility at time round t is*

$$U_i(\hat{\theta}^{\leq t}) = \sum_{\{p|a_i^p \leq t\}} \sum_{t' \in [a_i^p, d_i^p]} \sum_{j \in B} (s_{i,j}^{t'}(\hat{\theta}^{\leq t}) - \pi_{i,j}^{t'}(\hat{\theta}^{\leq t}) v_i^p)$$

$$- \sum_{\{p|d_i^p \leq t\}} (q_i^p - \sum_{t' \in [a_i^p, d_i^p]} \sum_{j \in B} \pi_{i,j}^{t'}(\hat{\theta}^{\leq t})) v_i^p. \quad (2)$$

The second term in Eq. 2 represents the loss of unsold and perished goods, which are calculated dynamically at the bid's departure time (i.e., when $d_i^P \leq t$). With the effect of the second term, sellers are motivated to lower their valuation in the bid when the departure time approaches.

Definition 3 (Buyer's utility). *Buyer j's utility at time round t is*

$$U_j(\hat{\theta}^{\leq t}) = \sum_{\{p|a_j^p \leq t\}} \sum_{t' \in [a_j^p, d_j^p]} \sum_{i \in S} ((\pi_{i,j}^{t'}(\hat{\theta}^{\leq t}) v_j^p - b_{i,j}^{t'}(\hat{\theta}^{\leq t}))$$

$$+ \pi_{i,j}^{t'}(\hat{\theta}^{\leq t}) r_j^p). \quad (3)$$

The second term in Eq. 3 represents that buyer j plans to make profit $\pi_{i,j}^t r_j^p$ by retailing the procured goods at price $v_j^p + r_j^p$. Since v_j^p represents the maximum budget allowed to buyer j, she has no incentive to bid with valuation higher than v_j^p. Within the budget limitation, buyer j is motivated to procure as much goods as possible up to q_j^p for satisfying the demand of her retail customers.

Agents are modeled as risk-neutral and utility-maximizing. As Eq. 2 shows, a seller gains profits by selling low-value goods at high prices but loses money if the goods perish without being sold. The seller's bidding strategy on valuation of the goods is intricate because she can enhance her utility in the trade by either raising the market price with high valuation bidding or increasing successful trades (i.e., preventing the goods from perishing) with low valuation bidding. Equation 3 reveals that a buyer makes profits by procuring high-value goods at low prices and retailing the procured high-value goods. Therefore, in this market, the buyer also has difficulty in finding the optimal bidding strategies since she can improve her utility by either lowering the market price with low valuation bidding or by increasing successful trades (i.e., enhancing retail opportunities) with high valuation bidding.

Based on the defined utility for sellers and buyers, our market's objective is not only maximizing social surplus produced by trade (i.e., $\pi_{i,j}^{t'}(v_j^{p'} - v_i^p)$) but also increasing retailing profits of buyers (i.e., $\pi_{i,j}^{t'} r_j^{p'}$) and reducing loss to sellers from unsold and perished goods (i.e., $(q_i^p - \sum \pi_{i,j}^{t'}) v_i^p)$).

We also require that the online DA satisfies the *budget-balance*, *feasibility*, and *individual rationality*. Budget-balance ensures that in every round the mechanism collects and distributes the same amount of money from and to the agents (i.e., an auctioneer makes neither profit nor loss). Feasibility demands that the auctioneer takes no short position on the commodity traded in any round. Individual rationality guarantees that no agent loses by participating in the market.

3 Market Design

In spot markets for perishable goods, sellers raise their asking price and buyers lower their bidding price as a rational strategy to improve their surplus as long as they can avoid possible trade failures. In such markets, agents have to manipulate their valuation carefully for obtaining higher utilities. Our goal is to design a market mechanism that secures desirable outcomes for both individual agents and the whole market without the need for strategic bidding by the agents.

The well-known result of [8] demonstrates that no Bayes-Nash incentive-compatible exchange mechanism can be simultaneously efficient, budget-balanced, and individually rational. Therefore, we aim to design an online DA mechanism that imposes budget-balance, feasibility, and individual rationality while promoting reasonable efficiency and moderate incentive-compatibility.

3.1 Allocation Policy

Many studies on the DA mechanism investigate a static market and use social surplus from successful trade as the objective function, with the assumption that agents never suffer a loss from trade failures. The ratio of achieved social surplus against the maximal social surplus at the competitive equilibrium is called *allocative efficiency*. The allocation policy that maximizes allocative efficiency in a static DA market arranges the asks according to the ascending order of the seller's price and the bids according to the descending order of the buyer's price, and matches them in the sequence. We designate this allocation rule as a *price-based* allocation policy.

The price-based allocation policy is efficient for the DA markets that assume trade in future markets or trade in durable goods, in which agents do not make any loss by trade failures. However, sellers of perishable goods in the spot market can lose the value of perished goods which are not sold during the trading period. Consequently, in addition to increasing social surplus, increasing the number of successful trades is also important in the spot market for perishable goods.

For static DA markets, several maximal matching mechanisms have been developed [9,10]. The basic idea is not to simply match high-valuation bids and low-valuation asks, but to match low-valuation asks with low-valuation bids that are priced no lower than the asks, and match high-valuation bids with high-valuation asks that are priced no higher than the bids. However, their methods cannot address the problem of an online market where each bid is valid only in its limited trading period. In the allocation policy of online DA mechanisms, *criticality* of bids must be evaluated and taken into consideration properly to increase the bids that can be traded successfully within their fixed trading period.

In this paper, we define criticality of asks as follows: Let M^t represent a set of all the pairs of bids that are matchable at time round t. At this time, buyers have as many as $\sum_{\{\hat{\theta}_j^t \mid (\hat{\theta}_i^t, \hat{\theta}_j^t) \in M^t\}} q_j^t$ quantity of bids that are matchable with seller i's ask $\hat{\theta}_i^t$. This value is used as the estimated matchability of the ask in calculating its criticality. At time round t, seller i in trading period p has as many as $q_i^p - \sum_{t' \leq t} \sum_{j \in B} \pi_{i,j}^{t'}(\hat{\theta}^{\leq t'})$ remaining goods to sell. Furthermore, at time round t, seller i has a slack time as long as $d_i^p - t$ till the unsold goods perish. We first define unsatisfiability of the ask as quantitative unbalance of supplies against demands as follows.

Definition 4 (Ask unsatisfiability). *Unsatisfiability of seller i's ask at time round t in trading period p is*

$$u_i^p(\hat{\theta}^{\leq t}) = \frac{q_i^p - \sum_{t' \leq t} \sum_{j \in B} \pi_{i,j}^{t'}(\hat{\theta}^{\leq t'})}{\sum_{\{\hat{\theta}_j^t \mid (\hat{\theta}_i^t, \hat{\theta}_j^t) \in M^t\}} q_j^t}. \tag{4}$$

Taking temporal limitation of the ask into consideration, we define criticality of the ask as follows.

Definition 5 (Ask criticality). *Criticality of seller i's ask at time round t in trading period p is*

$$c_i^p(\hat{\theta}^{\leq t}) = \frac{u_i^p(\hat{\theta}^{\leq t})}{d_i^p - t}. \tag{5}$$

Unstatisfiablity and criticality of bids are defined similarly as those of asks.

In the price-based allocation policy, bids and asks are sorted according to the value of claimed valuation and matched in the sequence. In other words, in the price-based allocation policy, the priority of bid is $\hat{v}_j^t$ and that of ask is $1.0/\hat{v}_i^t$, and bids and asks with larger priorities are matched accordingly. In our allocation policy, the priority of bid and ask is determined based on their unsatisfiability and criticality as follows.

Priority of bid and ask

1. If unsatisfiability of agent i's bid is larger than a predetermined threshold value $\mathcal{U}$, the priority of the bid is equal to its criticality $c_i^p(\hat{\theta}^{\leq t})$.
2. If unsatisfiability of the bid or ask are smaller than the threshold value,
   a) The priority of seller i's ask is set as $-\hat{v}_i^t$.
   b) The priority of buyer j's bid is set as $-1.0/\hat{v}_j^t$.

We call the above threshold $\mathcal{U}$ as *unsatisfiability threshold* and set its value as 0 based on the result of preliminary experiments [11].

In our allocation policy, we use the priorities of bids and asks as follows.

Priority based allocation policy

1. At the beginning of allocation, asks from sellers are sorted in descending order with regard to their priorities.
2. Then, starting with the ask of the largest priority, matchable bids with the ask are sorted in descending order with regard to their priorities.
3. The ask and a next bid in the sorted queue are matched. This process continues in the sequence until the quantity requested by the ask is satisfied or there are no matchable bids in the queue.
4. The allocation process continues until there remains no matchable ask.

When the unsatisfiability threshold is set as ∞, the allocation policy is same as the price-based allocation policy. When unsatisfiability threshold is set as 0, we designate the allocation policy as a *criticality-based* allocation policy.

The criticality-based allocation policy does not guarantee allocative efficiency. However, considering the possible loss by trade failures, the criticality-based allocation policy is expected to earn more profit for the agents by increasing successful trades in certain market situations. The criticality-based allocation policy tends to give a higher priority to a bid with a shorter trading period. Hence, agents have an incentive to divide their bid into multiple consecutive bids with shorter trading periods. This strategic behavior of agents can be easily prevented by charging an entry fee for bidding on the agents. Therefore, in this paper, we do not assume the agents adopt such bid-dividing strategies.

In online DA markets, quality of the allocation can be improved if we accumulate the bids without matching them immediately at their arrival and decide the allocation from the aggregated bids. However, deferring allocation decisions might prevent the existing bids from being matched, and hence, increase trade failures. In order to investigate the effectiveness of deferred allocation decisions in the online DA market, we define *elapse rate* as follows.

Definition 6 (Elapse rate). *Elapse rate of agent i's bid at time round t in trading period p is*

$$e_i^p(t) = \frac{t - a_i^p}{d_i^p - a_i^p}. \tag{6}$$

Using the elapse rate, the third step of our priority based allocation policy described above is enhanced to wait for additional bids before matching the existing bids and avoid expiration of the bids in the market as follows.

> **Priority based allocation policy enhanced with elapse rate**
>
> 3. The ask and the next bid in the sorted queue are matched *only when both their elapsed rates are not smaller than a predetermined threshold value $\mathscr{E}$*. This process continues in this sequence until the quantity requested by the ask is satisfied or there are no matchable bids in the queue.

We call the above threshold *elapse rate threshold* and set 0.9 as its value based on the result of preliminary experiments [11].

3.2   Pricing Policy

The pricing policy is important to secure truthfulness and prevent strategic manipulation by agents, which should promote stability of agent bidding and increase efficiency of a market. Nevertheless, obtaining truthfulness in DA markets while guaranteeing other desirable properties such as efficiency, individual rationality, and budget balance is impossible [8].

We impose budget-balance and promote reasonable efficiency in our online DA market, so we adopt k-double auction [12] as our pricing policy. And we set the value of k as 0.0 because of the following reasons.

1. Seller i does not have an incentive to overstate her true valuation v_i^p, because it does not change the clearing price without losing matching opportunities. She does not have a strong incentive to understate her valuation either, if our allocation policy can reduce the risk of loss caused by perished goods.
2. If the retail profit of buyer j, which is $\sum \pi_{i,j}^{t'} r_j^p$, is much larger than her surplus $\sum (\pi_{i,j}^{t'} v_j^p - b_{i,j}^{t'})$, which is usually the case in wholesale markets, she has an incentive to offer her true valuation for increasing successful trades.

With the above defined allocation policy and pricing policy, we speculate that our mechanism can make the online DA market for perishable goods yield a high utility with moderate incentive-compatibility while maintaining properties of budget-balance and individual rationality. Since our market model and mechanism are much more complex than traditional continuous double auctions, even for which theoretical analysis is intractable, we perform empirical evaluation of the market mechanism using multi-agent simulation.

4   Market Simulation

In the simulation, five sellers and five buyers participate in the market. For the simulations, we use two types of market depicted in Figs. 1 and 2, which have a common supply curve and different demand curves. Figure 1 depicts the market with a high risk of trade failures, where buyers' valuation distributes equally with sellers' valuation. Figure 2 depicts the market with a low risk of trade failures, in which the average valuation by the buyers is higher than that by the sellers. In the simulations, buyer j's retailing profit rate in trading period p (i.e., r_j^p in Eq. 3) is set equal to his true valuation v_j^p.

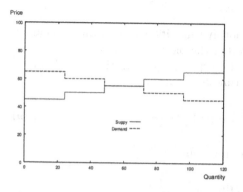

Fig. 1. Market with low demands

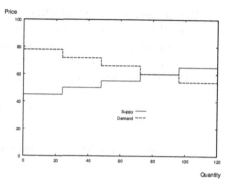

Fig. 2. Market with low demands

Each simulation runs for 12 days and the market is cleared every hour. Every day, the agents submit one bid or ask, each of which has 24 units of demands or supplies for the homogeneous perishable goods. Its arrival time is picked up randomly for every bid submission. The seller's ask departs the market 72 h after its arrival, which implies that a seller's goods lose their value in the market three days after their production because of perishability. The departure time of a buyer's bid is 24 h after its arrival, which simulates the situation of buyers procuring goods for retail sales of the next day. For each result shown in the following sections, 20 randomized trials are executed to simulate diversified patterns of agents' arrival and departure.

4.1 Bidding Strategies of Agents

Empirical analyses of complex markets necessarily focus on a restricted set of bidding strategies. In this paper, we prepare several types of bidding strategies for both sellers and buyers to simulate the behavior of different agents in their bidding, and investigate market outcomes in different situations.

The bidding strategies of agents used in the simulations are as follows.

1. Modest strategy (MOD)
   This strategy is only for seller agents. With this strategy, seller i always reports her valuation as

$$\hat{v}_i^t = 0. \tag{7}$$

   This strategy is developed to simulate one-sided auction markets where only buyers submit their bids.
2. Truth-telling strategy (TT)
   With this strategy, agent i always reports its valuation truthfully as

$$\hat{v}_i^t = v_i^p. \tag{8}$$

3. Monotonous strategy (MONO)

With this strategy, an agent monotonously tunes its report on valuation along with the elapsed time after the arrival of the bid in the market.

In trading period p, seller i and buyer j report their valuation as follows.

(a) Seller i's reported valuation at time round t is

$$\hat{v}_i^t = v_i^p(1.0 + \delta)\frac{d_i^p - t}{d_i^p - a_i^p}. \tag{9}$$

(b) Buyer j's reported valuation at time round t is

$$\hat{v}_j^t = v_j^p(1.0 - \delta\frac{d_j^p - t}{d_j^p - a_j^p}). \tag{10}$$

δ is a parameter to control aggressiveness of the agent's bidding behavior. In this paper, we set 0.2 as the value of δ.

4. Zero-intelligent aggressive strategy (ZIA)

With this strategy, by reporting the valuation randomly within a certain range, an agent seeks a larger surplus when there is little risk of trade failure and gives up making a profit when there is little time left until its departure. In trading period p, seller i and buyer j report their valuation as follows.

(a) Seller i's reported valuation at time round t is

$$\hat{v}_i^t = rand(v_i^p(1.0 + \delta)\frac{d_i^p - t}{d_i^p - a_i^p}, v_i^p(1.0 + \delta)). \tag{11}$$

(b) Buyer j's reported valuation at time round t is

$$\hat{v}_j^t = rand(v_j^p(1.0 - \delta), v_j^p(1.0 - \delta\frac{d_j^p - t}{d_j^p - a_j^p})). \tag{12}$$

$rand(x, y)$ is a function to produce a random value in between x and y. Thus, ZIA strategy is a randomized variation of MONO strategy.

5   Empirical Analysis of Market Equilibria

Sellers and buyers in the B2B market for perishable goods have different utilities and adopt different bidding strategies for maximizing their utility. In the experiments, we perform a limited strategic analysis by looking for Nash equilibria between restricted types of sellers and buyers based on the simplified market model in which all the agents on the seller side or the buyer side are homogeneous and follow the same pure strategy. The results obtained in the experiments is not completely accurate, but the degree of success achieved in predicting agent behavior and market outcomes can be used as a benchmark against which more sophisticated mechanisms of online DA can be judged.

Tables 1 and 2 show the payoff matrix between sellers and buyers in the high-risk market and the low-risk market, respectively. Each cell in the tables

Table 1. Payoff matrix in the high-risk market

Seller\Buyer	MONO	TT	ZIA
MOD	100%, 53.2 81,730.8 (399.5) -2,530.8 (399.5)	100%, 54.2 80,290.8 (399.5) -1,090.8 (399.5)	100%, 40.7 99,734.4 (1,161.8) -20,534.4 (1,161.8)
MONO	98%, 54.1 79,448.4 (677.9) -1,402.0 (256.4)	98%, 55.0 78,260.8 (708.2) -14.8 (264.1)	95%, 43.5 91,538.2 (1,507.6) -15,619.7 (1,210.2)
TT	80%, 56.0 66,286.1 (644.8) -11,315.6 (777.7)	100%, 55.0 79,092.0 (324.0) 42.0 (127.4)	58%, 53.1 53,844.9 (2,633.4) -25,866.4 (2,792.1)
ZIA	100%, 53.7 81,061.8 (298.9) -1,915.8 (260.7)	100%, 54.7 79,496.0 (579.2) -500.0 (368.3)	99%, 41.5 97,940.3 (1,353.3) -18,341.1 (1,181.5)

represents the result of interaction between the sellers and buyers with the corresponding strategy. The cell is separated into two parts: the upper part of the cell shows the average matching rate and the average clearing price, and the bottom left corner in the lower part of the cell reveals the average and standard deviation (inside parentheses) of the utility of seller agents and the top right corner shows those of utility of buyer agents.

In Table 1, two cells in gray are considered to be Nash equilibria. Between them, the Nash equilibrium (TT, TT) achieves the higher total utility (i.e., 79, 134). Furthermore, although it is difficult for the sellers to make profits in the high-risk market, the Nash equilibrium (TT, TT) achieves larger sellers' utility (i.e., 42.0) than the other results in Table 1. Hence, the Nash equilibrium (TT, TT) is preferable to the other Nash equilibrium (MONO, ZIA) not only because it saves the agents the cost of reporting strategically for more profits in the market, but also because it achieves a higher total utility and fair utility distribution among sellers and buyers.

Table 2 shows that there is no Nash equilibrium in this market, and the table also shows that the matching rate is almost 100 % and the total utility is around 11,000, which is distributed among sellers and buyers reasonably, regardless of

Table 2. Payoff matrix in the low-risk market

Seller\Buyer	MONO	TT	ZIA
MOD	100%, 64.1	100%, 65.1	100%, 48.7
	97,788.9 (479.4) 13,091.1 (479.4)	96,348.9 (479.4) 14,531.1 (479.4)	119,928.3 (1,435.0) -9,048.3 (1,435.0)
MONO	100%, 64.7	100%, 65.7	97%, 51.8
	96,861.3 (281.5) 14,018.7 (281.5)	95,455.2 (289.6) 15,424.8 (289.6)	113,289.8 (1,538.5) -4,562.4 (1,387.1)
TT	100%, 64.7	100%, 65.6	86%, 57.8
	96,938.4 (260.9) 13,941.6 (260.9)	95,670.0 (324.2) 15,210.0 (324.2)	94,997.1 (2,634.7) -2,100.9 (2,444.9)
ZIA	100%, 64.6	100%, 65.7	100%, 49.5
	96,881.7 (594.7) 13,874.1 (416.3)	95,417.4 (565.3) 15,367.8 (302.0)	118,684.1 (2,243.7) -7,968.5 (2,198.9)

the agents' strategy[4] except when buyers adopt the ZIA strategy. When buyers use the ZIA strategy, sellers' utility is largely damaged no matter what strategy the sellers adopt. Table 2 reveals that buyers lose incentive to adopt the ZIA strategy only when sellers use the TT strategy due to the resultant low utility and large deviation. Therefore, the best strategy for the sellers in this market is the TT strategy, and the best response of the buyers to the sellers' TT strategy is adopting the MONO strategy. The corresponding strategy profile (TT, MONO) is represented as the light-gray cell in Table 2. It should be noted that considering the value of standard deviation, buyers' utility in the light-gray cell does not significantly differ from the buyers' utility in the adjacent cell corresponding to the strategy profile (TT, TT). Hence, the buyers have a large possibility of choosing the TT strategy in the low-risk market.

From the above results, we find that our market mechanism for perishable goods succeeds in leading the sellers and buyers to behave truthfully for maximizing their utilities in both the high-risk market and the low-risk market.

---

[4] It should be noted that even when sellers use the MOD strategy, they can make reasonable profits in the low-risk market.

6 Conclusion

We developed an online DA mechanism for the spot market of perishable goods to achieve efficient and fair allocations among traders by considering the loss from trade failures. We explained that sellers have a high risk of losing money by trade failures because their goods are perishable and must be produced in advance to compensate for their unsteady yield and unpredictable quality. To reduce trade failures in the spot markets for perishable goods, our DA mechanism prioritizes the bids that have a smaller chance of being matched in their time period. Empirical results using multi-agent simulation showed that our DA mechanism was effective in promoting truthful behavior on the part of traders for realizing efficient and fair allocations between sellers and buyers in both the high-risk market and the low-risk market.

The results reported in this paper are very limited for any comprehensive conclusion on the design of online DA for perishable goods. For this purpose, we need to investigate other types of bidder strategies in a wide variety of experimental settings. Additionally, behavior of human subjects in the market must be examined carefully to evaluate the effectiveness of the designed mechanism. Furthermore, the current mechanism can be improved by incorporating some knowledge about future bids statistically predicted from past bidding records.

Acknowledgments. This work was supported by JSPS KAKENHI Grant Number 24300101.

References

1. Bastian, C., Menkhaus, D., O'Neill, P., Phillips, O.: Supply and demand risks in laboratory forward and spot markets: Implications for agriculture. J. Agric. Appl. Econ. **32**(1), 159–173 (2000)
2. Krogmeier, J., Menkhaus, D., Phillips, O., Schmitz, J.: An experimental economics approach to analyzing price discovery in forward and spot markets. J. Agric. Appl. Econ. **2**, 327–336 (1997)
3. Mestelman, S.: The Performance of double-auction and posted-offer markets with advance production. In: Plott, C.R., Smith, V.L. (eds.) Handbook of Experimental Economics Results, vol. 1, pp. 77–82. Elsevier, New York (2008)
4. Blum, A., Sandholm, T., Zinkevich, M.: Online algorithms for market clearing. J. ACM **53**(5), 845–879 (2006)
5. Bredin, J., Parkes, D.C., Duong, Q.: Chain: A dynamic double auction framework for matching patient agents. J. Artif. Intell. Res. **30**(1), 133–179 (2007)
6. Zhao, D., Zhang, D., Perrussel, L.: Mechanism design for double auctions with temporal constraints. In: Proceedings of IJCAI, pp. 1–6 (2011)
7. Gerding, E., Stein, S., Robu, V., Zhao, D., Jennings, N.: Two-sided online markets for electric vehicle charging. In: AAMAS-2013, pp. 989–996 (2013)
8. Myerson, R., Satterthwaite, M.: Efficient mechanisms for bilateral trading. J. Econ. Theory **29**(2), 265–281 (1983)
9. Zhao, D., Zhang, D., Khan, M., Perrussel, L.: Maximal matching for double auction. In: Li, J. (ed.) AI 2010. LNCS, vol. 6464, pp. 516–525. Springer, Heidelberg (2010)

10. Niu, J., Parsons, S.: Maximizing matching in double-sided auctions. In: Proceedings of Twelfth International Conference on Autonomous Agents and Multiagent Systems (AAMAS 2013), Volume arXiv:1304, pp. 1283–1284 (2013)
11. Miyashita, K.: Developing online double auction mechanism for fishery markets. In: Ali, M., Bosse, T., Hindriks, K., Hoogendoorn, M., Jonker, C., Treur, J. (eds.) Recent Trends in Applied Artificial Intelligence. Lecture Notes in Computer Science, vol. 7906, pp. 1–11. Springer, Berlin Heidelberg (2013)
12. Satterthwaite, M.A., Williams, S.R.: Bilateral trade with the sealed bid k-double auction: Existence and efficiency. J. Econ. Theory **48**(1), 107–133 (1989)

Designing Tariffs in a Competitive Energy Market Using Particle Swarm Optimization Techniques

Eleni Ntagka[1], Antonios Chrysopoulos[2]([✉]), and Pericles A. Mitkas[1,2]

[1] Electrical and Computer Engineering Department,
Aristotle University of Thessaloniki, Thessaloniki, Greece
[2] Informatics and Telematics Institute,
CERTH, Thessaloniki, Greece
{elntagka,achryso}@issel.ee.auth.gr,
mitkas@auth.gr

Abstract. The main challenge of the Smart Grid Paradigm is achieving a tight balance between supply and demand of electrical energy. A contemporary approach to address this challenge is the use of autonomous broker agents. These intelligent entities are able to interact with both producers and consumers by offering tariffs, in order to buy or sell energy, respectively, within a new energy market mechanism: the Tariff Market. Agents are incentivized to level supply and demand within their portfolio, in line with maximizing their profit. In this work, we study a profit optimization strategy that was implemented for Mertacor broker-agent, always considering the customized needs of his customers. The agent was developed and tested in the PowerTAC Competition platform, which provides a powerful benchmark for researching Tariff Markets. To fulfill the agent's objectives, two types of strategies were implemented: (i) a tariff formation strategy and (ii) a tariff update strategy. Both strategies are treated as optimization problems, where the broker's objective is maximizing its profit as well as maintaining an acceptable customer market share. To this end, Particle Swarm Optimization techniques were adopted. The results look very promising and there is a great future work potential based on them.

Keywords: Autonomous agents · Energy brokers · Electricity tariffs · Particle Swarm Optimization (PSO) · Power TAC

1 Introduction

The vision of the Smart Grid is mainly based on the concept of decentralized control mechanisms, which can contribute to maintaining the stability of the energy system in real time. Establishing and understanding such mechanisms is the cornerstone of an efficient, safe, and reliable energy system. This paper focuses on one of those control mechanisms, Intelligent Software Broker Agents, which

© Springer International Publishing Switzerland 2014
S. Ceppi et al. (Eds.): AMEC/TADA 2013 and 2014, LNBIP 187, pp. 129–143, 2014.
DOI: 10.1007/978-3-319-13218-1_10

assume the role of a broker between producers and consumers [8]. More specifically, broker agents interact with the available producers and consumers through a new market mechanism, the Tariff Market. In this mechanism, each agent offers tariffs in order to buy or sell energy, while at the same time it tries to: (i) persuade the customers into changing their consumption/production patterns and (ii) realize a profit. Additionally, the Tariff Market, by design, encourages broker agents to deal with the energy imbalances within their customer portfolio. Thus, broker agents play an important part in the stability of the grid, through monitoring their customers.

PowerTAC [9] is a competitive simulation platform, which provides a promising ground for conducting research on Tariff Markets. In particular, it models a liberalized energy market where competing broker agents try to maximize profit by trading energy in the wholesale and the retail market, susceptible to constraints and fixed costs, such as tariff publication and withdrawal fees, distribution fees, and penalties whenever an imbalance of energy occurs.

In this work, we study optimization strategies, implemented for the Mertacor broker-agent [2], in order to maximize profit; always with respect to the customized needs of its customers. To accomplish the agent's objectives, two types of strategies were implemented: (i) a tariff formation strategy and (ii) a tariff update strategy. Both strategies are treated as optimization problems, where the objective function maps to the broker's maximum profit, while retaining an adequate portion of the customers market share. Our approach involved the adoption of Particle Swarm Optimization (PSO) techniques as a core element.

The remainder of this paper is outlined as follows. Section 2 provides a review on the relevant literature, whereas Sect. 3 discusses the key modeling elements of Power TAC. Section 4 introduces the strategies developed for our agent, while Sect. 5 presents the experiments conducted. Section 6 summarizes our conclusions drawn and provides directions for future research.

2   Related Work

Up to date, the use of intelligent software agent technologies in tariff market simulations has been limited. Consequently, the published research on agents acting as brokers in such markets is relatively scarce. The PowerTAC platform [8] offers great opportunities for researching the current field as well as generating public policies. The studies [1,10] analyze the performance of agents participating in earlier trial competitions. The results presented support the idea of PowerTAC being a realistic simulation and a testbed for different agent trading policies.

In [15], Reddy and Veloso investigated several learning pricing strategies for one and for multiple autonomous broker agents using Markov Decision Processes (MDPs) and Reinforcement Learning (RL). However, the results seem to have limited application, as the market model used was a rather simplistic one. Specifically: (i) the tariffs defined only the consumption/production per kWh price, without considering other tariff parameters, (ii) the consumers' model was represented by a fixed consumption/production power load, which simplifies the broker's task and, (iii) the offered tariff was addressed to all consumer types regardless of their load quality or quantity. In [13], another class of broker-agents is proposed, also based on RL, but without the above restrictions. The experiments conducted demonstrate the superiority of this approach over earlier works. However, only the case of fixed rate tariffs was considered and the production tariffs were overlooked.

The PSO algorithm has been proven to deliver successful results in a large variety of applications. In power systems, it is usually employed on: (i) load and optimal power flow, (ii) reactive power and voltage control, (iii) power system reliability and security and (iv) economic dispatch. Moreover, PSO has been used to derive wholesale bidding strategies; such an example is given in [11]. However, trading in wholesale markets is vastly different from the Tariff Markets under examination [15]. In work that is more similar to our approach of broker agents, a PSO variant was used, the Evolutionary Particle Swarm Algorithm (EPSO), for deriving optimal strategic decisions for Energy Retailers [12]. The simulation used was a multi-agent energy market, based on an Intelligent Agent FIPA platform. The results showed that EPSO outperformed two types of Genetic Algorithms against which it was evaluated, as well as that EPSO is a flexible algorithm due to the particle movement rule borrowed from PSO.

3   The PowerTAC Tariff Market Environment

The PowerTAC competition constitutes a simulation of a liberalized retail energy market, where each competing broker has to make the appropriate transactions amongst retail and wholesale markets in order to maximize its profits, subject to certain fixed costs and constraints [9].

During the game, agents develop a portfolio of producers and consumers by offering tariff contracts for selling or buying energy, respectively. These tariffs are contacted to customers through the Tariff Market. The customers that participate in the Tariff Market are households, small commercial and industrial entities, many of which have also production capacity. With respect to the customer's tariff selection process, all customers are "utility maximizers" [9]. Each customer c evaluates an offered tariff i according to a tariff utility value:

$$u_{c,i} = f_c(p_{v,i}, p_{p,i}, p_{signup,i}, p_{withdraw,i}, x_c) \tag{1}$$

According to this equation, the utility of a given tariff i depends on: (i) the per kWh payments, $p_{v,i}$, (ii) the periodic payments, $p_{p,i}$, (iii) a sign-up payment, $p_{signup,i}$, (iv) a potential early withdraw payment, $p_{withdraw}$, in case the minimum duration of the contract has not been reached, and (v) an inconvenience factor, x_c, which represents the inconvenience of customer c in switching between tariffs. The exact definition of the function f_c may vary across customers, but it is defined as the normalized difference between the cost of the tariff given from the default broker (a broker used by PowerTAC for market stabilization, who is not competing with the other brokers), and the cost of the proposed tariff, minus the inconvenience factor [9].

Despite the fact that the tariff with the highest utility seems to be the most favorable offer, the customer's tariff selection process does not work in a deterministic fashion. In particular, each tariff t_i from the set of evaluated tariffs, $\mathbb{T}$, is assigned a choice probability, P_i, as follows:

$$P_i = \frac{e^{\lambda_c u_{c,i}}}{\sum_{t \in \mathbb{T}} e^{\lambda_c u_{c,t}}} \tag{2}$$

where parameter λ_c stands for the rationality of customer c: $\lambda = 0$, represents a completely irrational customer, whereas $\lambda = \infty$ represents a customer who always chooses the tariff with the maximum utility value [9].

4   Mertacor's PSO-Based Tariff Strategy

To operate effectively in the Power TAC environment outlined in Sect. 3, a broker agent has to make strategic decisions which can aggregate the solution of a highly complex problem. To address this challenging problem, Mertacor defines three policies:

1. **Tariff Formation Policy,** responsible for the publication of new tariffs
2. **Tariff Update Policy,** deciding whether to publish/revoke tariffs.
3. **Energy Prediction Policy,** determining the amount of energy that must be bought from the wholesale market.

In this work, we focus on the agent's behavior in the Tariff Market and thus we present only the first two policies. The third policy was developed for our previous edition of Mertacor and it is still used in this work; the interested reader is referred to [4].

4.1   Particle Swarm Optimization

The Particle Swarm Optimization (PSO) algorithm [6] is a population-based optimization technique, which has gained increasing popularity among researchers and practitioners as a robust and efficient technique for solving difficult optimization problems. The basic idea of PSO is the representation of potential problem solutions as the position of a number of individual entities, the particles. Each particle is composed of three D-dimensional vectors: (i) the current position $\overrightarrow{x_i}$, (ii) the previous best position $\overrightarrow{p_i}$, and (iii) the velocity $\overrightarrow{v_i}$, where D is the dimensionality of the problem's search space [14]. In original PSO, the aforementioned trajectory is accomplished through the position and the velocity update of the particles according to the following equations:

$$\overrightarrow{v_i} \leftarrow \omega \overrightarrow{v_i} + \overrightarrow{U}(0, \phi_1) \otimes (\overrightarrow{p_i} - \overrightarrow{x_i}) + \overrightarrow{U}(0, \phi_2) \otimes (\overrightarrow{p_g} - \overrightarrow{x_i}) \tag{3}$$

$$\overrightarrow{x_i} \leftarrow \overrightarrow{x_i} + \overrightarrow{v_i} \tag{4}$$

where $\vec{U}(0, \phi_i)$ represents a vector of random numbers uniformly distributed in $[0, \phi_i]$ which is generated at each iteration and for each particle, $\otimes$ is component-wise multiplication, and ω is an inertia weight [16] used to control the influence of the new velocity. Usually, we set $\phi_1 = \phi_2 = 2$.

According to Eq. (3), the velocity of a particle $\vec{v_i}$ is composed of three parts: (i) the momentum part, $\vec{v_i}$, which is the particle's previous velocity, impelling towards the direction that it has traveled so far, (ii) the "cognitive" part, $\vec{U}(0, \phi_1) \otimes (\vec{p_i} - \vec{x_i})$, which represents the tendency of the particle to return to the best position it has visited so far, and (iii) the social part, $\vec{U}(0, \phi_2) \otimes (\vec{p_g} - \vec{x_i})$, which represents the tendency of the particle to travel towards the best position found by its neighborhood, $\vec{p_g}$.

Eventually, the optimization process ends when some stopping condition is satisfied. Such conditions include a preset number of iterations or a sufficiently good predefined fitness value [14].

4.2 Tariff Formation Policy

The tariff formation policy constitutes an optimization problem, since its main objective is to create tariffs which would lead to maximum profit. Thus, when the broker needs to publish a new tariff, the particles of the PSO algorithm explore the problem's search space and choose the tariff which maximizes the predefined objective function. For better understanding of how the PSO was applied to solve the broker's tariff formation problem, we need to define: (i) how the problem's search space is formulated, and (ii) the objective function.

Search Space. In a tariff formation problem, the search space is composed of the parameters of potential tariffs. In this work, Mertacor offers two types of tariffs: *Fixed Rate Tariffs* (FRT), where there is only one fixed rate per kWh for all the hours of the day and *Time of Use Tariffs* (TOU), where the day is divided in two or three time zones, offering a different rate per kWh in each one of them. The offered tariffs are defined by: (i) a sign-up payment, (ii) an early withdraw payment, (iii) periodic payments and (iv) one or more additional different rates which correspond to different time zones. Consequently, if D is the problem's search space dimensionality, then each particle's position is a vector $x = <x_1 \ldots x_D>$, where $D \in [4, 6]$ depending on the number of time zones.

Objective Function. For achieving the agent's primary goal, i.e. the maximum possible profit, the tariff formation policy must adjust to different market conditions. Therefore, the objective function must be defined to take into account: (i) customer preferences, (ii) competitor tariffs and (iii) agent profit. Given the above restrictions, for a tariff $T_i \in R^D$, the objective function is defined as $f : R^D \to R$, where f is given by Eq. (5):

$$f_i = \sum_{j}^{C} profit_{i,j} \cdot p_{i,j} \tag{5}$$

where C is the set of the customers involved in the tariff market, $profit_{i,j}$ the agent's potential profit in case customer j chooses tariff T_i, and $p_{i,j}$ is the probability of customer j choosing tariff T_i.

In order to better approximate the parameter $profit_{i,j}$, its value is calculated according to the way the customers evaluate the offered tariffs. Thus, if customer j subscribe to tariff T_i, the agent's expected profit would be given by the next equation:

$$profit_{i,j} = \sum_{t=0}^{d_e} (C_{e,t,i} p_{v,i,t} + p_{p,i}) + (p_{signup,i} + F_d p_{withdraw,i}) \tag{6}$$

where $C_{e,t,i}$ is the customer's energy usage profile over the expected duration $t = [0..d_e]$ of a potential new subscription to tariff T_i, $p_{v,i,t}$ are per-kWh payments, $p_{p,i}$ are periodic payments, $p_{signup,i}$ is a one-time sign-up payment, and $p_{withdraw,i}$ is the expected cost of withdrawing from T_i, discounted by a factor F_d, that depends on the minimum subscription duration for T_i.

The energy profiles according to which the customers evaluate the offered tariffs for each customer are calculated based on the Bootstrap Customer data. This data includes information about the energy usage each customer had for every 1 h of the 14 days preceding the start of the simulation under the terms of the default tariffs [9]. Hence, our agent constructs a 24- h energy usage profile for each customer, where the usage for each hour is calculated as the mean usage that the customer had for that hour during the 14 days.

The estimation of probability $p_{i,j}$ is based on Eq. (2) according to which the customers choose tariff subscriptions. The calculation of the utility value for each tariff T_i is also based on the equations used by PowerTAC customers [9]. Hence, the utility $u_{c,i}$ which the customer c denotes to tariff T_i is given by:

$$u_{c,i} = n_{i,j} - 1 \tag{7}$$

where $n_{i,j}$ is the normalized cost difference of tariff T_i and it is calculated according to the equation:

$$n_{i,j} = \begin{cases} \frac{profit_{default} - profit_{i,j}}{profit_{default}} & \text{for consumption tariffs} \\[2em] \frac{profit_{i,j} - profit_{default}}{profit_{default}} & \text{for production tariffs} \end{cases} \tag{8}$$

The parameter $profit_{i,j}$ is given by Eq. (6) and $profit_{default}$ is the profit which the default broker would realize if customer j subscribed to his tariffs, without taking sign-up fee and withdrawal cost into consideration.

It should mentioned that the constant factor in Eq. (7) substitutes for the product of factors w_x and x_i, which exist in the equivalent customers equation, and they are not provided to brokers. $w_x \in [0..1]$ is an attribute of individual customers, and $x_i \in [0..1]$ is a linear combination of factors that penalize tariff features including variable pricing, time-of-use pricing, and tiered rates [9].

Therefore, in order to take into account the impact of these factors, we use their maximum possible product, leading to the worst case scenario.

4.3   Tariff Update Policy

The implemented Tariff Update Policy includes all the functions required to increase or maintain the agent's market share and total profit, always with respect to the prevailing market conditions in real time.

Market Share Assessment Using Fuzzy Logic. Initially, the agent evaluates its acquired market share, i.e. the customers subscribed to its tariffs. The assessment of this attribute is obtained using Fuzzy Logic primitives. In particular, Mertacor assesses its market share according to a fuzzy set defined as the number of consumers (producers) subscribed to its tariffs. The agent assumes that it has many consumers (producers) when their number exceeds the average number of consumers (producers) per broker. More details on the implemented methodology can be found in the paper describing for the previous edition of agent Mertacor in [4].

Algorithm 1. Tariff Update Algorithm for Consumers and Producers

---

if *(Consumers are* Few*)* **then**
  | minPosition *ctb-parameters = last Consumption tariff* ctb-parameters
  | Create new Consumption Tariff to publish
end

if *((Consumers are* Many*)* ∧ *(stabilization period has finished))* **then**
  | minPosition *ctb-parameters = 1.1 * (last Consumption tariff*
  | ctb-parameters)
  | Create new Consumption Tariff to publish
end

if *(Producers are* Few*)* **then**
  | minPosition *ctb-parameters = last Production tariff* ctb-parameters
  | minPosition *btc-parameters = 1.1 * (last Production tariff* btc-parameters)
  | Create new Production Tariff to publish
end

if *((Producers are* Many*)* ∧ *(stabilization period has finished))* **then**
  | minPosition *ctb-parameters = 1.1 * (last Production tariff* ctb-parameters)
  | minPosition *btc-parameters = 0.9 * (last Production tariff* btc-parameters)
  | Create new Production Tariff to publish
end

Upon assessing the market share, Mertacor must decide whether to publish new tariffs as well as the range of their terms to make them attractive. So, given the market share, the problem's search space boundaries are modified accordingly. These boundaries play a significant role in solving the problem, mainly because they dictate the minimum and maximum values of the tariff terms. Hence, the following vectors are defined: $minPosition = < minP_1 \ldots minP_D >$ which denotes the lower limit and $maxPosition = < maxP_1 \ldots maxP_D >$ which determines the upper limit of the search space. It should be noted that these vectors are different for each type of tariff. In particular, for the consumers of the Mertacor portfolio, the limits are modified according to the pseudocode in Algorithm 1, where ctb parameters refer to *customers to brokers*[1], as well as for the producers, where btc refers to *brokers to customers* payments.

If the agent possesses low market share, it moves the swarm toward more attractive tariffs. On the other hand, a high market share means that the already published tariffs satisfy the customers preferences. Henceforth, the agent must decide whether to take the risk and offer tariffs which may yield more profit or continue with its existing tariffs. The criterion for choosing over the other is a *stabilization period*, the end of which denotes that the agent's market share is consistently high. If the agent decides to take a risk, it is necessary to readjust the limits of the search, as outlined in the aforementioned algorithm.

Maximum Tariff Number. There is no hard constraint on the number of published tariffs in PowerTAC. Since the customers' evaluation process takes into account only the five most recent ones from each agent, Mertacor adopts this as an internal limit. Furthermore, considering the way the objective function was defined (and $p_{i,j}$ in particular), a large number of published tariffs would result in an increment in the complexity of estimating the new tariffs' parameters.

If the maximum number of tariffs has been exceeded, any redundant tariff is removed based on its *economic impact*. Thus, each tariff T_i is evaluated based on the normalized acquired profits (consumption) or normalized resulting costs (production) for the period the tariff was active tl_i (*tariff lifetime*):

$$n_{T_i} = \begin{cases} p_i/tl_i & \text{for consumption tariffs} \\ c_i/tl_i & \text{for production tariffs} \end{cases} \tag{9}$$

5   Experiments

The experimentation procedure had two primary goals: (a) to tune the various parameters of the agent's policy and (b) to study the agent's performance in different market environments. The experiments presented in this section were conducted sequentially so that the agent's optimal parameterization could be achieved. Based on this, the conducted experiments included: (i) **Pricing Policy Parameters Experiments**, (ii) **Market Conditions Experiments** and (iii) **The Power TAC 2013 Competition**.

An agent following the ZIP [3] policy was used as an opponent for the optimal parameter selection and the agent's evaluation, since this policy has been

---

[1] *ctb* payments are defined as negative numbers, thus their maximum values are represented by the *minPosition* vector and their minimum values by the *maxPosition* vector.

more effective than other common policies (ZI, RE, and GD) in Double Auctions environments [4]. It should be noted that all the competing agents are implementing the same strategy for buying energy from the wholesale market, in order to compare tariff formation and update policies on a common base.

In order to ensure the agent's robustness over various consuming patterns, the experiments were conducted for different groups of customers (households, offices and factored customers). The results given in the following sections are separated according to customers power types; i.e. Consumption (CONS), Interruptible Consumption (INT CONS), and Production (PROD). The metrics used are the mean market share of customers and the total profit of the agents participating, using ten-fold repetitions for each experiment.

5.1   Tariff Formation Policy Parameters Experiments

Acceptance Rate. For the estimation of the initial tariffs' acceptance probability, a Logistic Regression algorithm was adopted. The focus in these series of experiments was to create an estimator from a training set, where every element represents a tariff defined by: (i) a sign-up cost, (ii) an early withdrawal penalty, (iii) a periodic payment, (iv) a rate per kWh, and (v) the respective acceptance rate. The goal was to predict the term (v) of a possible tariff, given as many as possible combinations of the tariff terms (i) to (iv).

The problem was split in many sub-problems based on: (i) the consumer group the tariff referred to, since the consumer models of the platform differ on the consumption patterns, as well as on their tariff preference, and (ii) the dimension of the search space, D. As already mentioned, a TOU tariff may have one, two, or three different rates per kWh; thus, for $D > 4$, one or two more terms are added for calculating the energy cost. Figure 1 depicts two cases of an example experiment with household customers, where $D = 4$, the rate per kWh is -0.5 and the periodic payment assumes the values -1 and -0.5005.

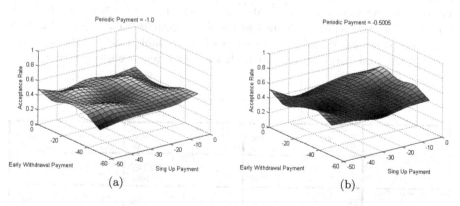

Fig. 1. Example of results from the acceptance rate experiments for Periodic Payment of (a) -1 and (b) -0.5005.

Parameters of the Tariff Formation Policy. The parameters that have a significant impact on the agent's performance are: (i) the parameters of the algorithm, (ii) the PSO variation, and (iii) the number of rates. In this work, the parameters that concerned the PSO algorithm were fixed, while the other two sets of experiments were conducted for two consumer groups: (i) household and (ii) office customers.

At first, the efficacy of the pricing policy was tested using: (i) the classic PSO and, (ii) the FIPS variation [7]. The results showed that in both cases, our agent surpasses the ZIP agent. As shown in Table 1, both variations have quite similar performance, which was expected as the FIPS variation does not differ significantly from the classic PSO. As a result, for the rest of the experiments the FIPS variation was chosen.

In the second set of experiments, the agent offered TOU tariffs, in which the day was divided into three time zones: (i) $0-8$, (ii) $8-22$, (iii) $22-24$. The above was based on the most common consumption patterns of the customers, with every time zone corresponding to different demand levels [5]. Experiments were conducted for the following variations: (i) one rate for all time zones, (ii) two rates, one for the high demand time zone, $8-22$, and a different one for $0-8$, $22-24$ and, (iii) three different rates, one per time zone.

Concerning the selection of the optimal number of rates, it was observed that the results tend to be similar (Table 1) but single-tier tariffs have slightly better performance. This may be attributed to the fact that every other participating agent offers tariffs with a single rate and the pricing formation policy is highly affected by the competing tariffs.

5.2   Market Conditions Experiments

Customer Behavior Experiments. The customer models of the Power TAC platform are enriched with a set of parameters that define their behavior in the market, and make them more realistic. The parameters that affect customer behavior as far as evaluating and selecting a tariff is concerned are: (i) *rationality*, which shows whether a customer always chooses the most advantageous tariff, (ii) *inconvenience*, which is defined as the linear combination of several factors that tend to punish volatility in tariffs, such as variable rates, TOU rates and tiered rates, and (iii) *inertia*, which shows how often a customer chooses to

Table 1. Results of PSO variant and number of rates experiments

| | Mean Market Share | | Total Profit | Mean Market Share | | Total Profit | Mean Market Share | | Total Profit |
	CONS	INT CONS		CONS	INT CONS		CONS	INT CONS	
PSO Variant	PSO			FIPS					
Households	97.76	96.99	153590	98.02	96.83	154820	-	-	-
Offices	98.4	99.18	43145	97.07	98.35	44090	-	-	-
Number of Rates	1			2			3		
Households	98.02	96.83	154820	97.39	96.6	132180	97.26	96.77	125290
Offices	97.07	96.83	44090	98.66	98.49	45423	97.65	98.4	32361

search for better tariffs. Based on these parameters, the following experiments were conducted to study the agent's behavior:

1. Rationality experiments where the performance of the agent is measured in a market comprised of: (i) extra rational customers (Rationality = 0.9), (ii) moderately rational (Rationality = 0.4) and (iii) almost irrational (Rationality = 0.1).
2. Inconvenience factor experiments, where the agent's performance is measured for the inconvenience factor values of 0, 0.5, and 1. As this factor approaches 1, it becomes increasingly difficult for a tariff to be deemed advantageous and, consequently, more difficult for an agent to attract customers.

The third parameter, the inertia factor, was fixed and set to 0.05, so that the customers would be very active. This value was chosen because an inert customer does not qualify as a challenging scenario for competitive agents. In order to examine the effects of the psychology parameters, the experiments were conducted on household customers.

The results of the first type of experiments showed that the less rational the customers were (Rationality = 0.1), the more money the agent earned. Nevertheless, it is worth mentioning that, for the extra rational sub-experiments (Rationality = 0.9), the agent attracted the most customers. Lastly, in reference to the inconvenience factor experiments, as shown in Fig. 2, while moving from a factor value near 0 to a value near 1, there was a gradual drop of 8 % in the agent's profits.

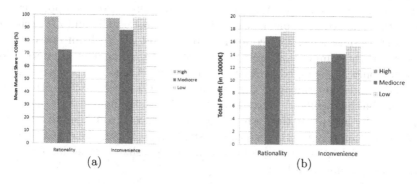

Fig. 2. Results for Mertacor agent for high, mediocre and low customer Rationality and Inconvenience factor values for (a) *Mean Market Share* and (b) *Total Profits*.

Experiments with Multiple Competitors. The next set of experiments aimed to assess the agent's performance in more advanced competition, placing it against more or better quality competing agents. At first, we ran a set of games where the broker agent was set against four agents that followed ZIP, ZI, GD and RE policy, respectively. These are some of the most common policies used in Double Auctions (DA) and TAC games. A second set of games was conducted against the previous Mertacor agent, implemented for Power TAC2011 [4], which follows a more competitive strategy than the agents above. The experiments included all the customer types of the platform. In order to measure the agent's performance on the consumers and producers separately, experiments were carried with and without production tariffs. In the results that follow, the current version of the agent is referred to as M13 while the previous one as M11.

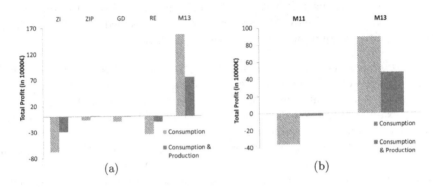

Fig. 3. Profits per agent from games against (a) ZI, ZIP, GD, and RE and (b) M11.

The results presented in Table 2 and Fig. 3 clearly illustrate that the agent's competitiveness is pushing towards biggest profits against multiple competitors (Fig. 3(a)) as well as against M11 (Fig. 3(b)). In reference to the opponents, we can see that the agents implementing adaptive strategies, GD and ZIP, achieved an almost six-fold lower loss compared to RE and ZI. Such an outcome was expected, as the competition provides to brokers a great amount of information, which can only be exploited by adaptive strategies. A closer inspection of M13's behavior reveals that the agent achieves almost 50 % lower profits in the games where production tariffs are offered. This was due to the fact that the agent had some difficulty attracting the desired share of producers, which led to a frequent tariff publication resulting in increased costs. Finally, it must be noted that M13 achieved the highest percentage of the mean market share, attracting more than 55 % of the consumers in both cases.

Table 2. Mean Market Share Per Agent for games with and without production tariffs

Broker Agent	CONS	INT CONS	PRODS
ZI	6.4	3.98	21.75
ZIP	4.75	1.13	17.62
GD	2.36	1.65	17.68
RE	31.36	11.48	17.84
M13	55.12	81.77	25.11

Broker Agent	CONS	INT CONS	PRODS
M11	37.23	13.72	-
M13	62.87	86.28	-
M11	40.87	16.34	60.87
M13	58.78	85.6	36.59

5.3   The 2013 PowerTAC Competition Results

Our agent participated in the PowerTAC 2013 Competition and was placed in the 6th place, which was not anticipated, considering the results of the experiments. Mertacor's placement in the competition does not constitute an objective criterion for evaluating the strategies developed, because during the final phase of the games some major connection problems emerged, causing Mertacor to become inactive after a number of rounds. Nevertheless, some conclusions can still be drawn on the agent's performance from the period it was still active.

In Fig. 4, two of the games the agent participated are illustrated, up to the moment the above problems arose. In Fig. 4(a), we can see that Mertacor (red line) got off to a good start and managed to preserve its upward course compared to its competitors: MLLBroker, CrocodileAgent and AstonTAC. Figure 4(b), shows the game of Mertacor against TacTex and cwiBroker, the two most competitive agent in the Tournament who received the 1st and 2nd place respectively. The fourth player in this game, INAOEBroker02, was placed last, making it one of the least competitive agents. Therefore, this game enables a more immediate comparison of Mertacor to TacTex and cwiBroker. From the line graph it can be seen that the agent holds the first place up to the middle of its valid game, where it is overcome by TacTex, while cwiBriker tends to gain ground.

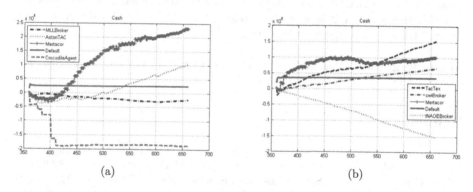

(a)   (b)

Fig. 4. Profits per timeslot from a game against (a) MLLBroker, AstonTAC and CrocodileAgent and (b) TacTex, cwiBroker and INAOEBroker (color figure online).

6   Conclusion and Future Work

The main challenge of the Smart Grid Paradigm is how to achieve a tight balance between supply and demand of electrical energy. A contemporary approach to address this challenge is the use of autonomous broker agents. In this work, we presented a profit optimization strategy implemented for Mertacor broker-agent, based on Particle Swarm Optimization techniques.

Based on the conducted experiments, the use of the policies implemented in this paper rendered the agent flexible and efficient in various conditions of the

Tariff Market. More specifically, the agent was able to adapt to different customer behaviors maintaining its good performance. The experiments showed the agent managed to display superior behavior in a multi-competitor environment as well as against an especially competitive adversary. In conclusion, it was proven that a Tariff Formation Policy based on PSO can have better results than ones based on Double Auctions theory (ZI, ZIP, GD and RE). In reference to the PowerTAC Competition, our agent was not able to demonstrate the same results that were supported by the experiments. This was due to various problems which prevented the agent from staying on-line until the end of the games. Nevertheless, a closer look at the agent's performance during the time it was active, confirms that the agent has good prospects of doing better in future competitions.

Further improvements can strengthen some aspects of the agent's functionality. First and foremost, action must be taken to eradicate the problems arisen throughout the last PowerTAC Competition and to reduce the high complexity of the algorithm. With respect to tariff formation policy, a better approximation of customer's energy usage patterns may result in more accurate predictions. Furthermore, the PSO algorithm can be modified to offer more tariff types and include additional game parameters (e.g. weather status), which could result in better decision making. Likewise, an effective modification could be the use of multiple swarms with different objective functions, the result of which would be combined to produce the final action. Additional experiments can be conducted in which the competing agents would offer TOU or Variable Rate tariffs, since no such tariff was available at the time.

Acknowledgments. This work was supported in part by the EU funded research project CASSANDRA (FP7-ICT-288429).

References

1. Babic, J., Podobnik, V.: An analysis of powertac 2013 trial. In: Trading Agent Design and Analysis, Workshops at the 27th AAAI Conference, pp. 1–9 (2013)
2. Chatzidimitriou, K.C., Symeonidis, A.L., Kontogounis, I., Mitkas, P.A.: Agent mertacor: a robust design for dealing with uncertainty and variation in scm environments. Expert Syst. Appl. **35**(3), 591–603 (2008)
3. Cli, D.: Minimal-intelligence agents for bargaining behaviors in market-based environments. Hewlett-Packard Labs Technical reports (1997)
4. Diamantopoulos, T.G., Symeonidis, A.L., Chrysopoulos, A.C.: Designing robust strategies for continuous trading in contemporary power markets. In: AMEC/TADA, pp. 30–44 (2012)
5. Jardini, J.A., Tahan, C.M., Gouvea, M., Ahn, S.U., Figueiredo, F.: Daily load profiles for residential, commercial and industrial low voltage consumers. IEEE Trans. Power Deliv. **15**(1), 375–380 (2000)
6. Kennedy, J., Eberhart, R.: Particle swarm optimization. In: Proceedings of the IEEE International Conference on Neural Networks, vol. 4, pp. 1942–1948 (1995)
7. Kennedy, J., Mendes, R.: Population structure and particle swarm performance. In: Proceedings of the 2002 Congress on Evolutionary Computation, CEC'02, vol. 2, pp. 1671–1676. IEEE (2002)

8. Ketter, W., Collins, J., Block, C.: Smart grid economics: policy guidance through competitive simulation (2010)
9. Ketter, W., Collins, J., Reddy, P., Weerdt, M.: The 2013 power trading agent competition. ERIM Report Series Reference No. ERS-2013-006-LIS (2013)
10. Ketter, W., Peters, M., Collins, J.: Autonomous agents in future energy markets: the 2012 power trading agent competition. In: Association for the Advancement of Artificial Intelligence (AAAI) Conference, Bellevue (2013)
11. Kumar, J.V., Kumar, D.V.: Particle swarm optimization based optimal bidding strategy in an open electricity market. Int. J. Eng. Sci. Technol. 3(6), 283–294 (2011)
12. Miranda, V., Oo, N.W.: Evolutionary algorithms and evolutionary particle swarms (epso) in modeling evolving energy retailers. In: 15th Power System Computation Conference, Liege, Belgija (2005)
13. Peters, M., Ketter, W., Saar-Tsechansky, M., Collins, J.: A reinforcement learning approach to autonomous decision-making in smart electricity markets. Mach. Learn. 92(1), 5–39 (2013)
14. Poli, R., Kennedy, J., Blackwell, T.: Particle swarm optimization. Swarm Intell. 1(1), 33–57 (2007)
15. Reddy, P.P., Veloso, M.M.: Strategy learning for autonomous agents in smart grid markets. In: Proceedings of the Twenty-Second International Joint Conference on Artificial Intelligence, vol. 2, pp. 1446–1451. AAAI Press (2011)
16. Shi, Y., Eberhart, R.: A modified particle swarm optimizer. In: The 1998 IEEE International Conference on Evolutionary Computation Proceedings, IEEE World Congress on Computational Intelligence, pp. 69–73 (1998)

Classification Driven Detection of Opportunistic Bids in TAC SCM

Anuj Toshniwal$^{(\boxtimes)}$, Kuldeep Porwal, and Kamalakar Karlapalem

Center for Data Engineering,
International Institute of Information Technology (IIIT), Hyderabad, India
{anuj.t,kuldeep.porwal}@research.iiit.ac.in,
kamal@iiit.ac.in

Abstract. The main objective of a bidding agent in TAC SCM is to get profitable orders and to get enough orders to keep the production going. There is a delicate balance that the bidding agent needs to maintain while deciding on which specific orders to bid and what bidding price to set. In this highly complex bidding problem with (i) many interdependencies, (ii) multiple information flows, (iii) historical data and knowledge, the bidding agent can bid for a few opportunistic orders at a reasonably higher price, which gives higher profit. In this paper, we use classification to determine opportunistic bids to increase our profit. Our solution is robust and adapts according to the dynamic changes in the market condition and the competition provided by the competing agents. Our results show that classification using our opportunistic approach contributes to a significant percentage of our agent's profit.

Keywords: Economic paradigms · Economically-motivated agents · Electronic markets · Innovative applications · TAC SCM · Automated agent

1 Introduction

In today's highly competitive market place, managing supply chains is one of the most challenging problems. Supply chains consist of heterogeneous subsystems and complex relationships requiring collective effort and constraint based optimization. In dynamic market conditions, it is very difficult to take both short and long term decisions simultaneously. A multi agent system, consisting of several autonomous agents can address this problem and take appropriate decisions.

The Trading Agent Competition for Supply Chain Management (TAC SCM) [1] was designed to capture many of the challenges involved in sustaining dynamic supply chain practices. This paper describes the bidding strategy of the *Iota* trading agent, which is one of the *winning* agents in TAC SCM 2012. In this paper we focus on the bidding sub-system, which is a crucial component. Bidding in TAC SCM can be considered similar to First Price Sealed Bid Auction in which the submitted bids against customers' request for quotes (RFQs) are compared and the bidder with the lowest bid wins the order.

Trading Agent Competition for Supply Chain Management.

© Springer International Publishing Switzerland 2014
S. Ceppi et al. (Eds.): AMEC/TADA 2013 and 2014, LNBIP 187, pp. 144–158, 2014.
DOI: 10.1007/978-3-319-13218-1_11

Agents participating in the game must simultaneously compete in two markets with interdependencies, and take their decisions based on incomplete information about the state of the market. In one market, agents buy their supplies and in the other, they sell their finished products. Supply and demand of each market varies dynamically not only by randomness but also due to competing agents' strategies. Agents have a limited time to take a number of decisions. All these factors make the problem quite challenging to address.

In this highly complex bidding problem with (i) many interdependencies, (ii) multiple information flows, (iii) historical offline data and knowledge, the *agent can bid for a few opportunistic orders at a reasonably higher price, which gives higher profit.*

We have modeled our agent as a *business entity* capable of using game theory, machine learning and data mining techniques. Our agent focuses on dynamics such as market trend, customer demand and changes in procurement costs to learn and adapt. We present a classification driven approach to identify opportunistic bids. Our agent classifies the customer requests received each day into different classes using a parameterized decision tree and bids accordingly.

The remaining paper is structured as follows. In Sect. 2, we discuss TAC SCM game specifications and describe the problem and related work. We present an overview of our agent's bidding module and focus on classification of customer requests in Sect. 3. In Sect. 4, we present the results showing performance of our agent in TAC SCM.

2   Bidding in TAC SCM

In this section, we describe the game overview and problem specifications. We also highlight some relevant related work that has been done on the problem.

2.1   TAC SCM Overview

In TAC SCM, six assembly agents compete in a simulated market environment constituting a supply chain. An agent's task is to procure components, manufacture personal computers (PCs) and to win customer orders (bidding subtask).

Each simulation day is of 15 s and the game consists of E days (in standard settings, $E = 220$). At the start of each day, all agents receive a Request For Quotes (RFQ) bundle specifying customer requests. Each RFQ specifies (i) product id, (ii) desired quantity, (iii) due date, (iv) reserve price and (v) penalty.

An agent must bid to satisfy both quantity and due date for the customers to consider the bid. Also, each day the agents receive a price report containing information about the lowest and highest prices for each type of PC ordered on the previous day. Full specification of the TAC SCM game is given in [1].

2.2   Problem Specification

The agent receives numerous RFQs from the customer each day, requesting different types of PCs. The total quantity of PCs requested on a given day is much higher compared to an individual agent's production capacity. Faced with this problem of plenty, the agent aims to identify and bid on a set of selected customer RFQs that maximize the profit subject to its factory capacity constraints [1] and component (current and expected in future) availability.

The profit depends not only on the RFQs being bid on the current day, but also on RFQs that need to be bid in immediate future. If these future RFQs are ignored while selecting the current day's bids, the agent might commit all available production resources on the current RFQs, leaving it unable to bid on more profitable future RFQs.

In a naive approach, the agent attempts to predict the highest winning price and bid on selected RFQs, expecting to win each one of them. But we follow a more viable opportunistic approach, which involves placing high bids on a subset of RFQs depending upon current market situation, expecting to win a few of them. Our agent tries and ensures that it balances this risky approach in such a way that it does not lead to low revenue while keeping its assembly line busy.

Design Challenges. There is a delicate balance that the agent needs to maintain while deciding on which specific orders to bid, and what bidding price to set. The agent does not want to acquire all orders but neither does it wish to underutilize its factory production capacity. Agents in the past have used varying approaches to solve this problem, but these approaches are highly complex and involve expensive computations.

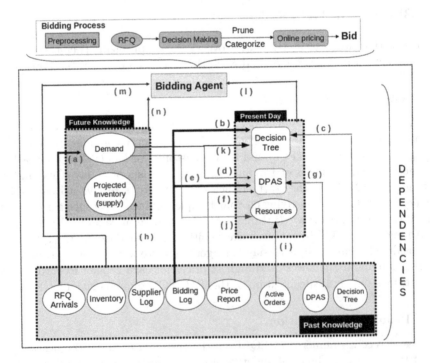

Fig. 1. Dependency model for bidding subsystem.

2.3   Related Work

Different techniques have been explored by agents to solve Bidding problem. Mostly statistical approaches are used to win sealed price based auctions. Some of the those approaches are discussed in the following survey [2]. A heuristic approach to search for the optimal set of bids is described in [3]. An approximate optimization procedure that uses values to decompose the decision problem is presented in [4]. Other examples of some important work include empirical game theory approach [5], mathematical programming approach [6,7], decision making [8–10], particle swarm optimization and policy search via adaptive functions [11]. Main disadvantage for most of these approaches that are based on learning from offline past bid data is that there are many dependent variables which make it difficult for the agent to map the current situation to a similar situation in the past data. There are numerous variables like competing agents, past and present market trend, agent performance, expected future demand, supplier factory settings - price, delivery time, capacity - and resource availability (component and factory cycles), which affect the decision making of the agent. It is very difficult to map all these parameters and settings to some previous game data and use it. Further, most of the models also fail to include current rivalry in the market while some algorithms fail to adapt quickly. In this paper we present a classification model which captures dependencies and can easily adapt to any runtime changes.

3   Bidding Agent

We have modeled our agent as a *business entity* capable of using game theory, machine learning and data mining techniques. Our agent focuses on dynamics such as market trend, customer demand and changes in procurement costs to learn and adapt. In this paper, we present only the classification subtask of the bidding subsystem.

Each day, the agent takes decisions based on past, current and expected future dynamics of the market. Our agent considers the daily market condition as a data stream and uses the information from the past k days window (we use $k = 5$). We follow trial and error approach with different window sizes to figure out the corresponding impact on agent's performance and fix the window size accordingly. Window size is an important parameter in our strategy, since our agent learns the current market situation based on information gathered in present window and adapts accordingly. Window size *not only* affects the bidding module, but also plays a crucial role in the pricing and procurement modules (which are *not* discussed in this paper).

In Fig. 1, we describe the dependencies between various subtasks of bidding. These dependencies are described below:

(a): Based upon the current arrivals of RFQs, agent predicts the behavior of future RFQ arrivals and demand (Sect. 3).

(b), (c), (k): Our agent's decision making criterion depends upon its previous criterion, it's bidding performance and future demand (Sect. 3).

(d), (e), (f), (g): Dynamic Profit Adjuster Scale (DPAS) is our price prediction module, used to decide the bid price. Our agent's pricing strategy depends upon it's previous state, bidding log, analysis of price reports and expected future demand.

(i), (j): Current availability of resources depends not only on current active orders, but also on demand in future.

(h): Projected components inventory of agent depends upon the past negotiations with suppliers.

(l), (m), (n): The bidding agent learns from the past, present and future knowledge as shown in Fig. 1.

Table 1. Daily execution loop for bidding

(i) At the start of each day, the agent does preprocessing of data involving:

– Demand Estimation.

– Price Report Analysis.

(ii) Classify the RFQs. Prune the non-profitable RFQs and *sort* the remaining RFQs.

(iii) Process the *sorted* RFQs, predict a bid price for each RFQ.

(iv) Send offer.

Table 1 describes the daily execution loop for bidding followed by our agent. Detailed description of pricing strategy and supplier negotiation strategies are not described in this paper.

3.1   Demand Estimation

Demand estimation is necessary to make important decisions like classification of RFQs, planning for future inventory levels and resource restriction.

Products are classified into three market segments – high range, mid range, and low range – according to their nominal price [1]. Correspondingly, customers exhibit their demand by issuing RFQs in each segment. Number of customer RFQs for day d issued in each market segment is determined by a draw from a Poisson distribution with mean Q_d. Demand evolves according to Q_d, which is varied using a trend τ given by daily update rule:

$$Q_{d+1} = min(Q_{max}, max(Q_{min}, \tau_d Q_d)) \tag{1}$$

τ is updated according to a random walk given by:

$$\tau_{d+1} = max(\tau_{min}, min(\tau_{max}, \tau_d + random(-0.001, 0.001))) \tag{2}$$

Whenever τ exceeds its min-max bound, it is reset to its initial value, which is equal to 1. The states Q and τ are hidden, but we know that Q_{d+1} is a deterministic function of Q_d and τ_d as specified in Eq. 1. This deterministic relation is exploited using a Bayesian Network Model in [12] to estimate the demand process based on the current observed demand. We use this distribution to estimate expected future demand as in [12].

We require a holistic view of demand. For this, we consider the sum of RFQs of the three market segments (Q_{sum}) and define net demand of a day d ($D_{net}(d)$) as follows:

$$D_{net}(d) = \begin{cases} low, & \text{if } Q_{sum}(d) < 130. \\ mid, & \text{else if } Q_{sum}(d) < 220. \\ high, & \text{otherwise.} \end{cases} \qquad (3)$$

The above values used for comparison are chosen through empirical analysis of large number of games and by analyzing the number of RFQs sent by customers each day which falls in the range of 80 to 320 RFQs per day.

3.2 Price Report Analysis

We define $H_{(d,p)}$ and $L_{(d,p)}$ for a product p at day d from High Price ($High\ Price_{(d,p)}$) and Low Price ($LowPrice_{(d,p)}$), received in price report at the start of each day. We use $H_{(d,p)}$ and $L_{(d,p)}$ to estimate the current trend and predict bid price accordingly.

Since we do not want to bias our decision on price fluctuation of a single day, we define $H_{(d,p)}$ as the weighted sum of High Prices of past k days window. Exponentially decaying weight factor ($\gamma/2^i$) is used to give higher weightage to recent days.

$$H_{(d,p)} = \sum_{i=1}^{k} \frac{\gamma}{2^i} * HighPrice_{(d-i,p)} \qquad (4)$$

Here, γ is the scaling factor such that ($\gamma * \sum_{i=1}^{k} 2^{-i} = 1$).
Similarly we find $L_{(d,p)}$ based on Low Prices of past k days.

If we increase the window size, the weight associated with most recent information decreases as the weight is distributed to include more days. This leads to slow adaptation by our agent which in turn affects our agents performance. Similarly decreasing the window size will bias our agent's decision towards most recent information leading to poorer performance, as shown in Results (Sect. 4) under Experiments subsection.

3.3 RFQ Classification

The vital aspect for winning any multiplayer game is that the agent must be alert to identify and grab any opportunity that comes along. Sometimes taking immediate rewards are better than waiting for long term rewards. On the other hand, sometimes the agent must think long term and be willing to take a dip in performance if it leads to a spike later, thereby improving the agent's performance. An opportunistic agent is one which is able to identify opportunities and act positively on them. But sometimes there are cases when there is no

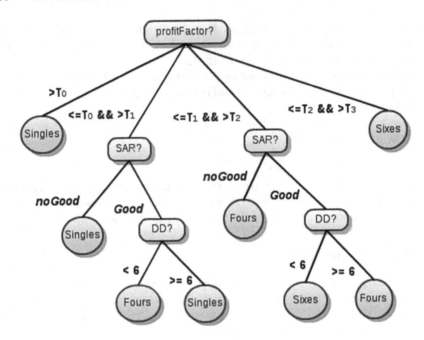

Fig. 2. Decision tree for RFQ classification

opportunity. Then agent should be flexible enough to choose the best possible strategy for that period too.

To identify and utilize opportunities, we classify the RFQs and bid accordingly, i.e. the agent predicts different bid price based on the assigned class of the RFQ to maximize it's profit. We use a parameterized decision tree model along with other learning algorithms like dynamic programming and heuristic based learning to solve this problem as elaborated below. We dynamically learn the parameters of the decision tree based on current agent performance and market conditions of past, present and future.

With the use of decision tree we prune the non-profitable RFQs and classify the remaining RFQs into three different classes namely *Singles*, *Fours* and *Sixes*[1].

- **Singles:** RFQs which are highly profitable, considering the manufacturing cost incurred by the agent. We need to try and acquire orders for these RFQs, even if we need to bid at a slightly lower price than desired, just to be sure that we win the bid. The profit margin, even at this lower price, is better than most other RFQs. The intuition here is that other agents might also try to bid on these RFQs and we must aim to outbid them.
- **Fours:** These are the RFQs for which our agent takes some risk. The agent bids on these RFQs, expecting to win a few of these. Such RFQs corresponds

---

[1] We use *Cricket* game analogy – *Singles* are used to keep the scoreboard ticking, while *Fours* and *Sixes* are highly risky but opportunistic.

to mainly two cases – (i) the expected profit margin compared to other RFQs is low, and (ii) profit margin is decent but the future demand is expected to increase, implying that the agent can earn more in the future. In either case, the agent takes risk knowingly and bids at a comparatively higher price in order to earn better profit. Also based on the acceptance rate of these bids, our agent analyzes the current pricing trend and competition in the market.

- **Sixes:** Remaining RFQs are classified as *Sixes*. We try for maximum profit and bid very close to the reserve price for such RFQs. Orders for such RFQs are like bonus -it is good if we have them, but it does not matter if we don't.

As we move from *Singles* to *Fours* to *Sixes*, the element of risk taken by the agent increases. In other words the chances of agent winning the order decreases. A 'steady flow' of orders corresponding to *Singles* RFQs is a must to ensure decent profit and sufficient factory utilization. Classifying all RFQs into Singles or Fours or Sixes is considered to be the pure strategy as each class has its own significance. But in SCM, market conditions are very dynamic and to adapt and utilize these conditions we have to use the proper mix of Singles, Fours and Sixes i.e. we have to be opportunistic.

We did thorough analysis to determine certain rules for building decision tree and for this we ran 1261 games with various parameters. These rules help us in selecting the attributes and in deciding the splitting conditions for various attributes of the decision tree.

Empirical Analysis Based Classification. After empirical analysis of 1261 games, we came up with certain heuristics and threshold values of the various parameters about the game. Using this we built the decision tree model. The decision tree is parameterized, where each parameter is learned/adapted dynamically based on market conditions of past, present and future. Thus, this decision tree is applicable for all types of games low, mid and high demand. Described below are the basic rules that we have obtained through analysis.

Rule 1: We increase the number of *Fours* and *Sixes* when either there is less competition in the market i.e. *Singles* acceptance rate is *Good*, or if the future demand is expected to be high. In the former case, the agent has the opportunity to take more risks; in the latter the agent knows it will get the opportunity to sell it's products at a comparatively higher price in the future, thereby bidding for more *Fours* and *Sixes*.

Rule 2: We decrease the number of *Fours* and *Sixes* when either there is high competition in the market i.e. if *Singles* acceptance rate drops below a certain level (*noGood* condition), or if the future demand is expected to be low. In both cases, we need to try and get more orders to increase revenue.

Rule 3: Closer the due date, the more difficult it is for the agents to fulfill the order in time, leading to possible late deliveries and penalty. Hence, RFQs with closer due date are classified as *Fours* or *Sixes* and priced a bit higher than normal. But if the expected profit is very good and resources are available, we take the risk with respect to late delivery and classify the RFQ as *Singles*.

Decision Tree. Decision tree (Fig. 2) has 3-attributes: $< ProfitFactor, DD,$ $SAR>$.

(i) *ProfitFactor* is used to consider the profitability feature of RFQs. It is the main attribute in classification. To define *ProfitFactor*, we first define *PriceFactor* for a RFQ as follows:

$$PriceFactor = \begin{cases} H_{(d,p)} - CostPrice_p, & \text{if Res} > H_{(d,p)} \\ Reserve - CostPrice_p, & \text{if Res} < H_{(d,p)} \end{cases} \tag{5}$$

Here d is current date, p is productID and *Res* is the reserve price of the RFQ. $CostPrice_p$ represents the minimum cost price of the given product, determined from the projected component inventory of agent available before the due date of the RFQ. We first find those set of components available in our projected inventory which sums up to minimum nominal price for the product and this price is considered as $CostPrice$. Say, if the due date for the RFQ is day 56. We consider components required for assembling the product, which are expected to be available by day 54 (one day is for production and the last day for delivery). From this set we find the components available with minimum cost and calculate the $CostPrice$ of product by adding the price of all 4 corresponding components.

We use *minimum* cost price to determine the *best* possible profit that we can get for each RFQ, by considering the inventory available. To normalize the *PriceFactor* corresponding to each RFQ we define *ProfitFactor* as follows:

$$ProfitFactor = PriceFactor/AssemblyCyc_p \tag{6}$$

$AssemblyCyc_p$ is the number of assembly cycles required to manufacture a unit quantity of the product.

(ii) *DD* attribute considers the due date of the RFQ. Due date plays an important role in pricing and resource allocation.

$$DD = (dueDate - currentDate) \tag{7}$$

(iii) *SAR* represents offer acceptance rate of *Singles* RFQs over previous k days. This attribute is used to evaluate the current market performance of the agent and the rivalry between the competing agents. High value of *SAR* implies that the agent is performing well by efficiently handling the competition from the rival agents and vice versa. We consider RFQs of only *Singles* category and not *Fours* or *Sixes* category for this factor, because of the critical importance of acquiring orders corresponding to *Singles* RFQs.

$$SAR = (singlesOrdered/singlesOffered) \tag{8}$$

where $singlesOffered$ is the sum of offers sent for RFQs treating them as *Singles* in previous k days and $singlesOrdered$ is the sum of orders received corresponding to these offers.

To implement the discussed rules in the decision tree we have to dynamically learn the thresholds to split *profitFactor* attribute.

Determining Thresholds. RFQs with *ProfitFactor* value less than T_3 are pruned. T_0, T_1, T_2 and T_3 thresholds are dynamically learned based on the following two factors:

(i) expected customer demand in the future (*futureD*). It is computed as follows:

$$futureD = mode(D_{net}(i)) \quad i = (d+1) \ to \ (d+k) \tag{9}$$

If the predicted future demand is higher than current observed demand, we increase the thresholds, since price is expected to increase when the demand improves and vice versa. Thus, if higher demand is expected in future, we can wait for the prices to rise, and at this time take more risks by bidding for *Fours* and *Sixes* RFQs. If lower demand is predicted in future, agent must try and acquire more orders now, before prices start decreasing. We define *demandEffect* for current day d as:

$$demandEffect = \begin{cases} -1, & \text{if } futureD < D_{net}(d). \\ 1, & \text{if } futureD > D_{net}(d). \\ 0, & \text{otherwise.} \end{cases} \tag{10}$$

(ii) offer acceptance rate of *Singles* RFQs (*SAR*). If *SAR* drops below a predefined lower bound static threshold *lowT*, we need to decrease the value of thresholds to try and get more orders. Similarly, if *SAR* is greater than upper bound threshold *highT*, we can afford to increase the thresholds and convert few RFQs from *Singles* to *Fours* and some RFQs from *Fours* to *Sixes* in order to get more profit. We have set *lowT* and *highT* values on the basis of a large number of training games' result logs. We define *sarEffect* as:

$$sarEffect = \begin{cases} -1, & \text{if SAR} < \text{lowT.} \\ 1, & \text{if SAR} > \text{highT.} \\ 0, & \text{otherwise.} \end{cases} \tag{11}$$

For day d, we compute T_i by using the following dynamic programming approach:

$$T_i(d) = (1 + (\beta * (sarEffect + demandEffect))) * T_i(d-1) \tag{12}$$

Here, β is the rate of change of threshold. β is a constant factor in the range $[0,1]$. Value of β is decided based on the confidence in determining *demandEffect* and *sarEffect* and is given by

$$\beta = 0.5 * \frac{TotalSingles}{TotalRFQs} + 0.5 * Pr(futureD|D_{net}(d)) \tag{13}$$

Here the *TotalSingles* denotes total number of *Singles* offered by agent and *TotalRFQs* denotes total number of RFQs received by agent in the current window. The probability term is determined through Demand Estimation process described above.

Once we update T_i's, we wait for a period of 3 days before making another update, to give time for the change in T_i's to work.

After classification, we first process the *Singles*, then *Fours* and lastly *Sixes*. In each category, the RFQs are ranked in descending order based on *ProfitFactor* of the RFQs. This method of ranking ensures that the profitable RFQs come out on top and are given more priority when allocating resources.

The agent has already committed some factory cycles in the future for the completion of it's active orders. Further, depending on the future demand, some of the factory cycles are restricted and not available for committing on the current day. For each RFQ, we check if sufficient free factory cycles are available to complete the order. If not, we check for any extra inventory which can be committed to the particular RFQ. But, if still unsuccessful, we demote the category of RFQ – from *Singles* to *Fours*; *Fours* to *Sixes*; *Sixes* to Prune.

Also to accomplish *Rule 1* and *Rule 2*, we convert some RFQs from *Fours* to *Singles* and some from *Sixes* to *Fours*. The intuition here is that some profit is better than no profit. But, we also ensure that we maintain the balance, as ultimately it is the profit that matters at the end of the game and not the revenue.

Our agent is flexible enough to know when there isn't any opportunity available. In that case, we can intuitively infer that rivalry is strong and it is better to increase number of *Singles*.

Table 2. Average scores of final round in TAC SCM 2012

Rank	Agent	Average score (final)	Average score (at end of 195th day)
1.	Deep Maize	11.46 M	8.118 M
2.	Punga2Bani	8.364 M	2.635 M
3.	Iota	5.835 M	3.226 M
4.	HEU2012	4.223 M	−4.058 M
5.	Mertacor	−1.367 M	−5.586 M
6.	Crocodile	−2.625 M	−7.897 M

Table 3. Experiment results (average of 50 games each)

	Strategy	Profit%	Utilization (in %)	Singles				Fours				Sixes	
				True	False	Offers	Orders	True	False	Offers	Orders	Offers	Orders
1.	Only *Sixes*	12.29	18	0	0	0	0	0	0	0	0	31681	429
2.	Only *Fours*	24.71	34	0	0	0	0	7154	20092	27246	2008	0	0
3.	Only *Singles*	58.38	71	15030	5887	20917	6524	0	0	0	0	0	0
4.	Window (=1)	58.79	57	15495	1290	16785	4474	5975	296	6271	734	2839	205
5.	Window (=3)	62.01	58	15909	1062	16971	4592	6118	208	6402	878	3639	308
6.	Window (=7)	61.64	60	16062	1152	17214	4501	6389	224	6629	833	3198	292
7.	Window (=9)	57.09	58	17980	1323	19303	4311	6634	308	6942	796	3402	187
8.	Opportunistic bidding	66.68	64	16690	845	17535	4812	4751	152	4903	1170	3651	443

4   Results

In this section, we evaluate the agent performance and compare the agent strategies under different experimental setups.

4.1   Agent Performance

To evaluate and validate the adaptive and dynamic techniques of our agent under different conditions, we took part in TAC SCM 2012 competition. The final score provides suggestive evidence regarding the efficacy of our strategy and approach. Our agent *Iota* finished third behind two other agents. This is mainly because our agent was not able to adapt well in the end phase of the game and fell behind the other top agents after 195th day. Table 5 shows that at the end of 195th day, the average profit of our agent was second highest. But during the end phase of the game, we were unable to hold our position and slip to third. To improve our performance in the end phase of the game, we need to improve coordination between the different modules of our agent. Apart from bidding module, pricing and procurement modules also play an important role.

In this paper, we focus only on the classification sub-task of the bidding subsystem. Pricing and procurement strategies are not discussed.

4.2   Experiments

We present the results of controlled experiments designed to compare different strategies of our agent and their impact on our agent's performance. We run 50 games for each experiment *against five of the best agents that have participated in TAC SCM competition* – TacTex [3], DeepMaize [4,12], Phant Agent [13], Maxon and Mertacor [11]. All five agents have finished first in atleast one of the previously held TAC SCM competitions. We use the binary codes of the agents available in TAC Agent Repository to run the simulations. Running each experiments 50 times basically covers different low demand, mid demand and high demand games and gives us a nice platform to analyse these results.

For the experiments conducted, Table 3 presents the comparison of average results of different parameters of our agent. Comparison is done mainly on the basis of *Profit%* among other factors.

$$Profit\% = \frac{Profit_R}{\max\limits_{\forall i \in agents}(Profit_i)} * 100 \tag{14}$$

$Profit_R$ indicates the profit of our agent and $Profit_i$ denotes the profit of agent i.

In Table 3, *False* indicates the number of RFQs which should have been classified differently and bid at a different price. If majority of the agents bid for a RFQ at a price, which is either 10 % greater or 10 % lesser than our agent's bid price, we term the RFQ as falsely classified. Lesser number of *False* offers indicates better strategy. Complement of the *False* set is the *True* set.

True offers are the offers corresponding to the RFQs which are classified and bid appropriately.

In the following experiments, we test the impact of our RFQ classification model on our agent performance. Strategy 8 is the final version of our agent, which we entered in the competition. We use the mixed strategy for Singles, Fours and Sixes RFQs classified using our parameterized decision tree. Window size is 5.

In strategy 1, we treat all the RFQs as *Sixes* and bid. Similarly in strategy 2 and strategy 3, we treat all the RFQs as *Fours* and *Singles* respectively and bid. Strategy 1, 2 and 3 are the pure strategies. Strategy 8 is our opportunistic bidding agent that does proper classification and is the mixed Strategy of Strategies 1, 2 and 3.

In 'Only *Sixes*' strategy (highly risky) and 'Only *Fours*' strategy (risky), profit and utilization are both less understandable. While in 'Only *Singles*' strategy (safe), the factory utilization is bit high, but profit is less compared to that in strategy 8, representing classification based on identifying opportunity. This is because the agent can maximize its profit by bidding reasonably higher on some RFQs, depending on the situation, expecting to win a few such orders.

In strategy 4, 5, 6 and 7, we change the 'window' size for our agent, keeping everything else the same as our opportunistic agent in strategy 8 where window size is set as 5. The results indicate that the agent is more robust with 5 as the

Table 4. Comparison of our strategy with top agents

Rank	Agent	Average score
1.	TacTex	8.49 M
2.	DeepMaize	6.62 M
3.	Iota	5.84 M
4.	Phant	5.67 M
5.	Maxon	3.31 M
6.	Mertacor	2.15 M

Table 5. Illustrating effect of rivalry due to competing agents.

Setup	Profit %	Singles		Fours		Sixes		Utilization (in %)
		Offers	Orders	Offers	Orders	Offers	Orders	
F(5), S(0)	66.68	17535	4812	4903	1170	3651	443	64
F(4), S(1)	70.11	15934	4902	5225	1286	3817	522	66
F(3), S(2)	75.36	15401	5136	5452	1367	4015	549	69
F(2), S(3)	83.07	15022	5201	5610	1508	4341	583	73
F(1), S(4)	90.88	14680	5315	5785	1587	4498	611	76
F(0), S(5)	98.79	14140	5699	6069	1634	4751	647	80
Dummy(5)	100	13633	5908	6518	1748	5051	706	93

'window' size. Keeping the window size small makes our agent biased towards a small change in market conditions. On the other hand, the agent adapts slowly to the dynamically changing market conditions if window size is large.

Table 4 illustrates the performance of our *Iota* agent against the five best agents of TAC SCM. In this experiment we compete against those agents for 50 games with equal distribution of low, mid and high demand games.

4.3   Adaptation

Table 5 shows that our agent learns and adapts according to the changes in market conditions and rivalry. *F(x)* in Table 5 represents *x* different agents, which have been finalists in previous years in TAC SCM competition (same agents as those in Table 4).

Similarly, *S(y)* represents *y* different agents, which got eliminated in the initial rounds in previous years SCM competitions while competing against agents of Set-F (*F(x)*), the agents are Crocodile, Botticelli, kshitij, Grunn and GoBlueOval (also taken from TAC Agent Repository). *Dummy* represents the default agent of TAC SCM, based on random bidding strategy. In short *F(x)* represents *x* self learning agents who provides tougher competition in the market while *S(y)* represent *y* self learning agents who had some strategy but can not provide good competition compare to agents in *F(x)*. So as we increase *x* in *F(x)* we increase the competition in the market and as we increase *y* in *S(y)* we decrease the competition in the market.

As the competition decreases, the opportunity increases and our agent is able to procure more orders. Also percentage of orders corresponding to *Fours* and *Sixes* increases, compared to high competition games. This leads to increase in profit. For each value of *x* and *y* we ran 50 simulations with equal distribution of low, mid and high demand games. Hence from Table 5, we can conclude that our agent adapts according to the competition provided by the fellow competing agents.

4.4   Summary

Tables 2, 3, 4 and 5 shows that our solution is able to perform effective opportunistic bidding by not only getting higher profit but also maintaining high utilization. Our agent is also able to adapt dynamic market changes. Thus there is scope for threshold based classification driven solution to address this important problem. The thresholds are computed at runtime to determine the RFQs to be bid. Our opportunistic agent has been able to get significant number of *Fours* and *Sixes* even with the top agents of TAC SCM.

Our classification model can be used for multiplayer game problems involving continuous iterations in a dynamic environment, with feedback from previous iterations. Real Time Scheduling System for Taxi [14] is one of the example where we can apply our model.[2]

---

[2] Demonstration for Taxi scheduling is out of the scope of this paper.

Future work involves further improving the performance of the agent in the end phase of the game[3]. Also, we must predict the set of possible future RFQs and bid appropriately.

References

1. Collins, J., Arunachalam, R., Sadeh, N., Eriksson, J., Finne, N., Janson, S.: The supply chain management game for the 2007 TAC. Technical report CMU-ISRI-07-100, Carnegie Mellon University (2007)
2. Vicky, P., Cassaigne, N.: A critical analysis of bid pricing models and support tool. In: 2000 IEEE International Conference on Systems, Man, and Cybernetics, vol. 3, pp. 2098–2103 (2000)
3. Pardoe, D., Stone, P.: Bidding for customer orders in TAC SCM. In: Faratin, P., Rodríguez-Aguilar, J.-A. (eds.) AMEC 2004. LNCS (LNAI), vol. 3435, pp. 143–157. Springer, Heidelberg (2006)
4. Kiekintveld, C., Miller, J., Jordan, P.R., Callender, L.F., Wellman, M.P.: Forecasting market prices in a supply chain game. Electron. Commer. Rec. Appl. **8**(2), 63–77 (2009)
5. Jordan, P.R., Kiekintveld, C., Wellman, M.P.: Empirical game-theoretic analysis of the TAC Supply Chain game. In: AAMAS'07, pp. 193:1–193:8. ACM, New York (2007)
6. Benisch, M., Greenwald, A., Grypari, I., Lederman, R., Naroditskiy, V., Tschantz, M.: Botticelli: a supply chain management agent. ACM Trans. Comp. Logic., 1174–1181 (2004)
7. Kovalchuk, Y., Fasli, M.: Adaptive strategies for predicting bidding prices in supply chain management. In: 10th ICEC, pp. 6:1–6:10. ACM, New York (2008)
8. He, M., Rogers, A., Luo, X., Jennings, N.R.: Designing a successful trading agent for supply chain management. In: AAMAS '06, pp. 1159–1166. ACM, New York (2006)
9. Collins, J., Ketter, W., Gini, M.: Flexible decision control in an autonomous trading agent. Electron. Commer. Rec. Appl. **8**(2), 91–105 (2009)
10. Ketter, W., Collins, J., Gini, M., Gupta, A., Schrater, P.: Detecting and forecasting economic regimes in multi-agent automated exchanges. Decis. Support Syst. **47**(4), 307–318 (2009)
11. Chatzidimitriou, K.C., Symeonidis, A.L., Mitkas, P.A.: Policy search through adaptive function approximation for bidding in TAC SCM. In: David, E., Kiekintveld, C., Robu, V., Shehory, O., Stein, S. (eds.) AMEC 2012 and TADA 2012. LNBIP, vol. 136, pp. 16–29. Springer, Heidelberg (2013)
12. Kiekintveld, C., Wellman, M.P., Singh, S., Estelle, J., Vorobeychik, Y., Soni, V., Rudary, M.: Distributed feedback control for decision making on supply chains. In: 14th ICAPS, pp. 384–392 (2004)
13. Stan, M., Stan, B., Florea, A.M.: A dynamic strategy agent for supply chain management. In: SYNASC'06, pp. 227–232. IEEE Computer Society, Washington, DC (2006)
14. Glaschenko, A., Ivaschenko, A., Rzevski, G., Skobelev, P.: Multi-agent real time scheduling system for taxi companies (2009)

---

[3] Need to improve coordination between the procurement module and the bidding module of our agent.

An Intelligent Learning Mechanism for Trading Strategies for Local Energy Distribution

Muhammad Yasir$^{(\boxtimes)}$, Martin Purvis, Maryam Purvis,
and BastinTony Roy Savarimuthu

Department of Information Science, University of Otago,
Dunedin, New Zealand
{muhammad.yasir,martin.purvis,
maryam.purvis,tony.savarimuthu}@otago.ac.nz

Abstract. Although most electric power is presently generated using fossil fuels, two abundant renewable and clean energy sources, solar and wind, are increasingly cost-competitive and offer the potential of decentralized (and hence more robust) sourcing. However, the intermittent nature of solar and wind power presents difficulties in connection with integrating them into national power grids. One approach to addressing these challenges is through an agent-based architecture for coordinating locally-connected energy micro-grids, each of which manages its own local energy production, distribution, and storage. By integrating these micro-grids into a larger network structure, there is the opportunity for them to be more responsive to local needs and hence more cost effective overall. In such an arrangement, the micro-grids have agents that can choose to resell their excess energy in an open, regional market in alignment with respect to their specific goals (which could be to reduce carbon emissions or to maximize their financial outcomes). In this study, we have investigated how agents operating in such an open environment can learn to optimize their individual trading strategies by employing Markov-Decision-Process-based reasoning and reinforcement learning. We empirically show that our learning trading strategies improve net profit loss by up to 29 % and can reduce carbon emissions by 78 % when compared to the original (non-learning) trading strategies.

Keywords: Renewable energy · Multi-agent systems · Power trading · Micro-grids

1 Introduction

A micro-grid refers to a local energy system that can generate and store its own renewable energy and also be connected to a main electrical energy supply grid [5]. The idea of a micro-grid is to utilize the distributed local renewable energy resources and satisfies power needs locally. It can also sell or buy power from an energy utility company. However, renewable energy sources (wind, sun) are intermittent in nature and vary hour to hour, even minute to minute, depending upon

© Springer International Publishing Switzerland 2014
S. Ceppi et al. (Eds.): AMEC/TADA 2013 and 2014, LNBIP 187, pp. 159–170, 2014.
DOI: 10.1007/978-3-319-13218-1_12

local conditions [5], which can compromise electric system reliability. Different energy management strategies are used to mitigate or eliminate the impact of supply variations, such as storage devices (batteries, fly wheel, capacitors, etc.), forecasting techniques, demand load management, and backup generators. One of the approaches to address this issue is the interconnection of nearby micro-grids which reduce the impact of non-steadiness of renewable energy sources, as communities having micro-grid can trade power with each other to satisfy their demands [5]. An agent-based architecture for local energy distribution among micro-grids is presented in Yasir et al. [16]. In this architecture, each micro-grid represents a community which has its own power generator based on the renewable energy sources and also has its own electric energy demand which varies from hour to hour. Every community has a coordinator agent which, when it has a power surplus or deficit, is responsible for power trading to other interconnected communities or to the utility grid. Each community may employ a different strategy for power trading depending upon either of two goals i.e. profit maximization, and reduction in carbon emission.

In this work, we study the trading activities of coordinator agents that can learn to adapt their strategies in an electric market. The learning trading strategies of the coordinator agents that improve trading performance by employing Markov Decision Process (MDP) and reinforcement learning. Our experimental results show that the learned trading strategies respond to changing conditions and lead to superior out-comes (with respect to financial rewards and reduced carbon emissions), when com-pared with fixed trading strategies.

The rest of the paper is organized as follows: In Sect. 2 we describe the electric market and the trading strategies, Sect. 3 covers the MDP learning framework. Section 4, shows empirical comparison of our learning trading strategies. In Sect. 5, we review related work in this area. Finally, Sect. 6 discuses some future prospects and also provides a conclusion.

2   Electric Market and Trading Strategies

In our work, we design an hour-ahead market and assume that on the hour of delivery, suppliers always provide the amount of power they had committed in the market. Also, there is one market for all the communities. The market mechanism in our work employs a double auction algorithm [8] to facilitate market clearing (determining the price at which a unit of energy is sold by matching bids and offers). All the sellers and buyers submit their offers and bids in certain time interval. Once the time is over, market clearing algorithm starts making match. In this algorithm, the buyer of the highest bid will be matched by the seller with the lowest bid. The clearing price (or unit price per kWh) is set as the mean of the (bid and offer) prices. Every match (i.e. a pair of seller and buyer)has its own clearing price. There is no one clearing price for all buyers and sellers. A coordinator agent typically buys from the market; and if no power is available in the local market or the price is high in the market, it buys from the utility gird.

As discussed above, a community employs a trading strategy for power trading. Some communities may be environmentally conscious and more interested in minimizing environmentally harmful emission, while others may be concerned about the maximization of financial benefits.

2.1 Trading Strategies

In this section, we describe the two main trading strategies that a community can use for trading described by Yasir et al. [16].

Altruistic Strategy (AS). The goal of a community that employs this strategy is the minimization of carbon emissions by using more green power (and thus not buy from the main utility grid, some of whose power is produced by fossil fuels). This strategy also encourages other communities to use renewable energy by selling its own (green) power in the market at the lowest price. So, the agent using this strategy:

- is willing to buy green power at high prices, if green power is available in the market, and
- sells green power in the market at a low price (lower than that charged by the utility), so that more communities can use its power.

Greedy Strategy (GS). A community using this strategy always wants to maximize its financial benefit by buying power at a low price and selling power at a high price in the market. GS always tries to

- Buy at a low price from any place (i.e. market or utility grid)
- Sells energy surpluses at a high price to any place.

Fixed Strategy (FS). A community that employs this strategy always offers and bids power in the market at a fixed price. For this paper, the fixed price is 21.5 cents.

Note that the generation cost of electricity is 7 cents per Kwh. So no strategy offers below 7 cents.

In [16] the authors empirically compared AS and GS strategies in term of two variables:

- Net profit/loss by community
- Carbon emission produced as a result of the strategy.

There are several limitations in this work. Although AS and GS adjust their current trading price based on the history of how they traded 24 h ago, they do not learn from past experience. As a result, these communities do not put optimal trading bids and offers in the competitive electric market and do not get the maximum profit or minimization of the carbon emissions. Similarly, above mentioned strategies make trading bids randomly by adding or subtracting small random numbers from their last bids. They do not know how much exactly they add or subtract from their last bids. Also, while making the bids they do not consider the current position of the market. By using the MDP model, we overcome all these limitations.

In this paper, we propose two types of learning strategies for trading that a community can use. One learning strategy is used to optimize the financial gain and the other leaning strategy is used to optimally reduce the carbon emissions to the atmosphere. The strategy that maximizes profits is called the greedy learner strategy while the strategy that minimizes the carbon emissions is called the green learner strategy. Both strategies learn an MDP policy using Q-learning. The learning algorithm uses a typical exploration-exploitation trade-off that explores more often in early episodes of simulation and progressively less in the later episodes of the simulation.

3   An MDP-based Learning Framework

Let T_s be the Learning Trading agent for which we develop an action policy using the framework of MDPs and reinforcement learning. The MDP for T_s is defined as:
$$M^{T_s} = (S, A, \delta, r)$$
Where:

- $S = si : i = 1....I$ is a set of states,
- $A = aj : j = 1....J$ is a set of actions,
- $\delta(s,a) = s'$ is a transition function, and
- $r(s,a)$ is a reward function

The state space should capture the two sets of features that are important to how Ts would set its trading prices:

- Last hour average clearing price (ACP) in the market
- Level of electric demand (DL) available in the market for trading for current hour.

The average market clearing price is difficult to represent because prices in the real world are virtually continuous. We restrict the range of prices from 10 cents to 36 cents per Kwh of electricity in New Zealand dollars [4] and discretizing the prices in 2 cents increments to get 13 possible values for the clearing price. Similarly we categorized the level of demand in to three bands: low, medium, and high. Information about ACP and DL is provided by the market to all communities participating in the market.

In the final representation, the state space S is the set defined by all the values of the elements in the following:

$$S = \{ACP_{t-1}, DL_t\}$$

Next, we define the set of MDP actions A. Each learning agent will generate its bid-ding prices by using the information of ACP_{t-1} and DL_t. The learning agent will either increase or decrease its trading price with reference to the ACP_{t-1}. After observing few real world electric markets [3,9], we found that price for the next hour electric power is either increased or decreased up to 2 cents per kWh as compared to the last hour. The action that an agent can do as a buyer or a seller is to increment or decrement certain amount from the last average clearing price. The range of increments and increments are between -2.5 and 2.5, with discrete options chosen by agents in 0.5 units, resulting in 11 possible actions. So the set of actions is the increment or decrement of last average clearing price from the range of price from 0 to 2.5 cents, and we discretize the prices in 0.5 units cents to get 11 possible values for the actions.

The transition function δ is defined by numerous stochastic interactions within the simulator. The reward function, r, is unknown to the MDP, and it is calculated by the learning agent depending upon its learning objective, i.e. maximize profit or minimize the carbon emissions.

Let T_{sP} be the learning trading agent that wants to maximize the profit. Then the reward function for the seller agent is:

$$r_{sp} = \begin{cases} Amt_{st}/Amt_{max-s} * (p_t - \Psi_{bt}), & \text{if traded inside market} \\ 0, & \text{if no buyer in market} \\ Amt_{st}/Amt_{max-s} * (\Psi_{bt} - ACP_t), & \text{if traded outside market} \end{cases}$$

The reward for the buying agent that wants to maximize its profit is:

$$r_{bp} = \begin{cases} Amt_{bt}/Amt_{max-b} * (\Psi_{st} - p_t), & \text{if traded inside market} \\ 0, & \text{if no seller in market} \\ Amt_{bt}/Amt_{max-b} * (ACP_t - \Psi_{st}), & \text{if traded outside market} \end{cases}$$

where: r_{sp} and r_{bp} are the rewards for selling and buying agents that want to maximize the profit, respectively, Amt_{st} and Amt_{bt} are the total quantities sold and bought from the market at time t by community Amt_{max-s} and Amt_{max-b} are the maximum quantities sold and bought from the market by community at any time. We use the denominator values to normalize the value of reward in certain range.

P_t is the price at which the quantity sold is/bought from the market at time t. Ψ_{bt} and Ψst is the price at which utility grid buys and sells at time t.

Similarly, let T_{sg} be the learning agent that aims to reduce the carbon emission as much as possible. The reduction in carbon emission is only possible if community buys (when it needs) power from the market. Being the green community, it also prefer to sell power inside the market. So the reward function for the selling agent is:

$$r_{sg} = \begin{cases} Amt_{st}/Amt_{available}, & \text{if traded inside market} \\ 0, & \text{if no buyer in market} \\ -1, & \text{if traded outside market} \end{cases}$$

The reward for learning buying agent for carbon emission minimization is:

$$r_{bg} = \begin{cases} Amt_{bt}/Amt_{needed}, & \text{if traded inside market} \\ 0, & \text{if no seller in market} \\ -1, & \text{if traded outside market} \end{cases}$$

where: $Amt_{available}$ is the total surplus power for selling and Amt_{needed} is the total power quantity required to meet its demand. The value of reward equals to 1 when all the power (available or needed) is sold or bought, from the market.

Since this is a non-deterministic MDP formulation with unknown reward and transition functions, we use the Watkins and Dayans [14] Q-learning formula:

$$Q_t(s,a) = (1-\alpha)Q_t(s,a) + \alpha[r_t + \gamma max_{a'} Q_{t+1}(s',a')]$$

4   Experiments

This section presents the results of four types of comparative experiments we have conducted using learning trading strategies.

4.1   Experimental Setup

In order to compare the above mentioned strategies, we set up forty micro-grid communities (C1 to C40). The communities have an average hourly consumption of 1150 kWh and a wind turbine of 2000 kW generation capacity. However, these values for an individual community will vary, since the communities are dispersed geographically, and hence have different wind speeds and patterns in their regions. Thus the power produced by each community is also different. Power generated by the wind turbine is calculated by using the formula [6]:

$$P = 1/2\rho A V^3 Cp$$

Where P is the power in watts (W), ρ is the power density in kilograms per cubic meter (kg/m^3), A is the swept rotor area in square meters (m^2), V is the wind speed in meters per second (m/s), and Cp is the power co-efficient. We obtained the synthetic wind speed (V) data of New Zealand from Electricity Authority New Zealand [7]. We also obtained hourly power consumption data of nine different places from the Property Services office of the University of Otago [11].

The assumptions made while running our experiments are as follows. All communities are situated at the sea level. So the value of is 1.23 kg/m^3. The blade length of the wind turbines is 45 meter (m). The cut-in and cut-out wind speeds of the turbines is 3 and 25 meters per second (m/s), respectively. Theoretically the maximum value of Cp is 59 %, which is known as Betz limit [6]. However, in practice the value of Cp is in between 25 %–45 % [6] depending upon the height and size of the turbine. The value of the power co-efficient (Cp) is 0.4

(i.e. 40 %). We also assume that the utility grid is always ready to buy power and sell power to the micro-grids at the rates of 18 cents per kWh and 25 cents per kWh, respectively. To trade into the market, a community uses the market-based trading mechanism discussed in Sect. 2.1. The value of learning rate (α) in our Q-learning scheme is 0.5, and the discount factor (γ) is 0.1. When exploiting the learned policy, we randomly select one of the possible actions that is within 20 % of the highest Q-value.

We computed the value of net profit/loss[1] and carbon emission[2] by varying the learning and non-learning strategies during simulation. We calculate the amount of carbon emission produced by using electricity emission factor of 0.137 (kg Co2-equivalent per Kwh) for New Zealand [7].

4.2   Results

We ran all experiments for 35,000 simulated hours. Due to space constraints, we have presented the results of only two representative communities: one that experiences net power deficits, and one that has power surpluses. One community (C1) has overall surplus power generation during 35,000 simulated hours, and the other community (C2) has deficit in power generation for the same period.

Experiment 1. In this experiment, first all communities in the simulation employ the fixed strategy (as described in Sect. 2.1) for the baseline scenario. To make comparison of learning strategies with baseline scenario all communities again employ the fixed strategy except communities C1 and C2, which use the two learning strategies (successively, one by one). Table 1 shows the results. The dollar sign ($) represents the net profit/loss and Kg shows the total carbon emission produced. The results clearly show that communities using learning strategies do better as compared to the communities that use only the fixed strategy. There is an improvement of around 10 % in net profit loss, and about 78 % reduction in the carbon emission by the employing learning strategies. Also the greedy and green learners perform better than fixed agent.

Table 1. Fixed vs. learning strategies

Community	Fixed strategy		Greedy learner		Green learner	
	$	Kg	$	Kg	$	kg
C1	1,430,788	495,151	1,558,207	137,067	1,531,480	108,986
C2	−1,503,315	870,403	−1,358,975	2,360,820	−1,449,140	185,688

---

[1] Net Profit/Loss = ((cash in - generation cost) - cash out).
[2] Carbon emission stores the amount of carbon di oxide emitted during electricity production, transmission and distribution.

Experiment 2. This experiment is similar to Experiment 1; with the difference being that all the other communities employ the GS strategy (in contrast to fixed strategy). Communities C1 and C2 used the learning strategies (again, one by one). Table 2 shows the results for the two communities using learning strategies in the presence of greedy strategies used by the other communities.

Table 2. Greedy strategy vs. learning strategies

Community	Greedy strategy		Greedy learner		Green learner	
	$	Kg	$	Kg	$	kg
C1	1,429,156	505,229	1,434,999	367,941	1,329,129	80,893
C2	−1,528,295	877,395	−1,503,213	616,847	−1,612,990	127,700

The results clearly show that communities using the learning strategies are better off as compared to communities using non-learning strategies (GS, AS, FS) in terms of net profit loss and carbon emissions.

Experiment 3. This experiment is also similar to Experiment 1 & 2, with the difference being that all the other communities employ the AS strategy. Communities C1 and C2 used the learning strategies (one by one). Table 3 shows the result for the two communities using learning strategies in the presence of altruistic strategy used by the other thirty-nine communities. By employing learning strategies in this setup, community improved up to 29 % and carbon emission reduced up to 31 %. It clearly shows that learning strategies obtaining their objectives even in the presence of the Altruistic strategy.

Table 3. Altruistic strategy vs. learning strategies

Community	Altruistic strategy		Greedy learner		Green learner	
	$	Kg	$	Kg	$	kg
C1	1,531,710	495,913	1,924,035	714,683	1,500,108	338,360
C2	−1,503,551	879,686	−1,060,448	1,321,194	−1,519,907	685,113

Experiment 4. This experiment consists of three parts: in each part all communities employ one of the strategies described in Sect. 2.1 (i.e. Fixed, Greedy, and Green) except C1 and C2 which use the greedy and green learning strategies. The results are shown in Tables 4, 5, 6, 7, 8 and 9. Tables 4, 6, and 8 show that both learning strategies perform better when compared to non-learner strategies (Tables 5, 7, and 9) even when they learn together in the same environment at the same time.

Table 4. Two learning strategies in Greedy strategy background

Community	Greedy strategy	
	$	Kg
C1 (Greedy learner)	1,422,662	391,738
C2 (Green learner)	−1,611,041	131,858
C1 (Green learner)	1,317,871	76,995
C2 (Greedy learner)	−1,509,336	643,874

Table 5. Non-learner strategies in Greedy strategy background

Community	Greedy strategy	
	$	Kg
C1 (Greedy strategy)	1399980	517,146
C2 (Green strategy)	−1,575,271	642,525
C1 (Green strategy)	1,350,825	364,804
C2 (Greedy strategy)	−1,533,322	902,284

Table 6. Two learning strategies in altruistic strategy background

Community	Altruistic strategy	
	$	Kg
C1 (Greedy learner)	1,912,356	730,615
C2 (Green learner)	−1,545,476	640,341
C1 (Green learner)	1,480,572	327,909
C2 (Greedy learner)	−1,067,943	1,337,009

Table 7. Non-learner strategies in altruistic strategy background

Community	Altruistic strategy	
	$	Kg
C1 (Greedy strategy)	1,838,603	804,407
C2 (Green strategy)	−1,504,681	873,256
C1 (Green strategy)	1,522,661	485,900
C2 (Greedy strategy)	−1,140,483	1,467,335

Table 8. Two learning strategies in fixed strategy background

Community	Fixed strategy	
	$	Kg
C1 (Greedy learner)	1,599,149	132,305
C2 (Green learner)	−1,437,841	181,317
C1 (Green learner)	1,541,371	101,318
C2 (Greedy learner)	−1,351,420	236,285

Table 9. Non-learner strategies in fixed strategy background

Community	Fixed strategy	
	$	Kg
C1 (Greedy strategy)	1,395,544	474,323
C2 (Green strategy)	−1,535,957	851,424
C1 (Green strategy)	1,396,106	474,270
C2 (Greedy strategy)	−1,540,306	872,806

Experiment 5. In Experiment 5, a community instead of using either the green or greedy learning strategy, uses a hybrid strategy of half-green and half-greedy learning strategies (HGGL) at the same time. A community using this approach splits its surplus or deficit into two chunks. It generates two different trading prices for these chunks and then enters into the market for trading. This way, a community learns to improve its profit and also learns to reduce its carbon emissions at the same time. Tables 10, 11, and 12 show the results of experiment 5.

These show that the community that uses use the half-green and half-greedy learning approach makes a compromised trade-off between the net profit/loss and the carbon emissions. It can be observed from the results that the resultant net profits and carbon emission produced by HGGL is between the Green and Greedy learner strategies.

Table 10. Half greedy, Half green learner in Greedy strategy background

Community	Greedy strategy		Community	Greedy strategy	
	$	Kg		$	Kg
C1 (Green Learner)	1,329,129	80,893	C2 (Green Learner)	-1,612,990	127,700
C1 (HGGL)	1,384,942	222,020	C2 (HGGL)	-1,553,823	400,220
C1 (Greedy Learner)	1,434,999	367,941	C2 (Greedy Strategy)	-1,503,213	616,847

Table 11. Half greedy, half green learner in altruistic strategy background

Community	Greedy strategy		Community	Greedy strategy	
	$	Kg		$	Kg
C1 (Green Learner)	1,500,108	338,360	C2 (Green Learner)	-1,519,907	685,113
C1 (HGGL)	1,647,174	411,278	C2 (HGGL)	-1,427,069	753,328
C1 (Greedy Learner)	1,924,035	714,683	C2 (Greedy Strategy)	-1,060,448	1,321,194

Table 12. Half greedy, half green learner in fixed strategy background

Community	Fixed strategy		Community	Fixed strategy	
	$	Kg		$	Kg
C1 (Green Learner)	1,531,480	108,986	C2 (Green Learner)	-1,449,140	185,688
C1 (HGGL)	1,551,825	113,224	C2 (HGGL)	-1,398,512	202,703
C1 (Greedy Learner)	1,558,207	137,067	C2 (Greedy Strategy)	-1,358,975	2,360,820

5   Related Work

Recently there has been increasing interest in the application of multi-agent systems to the power trading, management and control of distributed energy resources on micro-girds or smart grids. For example, Reddy and Veloso [13] presented a learning strategy for the broker agent in the smart-grid market. They used Markov Decision Process (MDPs) and reinforcement learning to train their broker agent about market tariffs. Peters et al. [10] also proposed a learning approach for the broker agent to learn the bidding price in the smart grid market. Similarly, Rahimi-Kian et al. [12] and Xiong et al. [15] proposed learning mechanisms for the electric suppliers to bid in the electric market. Alam et al. [1] introduced an agent-based model for energy exchanges among communities. In their proposed model, agents use a game-theory approach to form a coalition to exchange power. Fatimah Ishowo-Oloko et al. [4] presented a model for a dynamic storage-pricing mechanism that uses storage information from the renewable energy providers to generate daily, real-time electricity prices which are communicated to the customers. In addition Cossentino et al. proposed a multi-agent system for the management of micro-grids [2]. The prime responsibility of their proposed system is to provide an electronic market to the consumers and generators within a micro-grid. In case of any mismatches between supply and demand, their agent-based system will disconnect the loads or feeders depending upon the priority.

With respect to the above-mentioned proposed systems, none of the models considers the environmental concerns during energy trading or exchange. All models are concerned exclusively with profit maximization. In the model of Reddy and Velso [13], the goal of the broker is to maximize profit and avoid the balancing fee imposed by the utility grid in case of mismatch between production and consumption. In this model, the broker is an individual entity who does not represent any community and does not have its own power generating unit. The broker in this situation makes a match between the consumer and producers. Similarly in [10], the authors presented a learning strategy for the broker who makes a match between the producers of the wholesale market and the consumers of in the retailer markets. In two of the models [12,15], the bidding strategy for the electric suppliers (who trade in the wholesale market) is presented. Buyers haven't been considered. In Alam et al. model [1], they do not consider the profitability of the individual households as well as s the amount of carbon emission mitigated through coalition formation. In [4], there has not been much attention given to the consideration of robust energy distribution across locally-connected communities. Cossentino et al. [2] uses a trading mechanism among the internal agents of the micro-grid to balance supply and demand inside the micro-grids. In contrast, our research focuses on learning trading strategies for a community that not only supports inter-micro-grid power trading but also improves the financial benefits and reduce the carbon emissions of the participants in the proportions that the communities choose.

6   Conclusion

Interconnected micro-grids, with renewable energy sources and energy storage devices have already been shown to be effective respect to financial advantage, local autonomy, and more energy distribution [16]. We have presented the two learning trading strategies and have shown that a community can improve its financial benefit and reduce its carbon emission using an agent-based architecture. This has been accomplished by means of a multi-agent simulation that employs synthetic wind data, real electric demand, and current energy pricing data.

Based on the studies conducted, we found that if a community wants to maximize its financial gain then it should adopt the greedy learning strategy; and if a community is environmentally conscious, then it should employ the green strategy to reduce carbon emissions. A community can also maintain a balanced position between these two parameters by using, for example, a half green and half greedy learning strategy.

Agent-based system coordination and collaboration are inherently scalable. So in the future we intend to extend our analysis by conducting more elaborate tests with our agent-based modeling approach. We will then explore the following:

– Dynamic adoption of learning strategies (e.g. a community will choose by itself to become greedy learner, or green learner, or hybrid learner with varying mix of greedy-green strategies?, by looking at market conditions).

- Use of reinforcement learning for battery storing strategies.
- Extension of our model by considering power generating units at the consumer level (e.g. solar PVs).
- Reinforcement learning at the demand response management.

References

1. M. Alam, S. Ramchurn, and A. Rogers. Cooperative Energy Exchange for the Efficient Use of Energy and Resources in Remote Communities. In 12th Autonomous Agents and Multiagent Systems (AAMAS) Conference, pages 731–738, Saint Paul Minnesota, USA, 2013
2. Cossentino, M., Lodato, C., Pucci, M., Vitale, G.: A multi-agent architecture for simulating and managing microgrids. In: Federated Conference on Computer Science and Information Systems (FedCSIS), Szczecin, Poland, pp. 619–622 (2011)
3. IESO: Independent Electricity System Operator Canada. http://www.ieso.ca/. Accessed 10 Feb 2014
4. Ishowo-oloko, F., Vytelingum, P., Jennings, N., Rahwan, I.: A storage pricing mechanism for learning agents in Masdar City smart grid. In: 11th International Conference on Autonomous Agents and Multiagent Systems, Valencia, Spain, pp. 1167–1168 (2012)
5. Jacobson, M.Z., Delucchi, M.A.: Providing all global energy with wind, water, and solar power, part i: technologies, energy resources, quantities and areas of infrastructure, and materials. Energy Policy 39(3), 1154–1169 (2011)
6. Miller, A., Muljadi, E., Zinger, D.S.: A variable speed wind turbine power control. Energy Convers. 12(2), 181–186 (1997)
7. Ministry for Environment New Zealand: Guidance for voluntary corporate greenhouse gas reporting data and methods for the 2010 calendar year. Technical report, Wellington, New Zealand (2010)
8. Nicolaisen, J., Petrov, V., Tesfatsion, L.: Market power and efficiency in a computational electricity market with discriminatory double auction pricing. IEEE Trans. Evol. Comput. 5(5), 504–523 (2001)
9. G. Nordic Energy: Electricity Market Group. http://www.nordicenergy.org/. Accessed 08 Feb 2014
10. Peters, M., Ketter, W., Saar-Tsechansky, M., Collins, J.: A reinforcement learning approach to autonomous decision-making in smart electricity markets. Mach. Learn. 92(1), 5–39 (2013)
11. Pietsch, H.: Property service Division. http://www.propserv.otago.ac.nz/. Accessed 1 Feb 2014
12. Rahimi-kian, A., Sadeghi, B., Member, S., Thomas, R.J.: Q-learning based supplier-agents for electricity markets. In: 2002 IEEE Power Engineering Society Summer Meeting, Chicago, IL, USA, pp. 1–8 (2002)
13. Reddy, P.P., Veloso, M.M.: Strategy learning for autonomous agents in smart grid markets (2013)
14. Watkins, C.J.C.H., Dayan, P.: Q-learning. Mach. Learn. 8(3–4), 279–292 (1992)
15. Xiong, G., Hashiyama, T., Okuma, S.: An electricity supplier bidding strategy through Q-Learning. In: Power Engineering Society Summer Meeting, Chicago, IL, USA (2002)
16. Yasir, M., Purvis, M.K., Purvis, M., Savarimuthu, B.T.R.: Agent-based community coordination of local energy distribution. AI Soc. (2013). doi:10.1007/s00146-013-0528-1

Author Index